Sweet Judy Blue Eyes

Sweet Judy Blue Eyes

My

Life

in

Music

CROWN
ARCHETYPE
NEW YORK

JUDY COLLINS

All rights reserved.
Published in the United States by Crown Archetype,
an imprint of the Crown Publishing Group,
a division of Random House, Inc., New York.
www.crownpublishing.com

Crown Archetype with colophon is a trademark of
Random House, Inc.

Library of Congress Cataloging-in-Publication Data
Collins, Judy, 1939–
    Sweet Judy blue eyes : my life in music / Judy Collins.—1st ed.
      p. cm.
    1. Collins, Judy, 1939– 2. Singers—United States—Biography.
I. Title.
  ML420.C65A3   2011
  782.42164092—dc22
  [B]   2011014414

ISBN 978-0-307-71734-4
eISBN 978-0-307-71736-8

Printed in the United States of America

All photographs are from the author's private collection
unless otherwise credited.

BOOK DESIGN BY BARBARA STURMAN
JACKET PHOTOGRAPHY BY FRANCESCO SCAVULLO

10 9 8 7 6 5 4 3 2 1

First Edition

For my mother,

Marjorie Lorraine Byrd Collins Hall

(1916–2010)

Author's Note

I have made every attempt to quote the conversations with people in this book correctly. If I have failed to be exact, I've attempted to convey the sense and the meaning. At times I have also quoted letters, and those are verbatim.

In all cases, it is my memory of an event that supersedes the memories of other participants who might have been at the same party. There are no accidents in memory, for memory has its own reasons and its own logic. What I remember is what happened to me as I best recall it.

The Parade

How exhilarating it was to march
Along the great boulevards
In the sunflash of trumpets
And under all the waving flags—
The flag of desire, the flag of ambition.

So many of us streaming along—
All of humanity, really—
Moving in perfect sync,
Yet each lost in the room
Of a private dream.

—BILLY COLLINS

Sweet Judy Blue Eyes

Prelude

God of sun and moon, God of ocean tides,
You who drive the stars, you of perfect light
Teach me how to sing.

—JUDY COLLINS, "Singing Lessons"

*I*T's a Sunday night, and I am traveling from Hartford to New York City, heading in from a show. Rain pours down, and the driver of my sedan is battling the storm like a captain of a schooner in white waves. Thoughts of my life flow like the water around us: years of life, love and anger, rage and hope; the songs I have sung; the men and women I have loved.

"Suite: Judy Blue Eyes" is playing on the radio, softly, but I hear it through the steady sound of the rain and the hiss of the tires on the road. Unmistakable, Stephen Stills' voice floats above the harmonies of David Crosby and Graham Nash. Stephen's guitar cuts into my heart like an emotional arrow. Whenever I hear the song—in a grocery store, in an airport, on my own CD player—it resounds like a call from mystic lakes. It pierces the heart of this girl and all the other grown-up girls who think it tells their story. All great songs make you feel that way, as though they were written especially for you.

But "Suite: Judy Blue Eyes" really *is* my story. Stephen wrote it for me when we were both young and innocent, during our brilliant romance. The song never fails to transport me back to that thrilling and terrifying time we call "the sixties," when so many great songs proclaimed our grand, noble visions. We were reckless dreamers, hell-bent on finding our own personal happiness, determined to elevate all of humanity above the anger and violence of the past.

There is an old saying that every time you sigh, a drop of blood falls from your heart. It seems I sigh more now than I ever did, and that probably means my heart has lost many tear-shaped drops. I have lived my life, as we all do, between these sighs, between these drops of blood.

My life has taken me from innocence to rage and back again. Those precious early years seem oddly clearer to me now, at seventy. The people I knew and loved and the drama of that diamond-bright time move closer as they slip farther away.

Sweet Judy Blue Eyes will tell many stories I've never fully told, demons I have battled, and tragedies I've endured. In fifty years in the music business, there are also the blessings and grace I have found through it all.

I will tell how I found my way to my marriage to Louis Nelson and more than thirty-three years of living with a man who is my partner, my friend and lover, my solace and companion, whom I met when I thought I had lost everything that mattered.

I will talk of faith and money, sex and drugs and rock and roll, about learning to sing and tour, through all the days of shining sun as well as pouring rain. I will tell of my ongoing quest to become— and to remain—an artist.

With the passage of time, I am able to talk about circles that have been completed and old friends with whom I have reconnected. Many have died, each spiriting away a unique impression of me that no one else will ever have, each leaving a ghost of himself behind in my memory. These memories are my treasures— memories of singers and poets, rabble-rousers and rebels. The closest of friends, the dearest of lovers, family members who were a part of me. There are so many, including Marjorie, my mother, Chuck, my father, and Clark, my son.

Robert Richardson writes of the philosopher William James, "Trouble was for him a precondition for insight." I can only hope that the same is true for me, and that I have learned at least some of the lessons born not only of my own troubles and of those close to me but also of the people for whose causes I have marched and rallied, raised money, and gone to jail, and for whom I always, always sing.

I will speak of the wars of an emotional nature, against addictions, against suicidal depressions, against alcoholic drinking; these are not wars with fire and steel, but they are wars just the same, often with terrible prices to pay. No antiwar protest, no action against prevailing prejudice, ever was fought harder than these.

Through all these years, I have been eternally grateful for the gift of music. There are times when the sounds of the voices in my audiences, singing along with the old sweet melodies, are, for me, all that stand between despair and joy. When we sing, we can do anything—change the world, bring peace, be our best selves at last.

When we sing, our hearts can lift and fly, over the troubled waters and over the years.

Chapter One

Ruby-Throated Sparrow

I am yours, you are mine, you are what you are.

—STEPHEN STILLS, "Suite: Judy Blue Eyes"

NINETEEN SIXTY-EIGHT, the year I met and fell in love with Stephen Stills, was a leap year. In the Chinese calendar, it was the year of the monkey, a year destined to explode with creativity, social upheaval, and tragedy. The U.S. involvement in Vietnam had escalated into all-out warfare and was tearing the country apart. Martin Luther King Jr., in whom we invested so much hope, had been murdered in Memphis on April 4. The day after King's assassination, Robert F. Kennedy made one of the last speeches of his life at a political gathering in Indianapolis originally intended as a rally for his run for president, reminding the weeping audience of black and white mourners that he, too, had lost a brother to a white man with a gun and urging them, as the Greeks had put it, to "tame the savageness of man and make gentle the life of this world."

Many young people were marching against the war, and music captured our conflicting feelings of disenchantment and romantic idealism, from the traditional folk songs of the Weavers, "Wasn't

That a Time" and "Rock Island Line," to the powerful laments of singer-songwriters, Dylan singing "A Hard Rain's A-Gonna Fall," Phil Ochs singing "I Ain't Marching Anymore," and Joan Baez singing "Silver Dagger" in her haunting soprano. This incredible music was everywhere, playing on Top 40 and FM radio mixed in with the Beatles' "Lovely Rita" and "Eleanor Rigby," the Byrds sparkling with Jim McGuinn's twelve-string guitar on "Mr. Tambourine Man," and the Mamas and the Papas urging us to leave cold New York and dream of sunny California. "I'd be safe and warm, if I was in L.A.," they sang, their heartbreaking harmonies draping the airwaves with longing. There was the angst-filled psychedelia of the Doors with Jim Morrison begging us to light his fire, and Grace Slick, singing with Jefferson Airplane, her seductive voice drifting on the silky sound of her band: "One pill makes you larger and one pill makes you small." All these songs were hitting the radio waves side by side with the reports of casualties in Indochina.

The intermix of news flashes and this wistful and sometimes furious music made the atmosphere of the times seem almost otherworldly. "It's All Over Now, Baby Blue" cascaded across the country as Dylan put his lyrics to our tears and our rage.

It was a time of undeniable destructiveness as the war raged and the young trashed their bodies and their lives with the drugs many of us thought were so cool. I remember singing in the dusk of summer, the audience primed with wine, organic cheese, and fruit for a long night of music. I put fresh flowers in my hair and through the lace of my Mexican wedding dress. I had bought a full-length leather vest that had roses painted on it, and leather bottoms were stitched to my Levi's. I wore my hair straight and threw my head back. We were free, all of us, to be, to love, to live, in a world different from the one our parents had inhabited. We were going full steam ahead, and yet we floated like water lilies on a pond, dreaming of a billion suns.

It was a time of tremendous hope and of tremendous naiveté,

a pivotal period in which we would see how far we could push the wall. We knew we were the children of a new sun and a new moon. We were blessed with our music and our determination; we knew we would bring an end to the war.

I had been making records for seven years by now, finding my own musical place in anger and innocence, singing for love and against war. We had awakened to the horror of war; at the same time we reveled in this luminous era as folk music became popular and coalesced into a quest for a better world.

My first top-ten single, "Both Sides Now," was playing on the radio, with the sound of the silvery harpsichord on the ride-out and the guitars and sweet rhythm filling in behind the resonant beauty of Joni Mitchell's lyric. The song was climbing up the *Billboard* charts, and I was being hailed as an "overnight success," although by then I had been making records and doing concerts for nearly ten years. My creative side was blooming like the purple and pink crocuses poking through the last snows in the parks in New York City, where I had lived for five years. And now, for the first time, I had begun to write my own songs.

On June 1 I headed from New York to Los Angeles to make my eighth album for Elektra Records. John Haeny, my engineer, and David Anderle, my producer on this new recording, gave me a welcoming party so that I could meet all the new players. This was a band that would include many world-famous strangers, among them Stephen Stills, whom I had admired from afar when he played "Bluebird" with Buffalo Springfield. I had no idea what to expect, but I was already a little in awe of his great guitar playing and his lean, blond good looks.

It was a clear night in Laurel Canyon. Stars floated in a black sky as I drove west over the twisting roads from my rental on Mulholland Drive. I could feel a shimmer of promise in the air.

In the warmth of John's house the music flowed, as did the wine and the conversation. Candles sparkled in the darkened living room and a small fire crackled on the grate despite the early June weather. John got me a drink, and David Anderle introduced me to the players who would be on the sessions. I was dressed in a soft silk top and velvet pants. I was feeling thin—thin was always good! I was smoking a cigarette and looking through the wreath of smoke out the window when I saw a handsome man arrive, slam the door of a sleek Bentley, and stride up the walk to the house.

"Judy Collins," David said when he walked in, "meet Stephen Stills."

Stephen was wearing Levi's, cowboy boots, and a brilliant white shirt with the cuffs turned up and the top mother-of-pearl button undone at the neck. I could see the sinews of his throat as he took me in and bowed as if to royalty. His wrists were tanned, as though he had spent most of his days on a horse in the sun. He was possibly the most attractive man I had ever seen.

Then his eyes found mine, and we gazed at each other, transfixed. I knew then that he would change my life.

It was a good party. There was more than one moment of sudden silence as my eyes met Stephen's again and again. We talked and sang until late that night, and when the party was over, we found each other walking up the pathway to our cars. We didn't say much in parting, but the light of the fire that had been sparked glowed in our goodbye. We both knew we would see each other the next day, when the music began.

As we said goodnight, I felt that I already knew all that was important to know about Stephen. There was a sensation of bliss in my heart.

I knew I was falling in love.

I SETTLED down in Los Angeles to record the new album, making music all day and making love all night with Stephen. Everything about L.A. in those days was romantic. It was the rocking place to be. The Elektra Records studio was right in the middle of a fascinating neighborhood of thriving clubs and hotels that hosted many of the artists of the era as they came and went, recording the songs that were changing the musical landscape of the country.

Among the crowds pushing through the doors of the cafes and bars on La Cienega, you could usually find a star or two: Tim Buckley, with his wild, beautiful hair around his angelic face, drinking an afternoon Pernod; John Phillips, of the Mamas and the Papas, lanky and smooth-moving as a cheetah, wandering into the luxurious and notorious Chateau Marmont. You might see his bandmate Denny Doherty there, or Michelle Phillips, a beautiful blonde, the most elegant woman in the folk crowd, looking as though she had just stepped out of Bergdorf Goodman's (hippie) hair salon, her teeth white as snow, her smile bright, her figure slender, and her grace exquisite. We once took acid together, and even then she looked and spoke in a charming and loving manner. Her gifts included a voice that complemented the voices of John and Mama Cass and Denny, weaving its slightly dizzy way around the melody, a great part of the group's success. Michelle might be folding herself around a cup of hot chocolate or a rum toddy in the Chateau's big stone room with the fireplace.

There were days of music, lots of friends to hang out with, and the pleasure of my nights with Stephen.

Joni Mitchell often had David Crosby on her delicate arm. I had already recorded her beautiful song "Both Sides Now" and had gotten to know her a little. But she was elusive. With long blond hair and striking high cheekbones, she sang with a voice that seemed to be etched out of the Canadian landscape, sometimes haunting, sometimes soaring high as the Rockies. She smoked like a chimney, and there was always a cigarette between her thin fingers, but her skin was alabaster smooth. From time to time a certain look would pass over her face as she caught the eye of someone or noticed something she didn't cotton to, but then, like the sun peeking out from the clouds, she would break into a smile or even a song.

Farther up the hill from the Chateau Marmont, the Magic Castle twinkled all night among the low-slung pines and flowering plants. Close by was the Tropicana, hotel host to rock-and-roll bands. My friend John Cooke, whom we all called Cookie, usually stayed there as well. Tall and slender with an aura that always reminded me of an elegant waterbird, Cookie had a bright eye and a clever way about him. He was the son of Alistair Cooke, the English television journalist. Cookie played banjo and sang with a group called the Charles River Valley Boys, and was road-managing Janis Joplin and her band, Big Brother and the Holding Company, who also stayed at the Tropicana.

Cookie and I had been occasional lovers during those years, sometimes finding each other at lonely hotels on the road or in hot tubs in Marin County, even once in his apartment in Cambridge, Massachusetts. He was someone I trusted and felt comfortable with. Cookie had introduced me to Janis at the Monterey Pop Festival in June 1967, where ninety thousand people in the audience lifted her to the sky like a new star in the firmament when they heard the raw despair in her voice and the raging determination to make it through; both would soon find their way to the album *Cheap Thrills*.

Cookie was present at a strange encounter I had with Janis in the spring of 1968. It was at the Troubadour, a Los Angeles club owned by Doug Weston. I was there to hear Paul Williams the night before I was due to play a two-week gig. Cookie took me to the club, where Janis joined our table and she and I were reintroduced. We whispered hello to each other as Paul was singing "Rainy Days and Mondays," a song destined to become a huge hit for Karen Carpenter in 1971.

At the end of Paul's set, Janis pulled her chair closer to mine. Her already famous face was a little puffy and her eyes gleamed from under tired-looking lids, but her energy attracted glances and attention to our table. She had to shout over the roar of the crowd's attempt to get Paul back for an encore.

"I'm coming to hear you sing tomorrow!" she said in a loud voice. I responded, hoping she could hear me over the noise, that I was looking forward to my gig. As Paul left the stage and the room quieted down, Janis leaned across the table, speaking softly, intimately, into my ear.

"You know," she said, "one of us is going to make it. And it's not going to be me."

Janis' words have haunted me for more than four decades. I have never quite known what to make of them. We did not know each other well, and she could not have known how much I was drinking. But it has been my experience that a drunk can spot a drunk a mile away. Perhaps it was simply her reaching out into the world for company.

Janis and I laughed awkwardly then, strangely embarrassed, both of us, by the intimations of fate and the echoes of the early deaths of many artists. Janis' drinking and drugging seemed all of a piece with her dramatic, in-your-face lifestyle and persona. Her audiences expected her to behave badly, to live out there on the edge. They took all she gave them and seemed to protect her with their screams, with their outsized enthusiasm, with their passionate, loud approval.

The truth was, of course, that I was as close to the edge as Janis, but in the eyes of the public, I was the girl with wildflowers in her hair and, some said, a voice like a mountain stream. Janis was expected to fly too high and eventually to crash. I was expected to be the flower-child folksinger who might soar but would come softly to my feet in golden fields.

Two years later, on October 4, 1970, Cookie, who was still her road manager, would discover Janis' dead body in her room at the Landmark Hotel in L.A.

Sad times, sad girl, gone at twenty-seven. Janis defined the riotous rock-and-roll circus of the sixties, and she had been right— she did not survive it.

~~~

In 1969 I was traveling back and forth from New York to L.A. as my affair with Stephen progressed. Crosby, Stills and Nash was beginning to record, and Stephen and I were still working on my new album.

I found myself back in California in April for a concert at the Santa Monica Civic Center. Stephen met me at my hotel that afternoon; it was a time when our romance—thrilling but sometimes rocky—was difficult to manage, between his recording and my touring. He walked into my room that day at the Holiday Inn carrying a guitar case and smiling. We embraced, he wished me an early happy birthday, and I realized all would be well. I relaxed.

Sitting down on the bed, Stephen gently, lovingly removed an exquisite instrument: a gorgeous antique Martin guitar with a tone as smooth as buttery caramel. He ran his fingers over the strings while I melted, hearing that Stills sound, like no other.

Suddenly the big, ringing, open chords of his guitar and Stephen's clear tenor filled that blank, nondescript hotel room in Santa Monica.

> *It's getting to the point*
> *Where I'm no fun anymore . . .*

I knew immediately that the song was something special, something timeless, something for me.

> *Voices of the angels,*
> *Ring around the moonlight*
> *Asking me, since she's so free*
> *How can you catch this sparrow?*

Emotions surged and clashed as I listened to "Suite: Judy Blue Eyes." I heard for the first time, perhaps, that Stephen knew much more about my life than I had ever given him credit for. He understood the wrenching pain I felt about being in therapy for my anxieties and alcoholism, as well as my deep distrust of men and of commitment. He knew better than I that there were problems nothing in our relationship would solve. It was not that I did not love him, or that he didn't know I loved him. But there was the rupture that had occurred when my own determination met his—that I could not and would not give up control. It is all there in the lyrics, which were almost a self-portrait—perhaps a double portrait of two determined individuals, unable to come to terms with life together, and despairing of having to live apart.

It would have been enough that he could spell out the troubles in our love affair, but the song itself was so glorious, so transporting, that had it not been about me, I would have dreamed it might have been—it was a triumph of writing, of feeling, of his deep melodic gifts. I had heard a lot of songs, and sung some that had become hits. I knew I was listening not only to my story but also to a song that was going to be for all times, not just for ours. It was a classic, and it broke my heart.

I was in tears, my head in my hands and then my arms around his neck, our faces pressed together as though we could never be apart. There was nothing that was going to keep us together, yet nothing could part us. It was something I knew, but I didn't know what to do about it. The song made me weep, as it would for years to come.

When Stephen finished singing that afternoon in 1969, he held the guitar out to me.

"This guitar was made in 1930. I found it in an antique shop, and had it restored." Then he stepped over the luggage and the shoes that were strewn across my temporary one-night-stand hotel room as he was leaving.

"Now you have the song, and the guitar." At the door he turned back to me again. "And my heart."

Chapter Two

The Gypsy Rover

The Gypsy rover came over the hill
Down through the valley so shady

—Traditional, "The Gypsy Rover"

On a sunny afternoon in the spring of 1954, when I was fifteen, the Great Folk Scare, like a beautiful wild bird, flew into my living room and made a perfect landing.

I had walked the ten blocks from Denver's East High to where I lived with my family on Oneida, in East Denver. Ours was a house with stucco arches, a porch, a red roof of curved tiles, and a garden of roses and iris. Outside my window there was a small emerald lawn sheltered by a Russian olive tree whose pale lavender flowers gave off an exotic scent. I have often thought that this romantic place must have wooed the wild bird to win my heart, like a lover on the wing.

I arrived home and was standing next to our Baldwin grand piano, but instead of beginning my practice, I turned on our walnut-encased Emerson radio.

The announcer was discussing *The Black Knight*, a film set in the days of King Arthur, starring Alan Ladd. The sound track of the movie spilled into our living room, and the ballad called "The Gypsy Rover" stopped me in my tracks. It literally made me tremble. I knew at once it was meant for me.

The song called to me with its sweet story and lilting melody, and I fell into its arms. All the sonatas and études, nocturnes and concertos of those brilliant and challenging composers—the pieces I'd been studying and memorizing and weeping over most of my life until then—suddenly paled next to the simple beauty of this new sound. "The Gypsy Rover" told a tale of a girl who runs off with a dashing stranger, an age-old story that won my teenage heart, grabbed me by the soul, and changed my life forever.

That afternoon I raced to Wells Music, I plunked down my precious babysitting money, and I paid for the thin red vinyl slip of a record from the sound track of *The Black Knight*. The man behind the counter, whom I knew from visits to the store to buy classical piano scores, seemed pleased by my interest in the song. He told me there were dozens of versions of "The Gypsy Rover" and that many traditional singers had sung and recorded it. He seemed to know there was a world out there called "folk music," and pointed out the label on the record, which said that Leo McGuire, a Dublin singer, had copyrighted it in 1950. It was Leo's version I had heard, sung in the movie by Elton Hayes, who played the part of the minstrel in *The Black Knight*.

To me, "The Gypsy Rover" was as fresh as a new day. It was a song for a lover, for a dreamer, for a young woman yearning to move into other worlds.

As fate would have it, at home again I took the delicate red vinyl out of its sleeve and placed it on the chair by our Emerson. I turned around to do something, and somehow I managed to sit on it, splitting it into pieces. A disaster! I didn't have the money to buy another copy. I called Marsha Pinto and Carol Shank, my best friends and the dancers with whom I had performed the skit "Little

Red Riding Hood" all over Denver that year—the Lions Club, the Kiwanis Club, and the Brown Palace Hotel, where we met Rock Hudson—telling them I had found a new replacement for "Little Red Riding Hood," and asking them to get on the radio and listen for the song and write down the words. They were only too obliging; they, too, wanted something new to dance to. I described the song, and for a week we all turned on our sets as soon as we got home from school and listened for repeat plays. The movie was a big hit, so we heard the song many times that week. We wrote down the words, and I learned the melody, just as in the old and honored folk tradition, by ear and heart.

It would be the beginning of my new life.

My romance with songs began early. When I was four months old in 1939, "Over the Rainbow" was playing on the radio. My mother, Marjorie, told me I was named after Judy Garland, although my father assured me I was named after Judith in the Bible, the queen who had cut off the head of the evil King Holofernes to save her tribe. I loved that. I would be a warrior, a queen, and perhaps a Hollywood star!

I was surrounded by good music. My father, a successful radio performer and singer with shows in Seattle and Los Angeles, sang and practiced every day, and my parents started me on piano lessons by the time I was four. Daddy, blind from the time he was a little boy, was a fine musician whose daily programs were uplifting half hours of song from the Great American Songbook, readings from Ralph Waldo Emerson, old Mae West stories, and guest artists, whom he often brought home to dinner and who filled our house with joyful music. Even my godfather, Holden Bowler, who babysat me and changed my diapers, did so, I'm told, with an Irish tune on his lips.

We lived in Seattle, then in Los Angeles, and in 1948, when

I was nine, moved to Colorado, where my father had a new radio show. Denver was still a young city, and my eyes took in the grandeur of the "Queen of the Mountain Plains," a glittering cluster of clean-lined buildings framed by the majestic Rockies, rising white and rugged to the west.

When we moved to Denver, my brother Mike was five, and David was three. In Colorado my parents had two more children, Denver John in 1950 and Holly Ann in 1954. When I asked why she gave her fourth and fifth children two first names, Mom blamed it on the altitude.

Denver was a mile high and the mountains soared to fourteen thousand feet. In the winters, dry champagne snowflakes fell on the streets and on the aspen and pine trees that grew in the parks. Snow was new to us. We scooped it into snowballs and snowmen. My father said Colorado was the most beautiful place he had ever seen. He wrote a song called "Colorado Skies" in 1950, and we would hear him sing it on his radio show among other musical treasures— the songs of Rodgers and Hart, George Gershwin, and Cole Porter, and great old Irish ballads such as "The Kerry Dancers."

When I was ten, I contracted polio and was hospitalized for two months but recovered fully. I resumed the piano, practicing the classics, and my parents found me a new teacher in Denver, Dr. Antonia Brico, who believed I had the makings of a concert pianist— "the real thing," as she put it. I practiced diligently, and when I was thirteen I made my debut with Brico's orchestra, playing the Mozart Piano Concerto No. 10 for two pianos with another young pianist, Danny Guerrero.

Danny was sixteen and good-looking. He had wavy dark hair that was swept back from his face, and at our rehearsals his attractive figure was always decked out in a suit and tie. He could play the piano like an angel. Mozart had written this concerto to perform with his sister, Maria Anna, whom he called Nannerl, and Danny and I were charmed by the thought. We would be Amadeus and

Nannerl, at least for that night in February 1953 when we played the great concerto with Brico's orchestra in Phipps Auditorium.

My mother, who was a gifted seamstress and for many years made most of her children's clothes on her Singer sewing machine, spinning out calico shirts for the boys, velvet jackets, skirts, and flowered dresses for me (my sister Holly was still a glint in my father's eye), did something unusual for that performance. She bought me an organza dress, off the shoulder, long and flowing and white as the snow that fell the night of the concert—the biggest blizzard in a decade. Everyone—the dozen who made it through the snowdrifts—agreed that we had played well, and complimented me on my playing and on my beautiful dress.

For the next two years I would continue to study with Antonia Brico. But her dreams for my classical piano career were not to be.

I DISCOVERED very early in my life that I had an ear for melody. I could hear a song and play it on the piano, hear a piece of music I was attracted to and sing it, and find the harmonies that suited me. This talent was one that carried me easily into the performance of popular music, as well as driving my teacher nuts. She was used to classically trained musicians who studied the scores in order to learn the music, and she was convinced that my peculiar gift would lead me away from Mozart and Debussy.

In spite of the success and excitement of my young life, at fourteen I began to experience deep depressions and their brooding and debilitating effects. Perhaps it was because I was in hormonal upheaval, but I had no real idea why they happened. They came on at unpredictable times.

I had also already experienced the first of what would become a lifetime of migraine headaches, for which I was sent to a doctor and given all kinds of tests and a drug called Cafergot, which helped. My mother said my grandmother had suffered from migraines something terrible.

These depressions sometimes occurred before the migraines, but not always. Depression might hover on a day when I was alone, and I might dose it with sugar, to which I was already developing an addiction. The migraines as well as the depressions would usually pass in a few hours.

But one day my depression was utterly different. It seemed to take me by the throat and send me down into the deepest part of myself, where there was something I could not fight. For the first time I realized how I could escape these terrifying feelings. I had been fighting with Brico about not practicing enough, and my father wanted me to play a piece in public that I found far too demanding. (The onset of these feelings was often preceded by a paralyzing fear of not doing something perfectly.) That day I knew there was a way out.

I found an unopened bottle of a hundred aspirin in the bathroom cupboard and spent an hour downing the entire bottle, a few pills at a time. Almost at once I felt ill. I was eager to die, but not if it was going to make me throw up! I called my friend Marsha, who sent her father over. Dr. Pinto told me to make myself throw up, and that I would live.

Live! I had not planned on living, and now I would have to deal with the consequences.

I felt uncomfortable for a few days, but I had taken action, gone to the edge and over. I knew that the pressure needed to be relieved somehow.

Of course, no one talked to me about what I had done, not directly. There was no counseling, no therapy, no group that I might go to, no suicide or grief counselor who would be sent for. These were still the dark ages for mental health issues.

What I did must have been a terrible blow to both my parents. My father sent me a heartfelt letter of contrition in which he expressed regret at being so hard and demanding. My mother, Marjorie—beautiful and gifted—was not unfamiliar with trouble. She was slim, with auburn hair she curled into the fashion of the 1940s, high cheekbones, and big eyes in which I used to say I saw pieces of fruitcake. When my mother dressed to go out for an evening with my father, she looked to me like a movie star in her silk blouse and long skirt, her hair done and her makeup on, and the scent of Chanel No. 5 in the swirl of her satin cloak. Her life had not been easy, for in marrying a man who was blind she'd opted for a life that was both different and difficult.

Mother was one of nine and had seen her share of problems. She was pretty cool about most things, and my suicide attempt was no exception. But afterward I felt her watching me, her eyes scanning for trouble, her hands kind as she reached out to me, her smile more tender. She also stopped chasing me around the room with a broomstick when I misbehaved. I might have said it was almost worth it!

Music saved me, as it always had. I found a young guitarist, as well as a drummer and a piano player, for "The Gypsy Rover." My friends Marsha and Carol were dancing the parts of the young lass and her lover, and soon we were performing our new piece at all the usual haunts where we had done "Little Red Riding Hood." Our heads were filled with dreams of making it big and taking "The Gypsy Rover" to Las Vegas.

I convinced my father to get me a guitar. I started teaching myself to play, developing the necessary calluses on my fingers and silently panicking about the inevitable confrontation with Brico over my new musical love affair. My imperious teacher, a masterly pianist and a great conductor, obsessively pursued perfection both in herself and in her students. I knew from experience that she would fly into a rage when she found out I was playing folk music. I kept it from her for as long as I could.

And then, on another Saturday that spring, "Barbara Allen,"

sung by Jo Stafford, came over the radio and joined the battle for my heart and soul.

> *'Twas in the merry month of May, when the green*
> *buds were swellin'*
> *A young man on his deathbed lay for the love of*
> *Barbara Allen.*

I knew Jo Stafford's voice from her hits—"Shrimp Boats," "Hey, Good Lookin'," "I'll Be Seeing You," and "You Belong to Me." She had a voice as smooth as honey, rich in tone, and clear in diction. She had sung with the Pied Pipers as well as Frank Sinatra. In 1950, long before the advent of the "crossover" phenomenon, Stafford made the album *American Folk Songs* at the height of her popular success. In fact, the album was part of a folk music revival that was taking hold around the country. "Barbara Allen" was on that album, along with "Shenandoah" and "Black Is the Color." Before I ever heard of Woody Guthrie or Pete Seeger, Jo Stafford and Elton Hayes, the singer in the movie, put me in touch with the beauty and wonder of folk music.

Chapter Three

Lingo the Drifter

I am a poor wayfaring stranger
Traveling through this world of woe.

—Traditional, "Poor Wayfaring Stranger"

My evolution into a folksinger coincided with the arrival of Lingo the drifter, who came to Denver that year. This traveler, troubadour, and philosopher just showed up one day at my parents' house and changed all of our lives.

A singer of the songs of Woody Guthrie and Pete Seeger, Lingo had a radio show in Denver. He was a fan of Daddy's show, and stopped by to introduce himself and show his respect. Lingo strode into the house as if he had known us all his life, and dramatically doffed his Stetson, a worn and shapeless old thing with a small pine sprig sticking out of the brim.

He was a rugged-looking man with penetrating deep blue eyes under dark, long hair. He sang in a straight, clean, vibratoless voice, and sometimes I would join in. In his buckskin trousers and turquoise bolo and that godforsaken hat, Lingo would stake out his territory in our living room and proudly sing the songs of the new folk revival.

He seemed to make Daddy happy right from the start—perhaps my father sensed that Lingo shared his love of whiskey. They formed a friendship, I think, over their love of books and politics, as well as their love of alcohol.

Lingo soon was practically a part of the family. He said he was originally from Chicago. (Studs Terkel later told me that Lingo, whom he remembered as Paul Lezchuk, had lost his wife and child in an automobile accident, and had disappeared from the Chicago scene.)

During the many long Sunday afternoons he spent at our house, Lingo told us about his life. He said that he fought in the Battle of the Bulge in World War II and that his platoon was among the first to reach Hitler's death camps. He returned to Chicago, scarred by what he had seen, and enrolled at the University of Chicago on the GI Bill.

Lingo had by then founded what he would call the Dormant Brain Cell Research Foundation, an informal intellectual movement (perhaps a movement of one, at least at the start) that studied the human capacity to forget or ignore all our experiences and repeat the same tragic mistakes again and again.

Lingo came to Colorado and played the local joints around Denver. He quickly established himself as the hometown authority on folk music and radical politics. An admiring program director at a Denver radio station found a slot for him on Friday nights. Lingo filled the Denver airwaves with a mixture of traditional songs and the music of Woody Guthrie, which he performed live on his sweet old Martin guitar. He sang a lot of songs that I later came to understand were songs of the Almanac Singers, the first group Pete Seeger joined in New York in 1941 when he began writing music.

Lingo loved to drink Daddy's whiskey, wangle an invitation from my mother to stay for dinner, and talk philosophy and politics.

"Let me sing you a song or two by a couple of great American heroes," he would say. "This one is by Woody Guthrie." Woody's great song about Mexican immigrant farmworkers, "Deportee," might follow. Then he might sing a song by Pete Seeger, maybe "Hold the Line," which Pete wrote about the Peekskill riots in 1949, when Paul Robeson tried to sing for union members and heads were busted and bricks were thrown. Or maybe "Lonesome Valley":

> *You gotta walk that lonesome valley,*
> *You gotta walk it by yourself.*

There was history and passion in these songs, and when Lingo performed, his eyes blazed. I understood it as the light of defiance, the light of the true believer. My father and Lingo both believed, in their own ways, that music could save the world. With whiskey, the voices of Lingo and my father would rise, and as often as not, they'd belt out "Los Cuatros Generales," the bittersweet song of the Spanish nationalists that spoke of the loss of the good men and women of Spain, the loss of freedom, their political defeat that preceded World War II. The song's optimism is premature.

> *The four insurgent generals,*
> *They tried to betray us,*
> *At Christmas, holy evening,*
> *But your courageous children,*
> *They did not disgrace you.*

The song, with its soaring melody and urgent tempo, made me cry. It was a song of the people, trying to bolster them against their fears, trying to win the war with music, as we would always try to do.

Lingo was probably the first real hippie I ever met.

I was learning that this thing called folk music had been around for a long time, and that the roots of folk music are ancient, probably growing out of a troubadour tradition that had begun before written history. Kings and rulers from antiquity often had singers and troubadours in their pay who would put sagas and love poems to music and soothe the long nights with their lyricism. Blondel, Richard the Lionheart's troubadour, saved his master's life by hunting out all the prisons where he might be kept and singing a song outside the castle walls until he heard Richard's response. He then sent for help to free his king.

I knew from my classical training that composers often borrowed from the trove of traditional melodies when creating themes for symphonies or arias for great operas. But I hadn't realized how richly folk music had inspired twentieth-century classical music. Aaron Copland used a traditional shaker hymn, "Simple Gifts," in *Appalachian Spring*. Even Igor Stravinsky, though he contorted their harmonies, made use of the folk melodies from his Russian heritage to embellish his *Rite of Spring*.

In addition to the Dylan Thomas poetry they read together— Daddy from his Braille edition and Lingo from his ragged hardbound copy—the two men found common ground in politics. The war in Vietnam had begun with the use of "military advisers" after the fall of Dien Bien Phu. When the French got out of Indochina, the United States got in. Daddy and Lingo slung the fate of Indochina around our living room, swearing and shouting, their voices rising with the amount of whiskey they imbibed.

"We should not dig ourselves into a conflict we can never win," my father would say. "What do those sons of bitches think they are doing?"

Lingo and my father reinforced each other's point of view, though it often sounded like another argument. "Don't they know these people? They fought off the French, for God's sake!" Lingo would shout.

"As well as the Japanese and Genghis Khan!" my father would add. "And anyway, it's all about the natural resources. Everyone knows it!" And with a dramatic wave of his arm Daddy would knock over his glass for emphasis.

When she heard Lingo's remarks, my mother would just smile, and then with a kitchen towel she would pat the arm of Daddy's chair dry of the spilled whiskey and sometimes even bring him another full glass.

My sister, Holly, was only a toddler at the time, but when she got a new kitten, a beautiful blue point Siamese, my father named him Dien Bien Phu. Ironically, the cat managed to outlive the Vietnam War, but just barely.

My father convinced Lingo that, with his brains and insight, he should try to get on one of the new television shows coming out of Hollywood. Daddy even helped him get in touch with some of the people he had known there. In 1956 Lingo landed a spot on Groucho Marx's *You Bet Your Life*. Lingo always wore his same old buckskins on the broadcasts, looking like he'd just come down from the back side of a mountain in Colorado.

"I played the part of a backwoods mountain man to perfection," he told us, "because that is who I am!"

On a Saturday night in October, Lingo was on *You Bet Your Life* with Groucho throwing him questions. My family and I were all sitting around the TV set, happily watching the mountain man who had been a fixture in our living room. All of a sudden my father began pounding his chair and waving his fists, as he had always done in the shouting matches with Lingo about politics.

"Lingo does not, by God, know that answer! This show is rigged!"

Daddy believed he knew everything there was to know about the workings of Lingo's brain and was convinced his old buddy had been prompted. A few weeks later, *Twenty-One*, the ranking quiz show in Hollywood and on TV, was discovered to be leaking questions to Charles Van Doren, son of Pulitzer Prize–winning author, critic, and poet Mark Van Doren. (Later the scandal was chronicled in Robert Redford's film *Quiz Show*.)

Lingo earned a pot of money from his game show success and called a real estate agent in Colorado to ask if anybody had a mountaintop for sale. The agent found Lookout Mountain for Lingo, who bought the property with a rucksack full of cash and went up there with an axe.

"I built my place with a guitar, three chords, nine folk songs, and sixty-four thousand dollars!" Lingo told me. He invited my father, mother, and me to come up to his cabin on Saturday nights to hear the "folk music circle," a group of twenty-odd singers, pickers, storytellers, and assorted hippies. The air was so clear in those days that, from his aerie, the lights of Denver looked like sparkling diamonds.

We sang together under the stars at Lingo's mountaintop "This Land Is Your Land," "Roll On, Columbia" (about the dam on the Columbia River), and "Los Cuatros Generales." Lingo would feed us borscht and homebrew and we would muse about injustice and freedom and how we would fight for our beliefs. I had been primed for those politics in my family anyway; true-blue FDR Democrats, we were raised to be rebels, to be outspoken about politics. Each one of us Collins children was going to try to change the world.

Lingo taught me a great deal, sharpening my understanding of what the folk tradition was and what it wasn't. In a strange way, this eccentric singer guarded the door through which I was destined to pass. He knew the songs and held on to a ragged sense of hope despite the ups and downs of life. Like my father, Lingo possessed unbounded enthusiasm. He would leave his mark on me and help inspire me to pledge my life to folk music.

When my father and Lingo told me that I could change the world, I believed them.

Chapter Four

My Buddy

*M*Y father was a fiercely proud man. His sight began to fail almost from his birth on an Idaho farm in 1911. By the age of four, he was totally blind. On the farm, he did the chores, carried water, and hauled wood, and his parents had no idea that they should treat him differently than other children. There was work to do, and perhaps from that hardscrabble life came his determination not to appear handicapped. At seven, he was sent to a special school in Gooding, Idaho, and lived away from the farm with others who were "challenged." There he realized how different he was, and sought advice from his teachers on how sighted people held their heads, opened their eyes, and smiled their bright smiles. He put these into practice and was so convincing, even to these teachers, that they often asked him to escort others who could not hear, and often could not see, to go ice skating or take trips to town. When they remembered with a shock that he was blind, they just said, "Not to worry, Charlie knows where he is going!"

From his teenage years, Daddy always wore hand-painted glass eyes to cover the ravaged scar tissue left when he lost his sight as a child. They were a very beautiful blue and my mother ordered them from a little factory in Colorado. They arrived nested in what appeared to be an egg box, two dozen at a time. As distinctly as I remember the sound of his voice, I remember the sound of one of Daddy's glass eyes shattering against the bathroom tiles every once in a while as he put them in or took them out morning and night.

He discovered music early, learning the piano and honing his fine clear baritone as a young man. He combined those talents with his natural gregariousness and storytelling skills in a radio career that spanned nearly thirty years. He never shied away from politics. Daddy was funny, flamboyant, and theatrical, whether performing on the radio, sitting in someone's living room, or holding court at our piano.

He never had a seeing-eye dog to help him around, nor did he ever use a cane, and if he walked into your house, even drunk, you might think he had lived there all his life from the ease with which he made his way from room to room.

When he was sober, my father saw more than anyone I have ever known, and it was his inner vision that captivated all of us—strangers, friends, and his children alike. He was a hero of a man who overcame demons every day and was determined to live to the full. We knew we had a giant of a father, one who had been through his own fire.

Daddy's college experience loomed large in his memory, both for the friendship he found as a member of the Phi Gamma Delta fraternity and for the work he did while a student. He was already writing, to great success. He had a job with the Moscow,

Idaho–based *Bonner County Daily Bee* to cover the World's Fair in 1933 and rode the rails to Chicago with his friend John Spaulding.

I met with Spaulding in Bainbridge Island, Washington, in 2003, when he was in his nineties. John still couldn't get over the fact that he had jumped railroad cars from Moscow, Idaho, to Chicago and back with a blind man, but he said, "Chuck said he could do anything I could do, and we didn't have any money and he wanted to go to the World's Fair and convinced me we could go by train and never have to pay a cent. I thought he was crazy, but he was up for it, and soon so was I." All my father's old friends remembered Daddy's talent and energy and intelligence, and talked about the sheer delight of joining him on his adventures.

My father could captivate just about anyone. My mother, Marjorie, met him on a bus in Seattle on the day before his radio debut in 1937. She fell in love with him when she heard him sing "My Buddy" on his first radio show. She was listening with her best friend, Eileen, and by the time he had finished the song, she was in tears, telling Eileen she was going to marry that handsome Charles Collins. Indeed, they married quickly, and she remained smitten, even when he broke her heart.

My father's career in radio took off, and the young couple soon found themselves in Hollywood, where Daddy landed a show on NBC. In those years, between the ages of four and nine, I rode in childhood glory in the backseat of our slope-backed 1942 black Buick when Mother drove my father to work at the studios where many of the classic radio shows were produced. We met the Cisco Kid and were in the studio audience for broadcasts of *Let's Pretend*. We met the Shadow himself. We met Red Skelton, Bob Hope, and later George Shearing. Mercedes McCambridge—whom Orson Welles called "the world's greatest living actress"—was an acquaintance of my dad. My father's drinking was already a problem, and Mercedes and he would have a few drinks together. I think it was

Mercedes who told my father that if he wanted to quit drinking he had to go to AA.

We moved to Denver in 1949, and my father impressed everyone he met. Chuck Collins, father of five, husband of Marjorie, was famous there; people adored him for his beautiful voice, his wonderful radio show, and his uplifting optimism. He was a charismatic man. Sometimes he would perform the poems of Don Blanding, such as "Vagabond's House," a poem that evoked all my father's lost dreams and yearning. People would be in tears at the end of the poem, to which he played an improvised, rippling accompaniment.

> *When I have a house . . . as I sometime may . . .*
> *I'll suit my fancy in every way.*

As the years went by, my four siblings and I—his "little brood," as he called us—all basked in his popularity, his open-handed generosity, his welcome greeting to everyone he met. His elegant clothes were immaculately tailored to his slightly stocky frame, his shoes shined to a bright polish. He walked with his back straight and his head thrown back, and if he ran into a wagon or a skate on the sidewalk, so be it; to him, the cuts and bruises were badges of honor.

As children, we were always delighted that our father could read to us in the dark, from *Moby-Dick* to Hans Christian Andersen and the Brothers Grimm. When the lights went out we were comforted by the presence of our father's voice and the imaginary lantern that lit our way to other worlds.

Daddy decorated the landscape of his life with literature, music, and the allure of ideas. His every sense was delicately tuned to the world around him. He was, in many ways, a Renaissance man, well read, eager to learn, ready for the next insight, the next idea. He was also terribly vulnerable at times, and anyone who knew him had to beware of hidden pitfalls, such as his not wanting help from anyone. We all—friends and children alike—walked a delicate line between offering too much help and too little, knowing he could not see us but also aware he always knew where we were.

Still, I often felt that I was invisible. I think I have been trying all my life to get my father to see me.

He described his alcoholism as "periodic." Like the little girl in the nursery rhyme, he was good most of the time, but when he was bad he was horrid. Daddy was usually a solid citizen and managed to hold on to his jobs, but he could also come home roaring drunk and be abusive and violent. His moods could flash enthusiasm and joy and then plunge him, and everyone around him, into deep remorse and sorrow. I can remember his bubbling laughter about the feeling of the sun on his face or the taste of scrambled eggs in the morning. I remember his look of pride when my siblings and I brought home good report cards and his rage when our progress was not what he thought it should have been. And I remember the few times he took a hairbrush or razor strop to my behind.

My father's despair was tangible at times and lurked just under the surface of his hearty, good-natured laughter and his apparent success. When drinking, he could be a nightmare of bitterness and unpredictability. Many mornings after a bad night, I witnessed his climb over a terrible hangover—he'd mix wheat germ, molasses, grapefruit juice, and B vitamins in the blender, with a raw egg to boot. With a roar of determination not to be beaten, Daddy committed himself to the day ahead of him to make a living for his family. He did well, and until the early 1960s, he was winning the fight. Everybody said so. He never whined, never complained, and never felt sorry for himself—as long as he was sober.

It was in Denver that my father finally did go to AA—not to stop drinking, but because he had become addicted to amphetamines and it was scaring him to death. AA for him didn't last long; he told people he couldn't take "the God stuff" and never went back.

All along, my mother, so strong in many ways, had to wrestle with Daddy's rages and the knowledge that he was a skirt-chaser, especially when he drank. I knew about this because from the time I was old enough to listen, my father confided in me about his romances and sexual escapades. I was not shocked when he told me these things, and I understood that this information, usually imparted when he was drinking, was meant to create a wall between my mother and myself. I was already on thin ice with my mom much of the time, so my father's boundary breaking probably worked, at least while I was in my late teens.

But later, when I was nineteen and pregnant, my mother and I got rip-roaring drunk one afternoon over lunch at a restaurant in Denver's Cherry Creek neighborhood and talked about everything, including Daddy's affairs. Because of that soul-searching and brave meeting, engineered by my mother, we settled all our past differences. From that moment on, my mother and I were the best of friends, able to talk over everything in our lives. We had a loving relationship from then on, for which I will be eternally grateful.

And in spite of it all, her love for him never wavered. Marjorie Lorraine Byrd was as smitten with my father as she had been the day they met. She was never unfaithful over all those years.

And she forgave him everything.

Chapter Five

The Blizzard

Colorado, Colorado, when the world leaves you shivering
And the blizzard blows,
When the snow flies and the night falls
There's a light in the window and a place called home
At the end of the storm.

—JUDY COLLINS, "The Blizzard"

I TURNED sixteen on May 1, 1955. That year, J. R. R. Tolkien's *The Lord of the Rings* was published, and someone gave me the trilogy, which I read under the covers when the lights went out. Marilyn Monroe had married Joe DiMaggio the previous year, and my father thought it would ruin the baseball star's career. One of my most vivid memories is of my father listening to the games, slamming his fist on his armchair when things didn't go well for whatever team he happened to be rooting for—usually the Yankees. I can hear the sound of the crowd pouring out of our Emerson radio, the cheers and the boos on a Sunday afternoon and the tinkle of the ice in my father's whiskey glass. I began reading books other than the *Count of Monte Cristo* and *Nancy Drew*. My friend John Gilbert had turned me on to Albert Camus, the French writer and existentialist, who drank too much and broke my heart when he died a few years later in a car crash. Bill Haley and the Comets had one hit after another on the radio, followed by Elvis.

America was still reeling from the Korean War and the divisiveness of Joe McCarthy's Red Scare. But even as Washington looked to the Eisenhower administration to restore stability, new voices and new faces were rising. The new power of television had helped propel John F. Kennedy, the young senator from Massachusetts, to national prominence, and many of us began to agree with his father, Joe, that his son would one day be president.

*T*HE country was falling in love with folk songs, as was I. I looked for material wherever I could, haunting the record stores with my precious babysitting money in hand, buying records of old sea chanties and English folk songs. I didn't know then that the folk music for which I had conceived such passion had already taken root in eclectic clubs such as the Gate of Horn in Chicago, the Village Gate in New York, and the Purple Onion and the Hungry i in San Francisco, all of which regularly gave over their stages to the solitary singer with a guitar.

I found the Denver Folklore Center, where I spent every cent I had on records. I met other singers, whose lives were all about learning, trading, sharing, and finding songs. I suddenly understood that my father's repertoire of music included much more than Rodgers and Hart and Irving Berlin. In the morning, rain or shine, hungover or stone cold sober, he would warm up his rich, clear baritone with Rodgers and Hart, and then burst into "Danny Boy" or "Kerry Dancers," "Kathleen Mavourneen" or "Galway Bay."

I continued going to Lingo's mountain retreats to drink homebrew and learn folk songs. Dick Barker was often at Lingo's; he was a redheaded cowboy with a sweet, haunting voice. He was the first person I heard sing "Ten Thousand Goddam Cattle." He sang a beautiful song about a town in the mountains forty-four miles from Telluride, on the Delores River.

> *In the country down below, where the little pinyons grow*
> *and it's always nearly half a day to water,*
> *There used to stand a town, where a brook come tumblin'*
> *down,*
> *From the mesa, where it surely hadn't ought to.*

It was a magical song, and as I watched Dick sing it, of course I fell a little bit in love with him. He wore cowboy boots and lived on his family's ranch, west of Denver, cleaning out the horse stalls and spreading manure around the gardens and fields. He rode horses every day. I was enthralled.

We fooled around in the back of his truck a couple of times— hot and passionate petting with our boots on. Dick would end up buying a ranch in Moose, Wyoming, and running a float trip company on the Snake River. He lives there to this day and hangs with the local folksingers, including my friend Cookie, who goes to Dick's Friday night "hoots."

Nineteen fifty-five was also the year I fell in love with Peter Taylor. Peter had been born and raised in Colorado, and he arrived in my life like fireworks in the mountain air. It had been his stepfather, Hal Clark, who hired my dad for his radio show in 1949. Hal was about to marry Margaret Taylor, a widow with three children, Hadley, Peter, and Gary. My father told me later that the children's father, James Gary Taylor, had taken his own life the year before. At nine, I had never heard of anyone who had died by his or her own hand. I found the knowledge strangely haunting.

In the summer between my sophomore and junior years of high school, I was teaching piano to Peter's sister, Hadley, overseeing her technical training for Dr. Brico, who would take her on as a student in the fall. I had not seen any of the Taylor children in the ensuing years, and it was a fluke that Brico wanted me to work with Hadley, who during one of our lessons said she thought I should meet her brothers.

Hadley had a summer job at Sportsland Valley Guest Ranch, on the other side of Berthoud Pass from Denver, and helped me get hired. Her handsome and articulate older brother Peter gave me a ride to the mountains. Our eyes met in the mirror as Peter drove over the pass, and by the time he took my hand to help me out of the car at the ranch, I was in love.

Sportsland Valley Guest Ranch stood among meadows surrounded by ponderosa and blue spruce. The air was fresh and the light glittered off the lingering snow on the peaks. The ranch had space for about fifty guests, for whom I washed dishes, served meals, and cleaned cabins. When the day's work was done, I sang folk songs in the big main room, where the guests gathered for mulled wine after a day of horseback riding. Hadley and the other girls, her brothers, Peter and Gary, and the guests would sing along on "Black Is the Color" and "The Gypsy Rover" and "Loch Lomond." Gary's girlfriend, Hillary, was Scottish and knew all the songs. There were stolen glances and firelight, sweet walks through shadowed forests, rides together through the woods on horseback, and days overflowing with romance.

> *So you'll take the high road*
> *And I'll take the low road*
> *And I'll be in Scotland afore ye.*

It was August 1955 and it seemed the whole world was in love. I might have known that love could break your heart, but I was more than willing to take that chance.

When I came down from the mountains, though, I was still in high school, still had to go to class and do homework, still had to help my mother with housework and look after my siblings—Mike, David, Denver John, and Holly Ann.

One day when I was visiting Peter's house on a Saturday afternoon, his mom, Margaret, was sorting through some photographs, looking for baby pictures of Peter and his siblings to show me. Suddenly she pulled out a photograph of a very tall, good-looking man.

"That son of a bitch!" she said, allowing me only a glimpse of the man in the photo before she tore it into little pieces and threw them into the trash. I asked her who he was. She told me in an angry voice that he was her husband and Peter's father, James Gary Taylor. I did not say I knew the family secret, that James Gary Taylor had taken his own life.

"He was a bastard," she said. It was the first and last time I ever heard Margaret talk about Peter's father.

The two of us went on looking at the family photos in silence. I could not concentrate on the pictures of my tall, good-looking boyfriend as a cute little boy throwing snowballs, laughing under a Christmas tree, standing with Gary and Hadley in his little sailor suit in the park. Margaret went on as if she hadn't seen a ghost pass through the room.

My romances—with Peter and with folk music—swirled through my life as if I were a normal 1950s teen. I loved *Your Hit Parade* and my Saturday nights were often spent watching Dorothy Collins, with her little upturned nose and hairdo, those funny skirts and tight, wide belts. I danced to songs such as "The Great Pretender," "Blueberry Hill," and "Earth Angel." Sometimes Carol, Marsha, John Gilbert, my one male friend, and I would play Elvis' rockabilly songs at our favorite diner in Colfax, where I learned to smoke cigarettes, choking at first but keeping at it. We put away burgers and fries while we pumped dimes into the jukebox.

There is a time for everything, as Pete Seeger says in "Turn!

Turn! Turn!" Rock and roll will always be a part of my life, but it never lured me from what I know now was my predestined path. I knew I had to sing those sweet, haunting folk songs, the ones that told stories about railroad men and murderous strangers and women with their hair pinned to the ground (from the traditional song called "Two Butchers," about a traveler who is lured from his journey by a woman who placed herself along the road with her "hair pinned to the ground," distracting him so that her accomplices could rob him). There were songs about human nature, political songs by Pete Seeger and Woody Guthrie, songs by the long-lost troubadours, songs about war and peace, love and heartbreak.

THROUGHOUT the next year Peter and I saw each other when we could, and we became more strongly attached, even though he was in college at Boulder and I was still in high school. We talked of books and hopes and ideals, and wrestled, each of us, with the conflicts in our lives. I fretted about turning my back on the piano and about my perceived betrayal of Brico. At my last lesson with her, when I told her that I was not going to pursue the career she and my parents had planned for me, she was furious, and we both were in tears. Brico knew I was ambivalent about my decision, but she also knew I was determined. In spite of my love for the great music I had studied with her, I broke her heart—but I also knew I had made the right decision.

Peter was torn over his own future. We were against the war in Vietnam, and the draft was on. Peter knew he would, at some time in the future, have to do his time in the service, even as he dreamed of going on with his studies at the university.

I had another year in school and another great summer at Sportsland Valley. I performed "The Gypsy Rover" at concerts all over Denver with my friends Marsha and Carol. Peter enlisted in the Naval Aviation Cadet Program in 1956 and came to Denver only occasionally, when he had leave. When he did, we hung out with my father and Lingo, spending time going to movies, having meals with our families, and getting to know each other better.

I graduated from East High in June 1957 and had to find another job for the summer. After two summers at Sportsland Valley, I knew I wanted to return to the mountains, and had written letters to a few lodges in the Rockies. The job I got was at Lemon Lodge in Grand Lake, a pretty mountain haven in Rocky Mountain National Park. The lodge was run by a widow, Jenny Lemon, who had a great property and two rowdy but cute kids, six and eight, who ran rings around me all summer.

Peter and I didn't see each other very much. When he was home on leave, we danced around the edges of sex but didn't go "all the way." Lonely in the mountains, I would go to the local dance hall in town, a smoky club where they served big drinks and everyone seemed to be having a good time.

There was a cowboy from one of the stables in Grand Lake whom I got to know when I went riding at his father's stables. Jim, as I will call him, would sometimes come fetch me at dawn, a saddled bay pony behind him as he rode his own cutting horse and whistled under my window. I would be dressed and waiting at five-thirty and we would spend a couple of hours together riding our horses in the long grass of the high meadows, rounding up the saddle ponies for their workday at the stable in Grand Lake. I felt a little like the girl in "The Gypsy Rover." It certainly wasn't love, but it was romantic and exhilarating. "Love the one you're with," as Crosby, Stills and Nash would later sing. One night after one or ten too many drinks—which was becoming a habit in my life—we went down by the lake and necked like mad. I went to sleep yearning to see Peter.

I loved being on Grand Lake on those long summer days,

working hard for Jenny, cleaning cabins and making beds, and then water-skiing behind her boat in the afternoon with her two kids laughing at my efforts (when it was smooth, I would tumble into the mirrorlike water; when it was rough, waves lapping against my bare legs, I was fine). Still later, I played my guitar and sang my songs in front of the great stone fireplace. I was barely eighteen, happy, in love with the mountains, the music, and dreams, and Peter Taylor.

PETER came to see me that summer, when he had leave. He had quit the flight training program because his entire body would break out in hives when he had to fly in close formation. In that type of flying, his safety depended on total trust, a certain intimacy with the other pilots. Peter Taylor was normally a stand-up, go-for-it kind of guy, and perhaps the secret in his family had something to do with this out-of-character reaction to wingtip-to-wingtip flights as a Naval Aviation Cadet. In any case, he wound up going from flying jets to cruising on a tin can in the Atlantic.

After those few short days of summer leave, Peter was off to sea and I was off to my first year at a little college in Illinois called MacMurray. I struggled through the cold midwestern winter, singing folk songs, cadging socks and cigarettes from my roommates, as poor as a church mouse. I worked in the library to supplement the tiny scholarship given to me by my mother's women's group, P.E.O.

That March on spring break, I took the California Zephyr home, drinking scotch-and-water in the bar car all the way to Denver. Two days later, Peter was back for good from the Navy. We drove to Arapahoe Basin, an hour west of Denver, where we froze our asses off skiing in a snowstorm all day. The snow was so thick that all I could see was Peter's red parka in front of me. I followed it down, inhaling snow with every breath, cold and scared but also excited, knowing we would not go back to Denver at the end of the day.

When we got to the hotel, I hid my ring finger as we strode past the desk clerk to a single room. I was woefully unprepared. The only thing I knew about birth control was the rhythm method, which had worked so well for my parents—five times at least. There, in a romantic night of a new and totally undreamed-of physical freedom, Peter and I conceived our son, Clark.

I remember in the morning the waiter in the restaurant warmed our cups with boiling water and dried them off before pouring the steaming coffee.

Back at school in the late winter in Illinois, I was pregnant and terrified. When the term ended in May, I took the California Zephyr back to Denver, where Peter was waiting for me. We talked and worried about what to do, but before we could make any clear decisions or come up with any real plan, Peter had to return to Estes Park, where he had found a job. Driving back through the mountains at night—and probably drunk—Peter crashed his car, but walked away from the wreck unscathed. His narrow escape brought us to the sudden realization about what we both wanted: this child, a marriage, and a life together.

In June 1958 I let go of my anxieties and my fear of commitment. Peter drove down to Denver, and we told our families about the baby. The panic I had been feeling evaporated as soon as we discussed it. Suddenly I felt for the first time that I knew where I belonged. Peter and I moved to the mountains, looking for a place to live and work. What we found was paradise.

We were offered the job of running Fern Lake Lodge in Rocky Mountain National Park by Jim Bishop, the owner of both Fern Lake and Bear Lake Lodge. The only real requirements for the job were that Peter should be able to chop wood and make sure that the water kept flowing through the outdoor pipes that trapped it from the higher elevations, and that I should be able to bake bread and pies in a woodstove. There was no electricity, and part of my job would be to serve lunch to the hikers pausing in their nine-mile hike from Bear Lake Lodge to the moraine on the other side of the national park. In the traditional manner of mountain hospitality, we would, Jim said, serve up homemade lunches, and Peter and I said we could do all of that and more. No problem!

On our eager promises, Jim hired us and put us up the first week at Bear Lake Lodge, at the foot of the mountain trail, while we waited for the snow to melt. Fern Lake Lodge had not been open for a couple of years, since no one wanted to be up there, miles from anywhere, without electricity. We knew it would be just the thing for us. We couldn't wait.

Over grilled buffalo steaks by a roaring fire that first night at Bear Lake, Jim told us the history of Fern Lake. For over fifty years, he said, the lodge, with its twelve surrounding cabins, three wood-burning stoves, featherbeds, and stores of knives and forks and plates for a hundred, had been hosting guests winter and summer. Pack horses brought visitors in with their steamer trunks, snowshoes, skis, and skates. They glided the frozen lake and used crampons and picks to climb the Little Matterhorn, the peak that towered twelve thousand feet above. Flames burned high in the huge fireplaces. In summer there were wildflower hikes and treks to the tundra from the lodge. Some years three chefs manned the stoves.

Over time, the lodge had acquired a certain mystique. Anyone whose name meant something in the lore of the Rocky Mountains had passed through it: the Earl of Dunraven, who hunted in what had previously been the wilderness of Rocky Mountain National Park; F. O. Stanley, who brought his Stanley Steamers into Colorado; Frederick Chapin, who wrote *Mountaineering in Colorado*; and Isabella Bird, who wrote *A Lady's Life in the Rocky Mountains*. Even Enos Mills, one of the founders of the park, who had explored the wilderness for Theodore Roosevelt, came for winter and summer holidays, roughing it in the Rockies.

Fern Lake Lodge had a colorful, deep Colorado history, and we were going to be running this special place.

While we waited for the trails to be clear of snow, the chef at Bear Lake Lodge taught me how to use a woodstove. For those few precious days and nights Peter and I drank the owner's Jim Beam and made love with abandon under the eaves of our bedroom on the top floor of the lodge.

At the end of that week, on July 4, the snow had melted on the trails enough so that we loaded our gear into our backpacks, each carrying nearly fifty pounds, and set out. We hiked the five miles to the top of the grade, where Fern Lake Lodge sat at the edge of a dark blue mountain lake, sparkling and freezing cold. We settled into our cabin, unpacked food and clothes, and made ready for the daytime visitors who would be surprised and pleased to find us there in the mountains. We welcomed them with home-made cherry pies and fresh-baked bread.

I began cooking on this ancient relic of a stove, learning quickly how to manage temperatures. I would bake rolls rather than loaves, and find ways to prepare even exotic Mexican meals with our weekly supply of hamburger and our favorite tortillas. My mother said I must be nauseated by having to cook and bake when I was pregnant, but it never for a minute bothered me.

Peter constructed a "Girl Scout cooler" under the pine trees outside the kitchen, hooking up a pipe to bring freezing spring water from the upper mountain. We bathed in a big tub on the floor of our kitchen, with water pouring from another tub filled with holes and hanging from the ceiling on metal hooks. Water moved into that tub through pipes in a radiator strapped to the back of the living room fireplace and flowing to the kitchen. The evening fires with their flames licking the radiator kept us in hot water every night.

Friends came up the mountain to visit, bringing us fresh avocados and fruit, and sometimes mail. We sang old English and Scots rounds with them in front of the big fireplace in the living room. My family trekked the nine miles of wilderness, my father carrying one end of a pine branch with my mother hanging on to the other end—a fitting metaphor for their marriage. Inside the lodge, Daddy reached down to run his fingers over the rounds of pine on the floor.

"Puncheon," he said, "this is a puncheon floor!" No one else had known, all the others who could see so well.

The scent of pine in the fresh morning air filled my head, and the sound of the axe smacking into the chopping block promised a fire to bake bread and provide warmth. To the sound of night birds, Peter and I made love in the old cabin down by the lake. The comfort of this easy, intelligent man in bed next to me meant I was safe; the sex was sizzling and the days were filled with wood fire and heart's fire; the baby was growing and I was blossoming in some way that I couldn't even fathom. My heart relaxed, perhaps for the first time ever.

There were no tense moments between my parents. My anxieties about performing and practicing and being up to the mark, pleasing both Brico and my father, were banished to the wilderness, relieved by the pleasure I took in my guitar and in my life with my husband, the man I had now loved for many years.

It would be ages before I would again feel as safe and calm and comforted as I did that summer. The real comfort was still far off, and there would be rivers of tears and oceans of booze to travel before I found it. Perhaps I had a glimpse of the future, of the plan that was being worked out for me.

By now I was several months pregnant, and my belly jutted against my steel-faced Guild guitar as I sang to the guests, my voice ringing out across the lake. I ran through all the folk songs I had learned by then—"The Lavender Cowboy," "Ten Thousand

Goddam Cattle," "Maid of Constant Sorrow," and "The Gypsy Rover"—before people headed back down to Bear Lake Lodge at the other end of the trail.

It was romantic in every way.

Peter and I made $300 for the entire summer, and it was just about all we had to our names. After Labor Day we stowed our gear and headed down to Bear Lake and Estes Park again, each carrying a heavy pack, my guitar and our luggage slung across the flanks of the packhorse, winding our way back from our mountain Eden. We left talking excitedly about ways to buy or lease the lodge and make this our life. I felt wholly complete.

But we never lived out our dream. Both Fern Lake Lodge and Bear Lake Lodge would be dismantled from the inside out the following year as part of a government mandate to remove commercial enterprises from the national parks. The old photographs of hikers and skiers in furs and sealskins, the wood-burning stoves from the cabins around the lake, the Coleman lanterns, the quilts and stores and knives and cooking implements and pipes for the mountain spring-fed water supply—every bit of it would be either pillaged or legally hauled down the mountain on pack mules.

My family and I continued to hike up the Fern Lake trail for reunions even after my father died, when there was little left of the lodges but the puncheon floors. I have a photograph someone took of the lodge, deep in snow, some Colorado winter.

It was a dream place and a dream job. If I had been able to find a way to make a life in the mountains doing what I was doing that summer, I would probably still be there.

It still feels to me like paradise lost.

Chapter Six

So Early in the Spring

So early, early in the spring
I shipped on board to serve my king
I left my dearest dear behind
She oftimes swore her heart was mine.

—Traditional, "So Early, Early in the Spring"

On the eighth of January 1959, in the bitter cold of a Colorado winter after twenty-eight hours of labor in the Seventh-Day Adventist Hospital in Boulder, my son, Clark, was born, a perfect, beautiful boy, my little shining light. He had blue eyes and soft red hair and the temperament of an angel.

Peter and I were just starting out in our life together, a young couple content to spend the cold winter huddled in front of our electric heater, happily watching our son grow. We were barely squeaking by financially. I had a job filing papers at the University of Colorado there in Boulder, and Peter was studying at night, delivering newspapers at four in the morning before going off to the university, where he was working on his bachelor's degree in English literature.

I came up with ingenious ways to live within our meager budget. I remember one month spent making steak and kidney pie and freezing it; we had steak and kidney pie for six weeks. I had also started combining sugar and mash into a very fine homebrew as an alternative for the 3.2 horse piss that called itself domestic beer. It was potent stuff, if it got the chance to age; more than one bottle exploded in the closet of our tiny apartment.

At six o'clock on a freezing winter morning in March 1959, I was still huddled down among the covers, luxuriating in those last moments of sleep before I had to feed the baby and get the day started. Peter had returned from delivering his papers and was stomping the snow off his boots and making my morning coffee.

"I just had a thought," Peter said, handing me a big mug of steaming coffee. I sipped it and looked at him gratefully. Coffee was already my second drug of choice.

"What is that?" I asked.

"Why don't you get a job doing something you know how to do? Like singing?"

The suggestion excited and energized me. I called my dad in Denver and through Al Fike, an entertainer he knew, I was able to get an audition at Michael's Pub.

There were three clubs in Boulder at that time—Tulagi's, a relatively unremarkable place to hang out over a few beers; the Sink, a reeking, seedy spot mostly for students who just wanted to get drunk; and Michael's, a pub that served pitchers of 3.2 percent beer and "real Italian pizza." Sometimes you could hear music—an accordion player or maybe a barbershop quartet or some ragtime piano at Michael's. But none of the three clubs had ever featured— or had even thought of featuring—folk music.

The night of the audition I fed Clark his dinner and put him in his father's arms. With the folk songs I had collected and polished ringing in my head, and dressed like a troubadour, with my tight black pants and red silk top that came to my knees, my old roughed-up Guild guitar in its case, I drove down to Michael's Pub in the cold. My hair was in a pixie cut just below my ears, a cut my husband Peter had given me by putting a bowl on my head and me praying as he slid the scissors around my head, that he wouldn't cut off my ears.

The owner, Mike Bisesi, quieted the college kids in the big, smoky room and announced me.

"Surprise! A folksinger will now entertain everyone with her"—he looked over at me with a wink—"folk songs!"

I could hear people ordering more beer or going on with their conversations as I stepped up onto the stage and into the spotlight, my guitar tuned and my heart in my mouth. I waited. And waited a while longer, until the talking quieted down. I suppose they figured they'd better quiet down or I'd never go away, and that after I had sung, they could get back to the business of enjoying a night out.

The smell of beer and pizza filled my nostrils, and the cigarette smoke hovered over the entire room. The sound system was good, and as I started to sing and to play the guitar, the eyes of sixty or so college students began to focus on me, listening to the songs. The crowd would sing along on the choruses of songs they knew, such as "The Gypsy Rover," but otherwise the room was silent except for my voice and guitar. When I finished, thunderous applause filled Michael's. I had to go back for an encore, now no longer nervous but pleased and happy. Mike took my elbow as I came off the stage after the second encore and I was smiling at my apparent success.

There was still loud clapping in the room, and many people were getting up from their tables, coming over to tell me how much they had enjoyed the music. Mike pulled me toward the kitchen in the back.

"First I have to tell you that I absolutely hate folk music!" he said. My face fell. But Mike was not finished.

"You are hired. Five nights a week, three shows a night, a hundred dollars a week. You start tomorrow." He smiled at me, this time with real pleasure.

I was thrilled! I had a job. I would be able to support my family and do what I loved. I felt like the luckiest woman in the world!

I practiced and learned more new songs, listened to recordings, and sought out other people who were doing the same. I had no illusions about my singing or my voice. I knew I could sing well enough when playing the guitar or the piano, but I thought of myself mainly as an interpreter, a teller of stories.

Mike kept hiring me, week after week. He put signs in the windows and ads in the Boulder paper, and the people came to see me. The girl in the tights had broken the barrier. Boulder, Colorado, had a folk music club.

I was, officially, a folksinger.

And I would never have to audition for a job again!

Chapter Seven

The Gilded Garter, the Exodus, and the Excess

'Twas a balmy summer evening
And a goodly crowd was there
That well nigh filled Joe's barroom
At the corner of the square.

—HUGH ANTOINE D'ARCY,
"The Face on the Barroom Floor"

AFTER the Michael's Pub run in Boulder, I was hired for my second job at the Gilded Garter in Central City, Colorado, on Clear Creek Canyon, just up the hill from the then tiny town of Blackhawk. We packed our few belongings (I think everything we owned fit into two or three suitcases) and my big homebrew clay jug and moved deeper into the mountains for the summer. Peter and I found an apartment in Blackhawk, across the road from a barn with a huge Bull Durham sign. I always thought that bull was peering into our apartment with a smile on his hairy face: *It is smart, fashionable, correct, upon all occasions to "roll your own" cigarettes with "Bull"*

Durham tobacco . . . It's the smoke of the service in barracks, camp and field, the smoke of clean-cut man-hood the world over!

Grabbing for purchase on the rocky terrain of the foothills, Central City had been a silver-mining center in the 1860s, and tourists could still explore a number of abandoned mines, riding on the backs of long-eared mules who were used to the dark, scary-looking tunnels. Before my show, we might walk up with Clark in his backpack for drinks and maybe a dinner of roast chicken and fries at the Glory Hole, a bar that livened up the town's three dusty streets. Central City had a crowd of talented kids around my age waiting on tables, washing dishes, ushering at the Opera House. Clark was learning to crawl and we began having friends over for dinners on the deck, spending our free evenings spinning rock-and-roll records on our precious turntable, twirling under the stars, listening to Pete Seeger and Buddy Holly.

In the summer of 1959, you could hear a lot of rock and roll on the radio, and the war was becoming even more of a worry to all of us. More "advisers" were being sent to Vietnam, and there was an active antiwar movement gaining traction at the University of Colorado. Popular music had begun to shift and expand, infused with new elements of folk and country and R&B. Elvis was about to get out of the army and marry Priscilla. Meanwhile, we still listened to Frank Sinatra ("It's a quarter to three, there's no one in the place except you and me"), Johnny Cash, and the Kingston Trio. One of our favorite albums, played over and over on our treasured $33\frac{1}{3}$ rpm record player, was *The Genius of Ray Charles*. We listened to a pianist named Don Shirley, and to a recording of *The Moldau* by Smetana and Respighi's *The Pines of Rome* and *The Fountains of Rome,* which we played at earsplitting volume.

We read James Michener's new book, *Hawaii,* and *Doctor Zhivago*, and of course *Lady Chatterley's Lover,* which had finally been made available in the United States that year. We kept up with the world through newspapers and by listening to the radio. We knew that both Alaska and Hawaii became states, that the Chinese invaded Tibet, and that the Dalai Lama, head of the Buddhist movement in Tibet, escaped to India.

Buddy Holly, born Charles Hardin in Lubbock, Texas, in September 1936, was known as the single most important force in rock and roll. He had died on February 3, 1959, a little under a month before the start of my singing career at Michael's Pub. His death was still being talked about and written about that summer as "the day the music died." His small chartered plane had gone down in a snowstorm in Iowa, killing everyone on board, including his band and the pilot.

Buddy was three years older than I and had been singing with the Crickets, his band, since 1957. I had first heard him on *The Arthur Murray Party* singing "Peggy Sue" when I was home from MacMurray that year. "That'll Be the Day" had been a big hit and put him on *The Ed Sullivan Show,* and in 1958 I heard him sing "Oh Boy," again on *Sullivan.* He was good-looking and slim, with a voice that cut through on the radio, a sexy man in his horn-rimmed glasses.

I have often thought of Buddy and his band on that cold night when I have had to charter planes to get in and out of the cities I play in. This was a terrible piece of news for anyone who was a fan of Holly's, and for anyone at all who had a heart. It hit me very hard; I felt nauseated and frightened when I heard the news.

In Central City, I held down two jobs—waiting tables during the day at the Tollgate Hotel and Bar in town and singing at the Gilded Garter at night. Peter had a job at a gas station until he got into a fight with the guy who owned the place and got fired. We didn't watch television; in fact, we didn't have the money to buy a TV. Gas cost 25 cents a gallon and a loaf of bread was about 20 cents, although I was still baking most of our bread. Nylons were a buck a pair, but I mostly wore tights in the winter and went bare legged in the summer. I had yet to burn my bra, but that was coming. You could get a radio for fifteen dollars, and it cost 4 cents to send my folks a letter from Blackhawk to Denver.

On the floor of the Teller House in Central City, a few doors down from the Gilded Garter, is painted "The Face on the Barroom Floor," which you could look down at or step over before they blocked it off with a silken rope. It was said to have been painted by a heartsick man and was inspired by a poem of Hugh Antoine D'Arcy about a man who crawled into the bar drunk and offered to paint a picture of the woman who had done him wrong. After a night of singing at the Gilded Garter, I would meet friends at the Teller House bar—sometimes Terry Williams, who taught English at the Colorado School of Mines in Golden, and his wife, Nancy, and often Angelo Di Benedetto, a jeweler and well-known artist who made me a gorgeous cast silver bracelet with an onyx stone. We would drink a lot and gaze at the painting on the floor through a melancholy haze of alcohol. I heard the story of Baby Doe Tabor, from Leadville, who had married Horace Tabor and become a millionaire before losing everything when Horace died amid the downturn in the silver market at the turn of the century. She lived for thirty-five years in a shack on the Matchless Mine property until she died of a heart attack during a heavy snowstorm.

At the Gilded Garter I opened for a rock-and-roll singer named Donna St. Thomas. It was a strange set. I came out in my tights and Robin Hood silk top to sing "The Gypsy Rover," "Maid of Constant Sorrow," and other songs for an hour, followed by a short break where people could order more drinks. Then Donna sang "Rock Around the Clock," "Blue Suede Shoes," and "Heartbreak Hotel," shaking her body and showing off her well-endowed figure. Donna was married to Warren St. Thomas, who owned both the Gilded Garter and the premier strip joint in Denver, the Tropics, where a remarkable woman who called herself Tempest Storm was taking off her clothes and creating quite a stir. One

Sunday night Peter and I got Clark a babysitter and went down to Denver to see Tempest Storm's show.

The redheaded Tempest Storm was known as the "girl with the fabulous front." I expected her show to be tacky, even a little seedy, but Tempest put on a pretty classy act. She was also gorgeous and carried herself elegantly onstage. She didn't take all her clothes off at once, leaving tantalizing remnants and using her fingers to suggest total nudity as she shivered off the shawl, shoes, scarf, and another shawl, revealing smooth, silken skin and, finally, most of her fabulous front. I had never seen a woman naked, except myself in the mirror when I was trying to figure out why *I* did not have a fabulous front! We went to meet her after the show, and I could barely speak. She was dressed demurely, and I remember thinking that *she* wouldn't have to sing for her supper, ever.

Still, I had come to love singing for my supper and was happy to spend the summer at the Gilded Garter. I didn't know it then, but one of the people who would come to hear me in Central City was a young man from Minnesota named Robert Zimmerman. He sang a lot of Woody Guthrie blues, and no one had ever heard of him.

eAFTER our return to Boulder, with Peter in his last year of studying for his bachelor's degree, I got my third professional gig at the Exodus in Denver, around the corner from Antonia Brico's sprawling stone studio, where I had spent so many years studying the piano. Hal Neustaedter had opened the club in 1958, and by the time I worked there for the first time, in the fall of 1959, it was *the* club in the Rockies for folk music.

I drove a long, dark forty miles every night from our house in Boulder to get to the Exodus. Often I had quite a few drinks in me, especially on the way home after a show. I was beginning to

feel that hollow place in my heart that told me I had the same problem as my father, but still I believed I could control it. After all, at
least I could see, I would tell myself, rationalizing that it was the
blindness that made my father lose control when he drank. Sometimes I was very drunk, drunk enough that I had to keep one eye
closed to make sure I was focusing on the road. One friend of mine
had driven off that highway on a dark night at a very high speed
and was paralyzed as a result. Another had been sideswiped at midnight, and his girlfriend, a cellist from Brico's orchestra who was in
the passenger seat, had been killed.

At the Exodus, the roster included a combination of better-
known singers, including Bob Gibson, the Tarriers, and Josh White.
I got to listen to and learn from seasoned touring professionals,
masters of their art and craft. It was thrilling, and at times very
scary.

One of the first groups I worked with was the Tarriers, a
group that included Eric Weissberg, Bob Carey, and Clarence
Cooper. Bob Carey was a neat-looking man with a slight build—
not more than five foot six—who always had a smile on his face.
I liked Bob—he was basically a gentle man, and was always sober
enough, though later he fought a terrible battle with drugs. He
lived on the edge and went over, as many would as the years went
along. His body would be discovered in 1976 on a park bench in
New York, a victim of drugs and alcohol.

The Tarriers originally consisted of Bob Carey, Alan Arkin
(the great film actor who would later star in *The Russians Are Coming, the Russians Are Coming*), and Erik Darling. They had started in
1956 and landed a big hit on the radio that year with "The Banana
Boat Song."

In the second week of my job at the Exodus, I worked with
Bob Gibson. I had listened to his albums in high school and knew
his rich, clear tenor and engaging playing well. I fell in love with
Bob's finger-picking wizardry, so crisp and free.

Bob was in his late twenties. He stuck out his hand to shake mine, and I saw a cute guy with sparkling eyes, his hair cut short like the Kingston Trio's. He looked a bit like James Cagney, with the same sort of offset, crooked smile.

A Brooklyn-born folksinger and guitar player, Bob had heard Pete Seeger for the first time in 1953. He was inspired to use his rent money to buy a banjo and quickly started singing in Florida at local clubs, then made his way to the Green Door in Michigan City, Indiana, fifty miles from Chicago. He got a job at the Offbeat, a folk music club in Chicago, singing folk songs about boat captains and seafarers, accompanying himself on the banjo.

When Albert Grossman and Alan Ribback, two music-loving entrepreneurial young guys from Chicago, opened the Gate of Horn in 1956, they hired Gibson for an eleven-month run at the new club. By the end of his run, Gibson had graduated from opening act to main attraction. He became a star in Chicago and earned himself singing engagements at clubs around the country, a record contract, and a management contract with Albert Grossman. Bob was Grossman's first client. (Later Grossman would manage Peter, Paul and Mary, Bob Dylan, Jimi Hendrix, and Janis Joplin.) After his long run at the Gate of Horn, Gibson would almost single-handedly start the revival of folk music in Chicago.

Bob's energy was razor sharp; perhaps it had something to do with the speed he took and the booze he drank. But Gibson's bad habits did not seem to be a handicap when I knew him. We would knock a few back, then have a good laugh about drinking too much and whether or not I was sober enough to drive home. His wit was cutting but always backed up with a gentleness that softened its impact. He was eight years older than me, and by the time I met him he was already a force of the folk revival as well as a touring powerhouse.

At the Exodus, where I opened for him, he would haul out his banjo, open his mouth, and charm the birds out of the trees.

He was successful, a great force on the stage. Bob would become addicted to heroin in the mid-sixties and would spend the rest of the sixties and seventies trying to get clean. But when I met him, Gibson was golden.

Bob would listen to me every night we played together at the Exodus, and he would offer me encouragement afterward.

"You are a fine performer and you have a great career in front of you," he would tell me. "You just gotta be patient, that's all, and don't be afraid of the work." He gave me his enchanting grin. "And try to smile, just a little?"

He had a point; I was grim, tight-lipped, all business, wanting to get the story told. The smile would take me a thousand miles, and Gibson knew it. "You gotta smile! You're killing 'em with all those serious songs. Make 'em listen, give 'em contrast!"

I would sing "The Great Selchie of Shule Skerry," which I had learned from one of the albums of Scottish ballads I had started collecting in high school. It was a strange, otherworldly story of a seal, a hunter, and the woman who bears the seal's child:

> *In Norway there sits a maid*
> *"By loo, my babe," this maid begins*
> *"Little know I my child's father*
> *Or if land or sea he's dwellin' in."*

Bob would weep whenever I got to the part where the hunter shoots the baby Selchie and the father. When we finished our engagement at the Exodus, he went back to Chicago, where he told Alan Ribback about me and the song—and Alan booked me for six weeks at the Gate of Horn.

Bob's role in establishing the singer-songwriter tradition is never properly acknowledged. His eye for talent, his unquestionable taste in songs, his enthusiasm, even his friendships—with

Albert Grossman, with Odetta, with Joan Baez, with me—have slid somehow under the radar. His influence and insight have earned him a place in the folk music pantheon.

Back at the Exodus in the winter of 1959, I was opening for Josh White. Josh had it all: good looks, genuine charm, a great sense of humor, an incredibly seductive energy, and a rollicking, all-embracing laugh that seemed to take in the whole room and the whole world. He had snow-white teeth and smiled much of the time in spite of a fungus in his fingernails that caused him pain on a regular basis. He seemed to carry the sun around with him, and if you were anywhere near him you felt that warmth.

The stage at the Exodus was set in the middle of the room, with the audience in front of you as you sang, and the bar behind you. I would start the first of three shows a night, six nights a week, still dressed in my tights and Robin Hood top and boots, my hair long and straight, wearing practically no makeup. The audience was friendly and welcoming, and I finished with a flourish to the sound of great applause.

In the intermission after my set, waiters swirled through, bearing pitchers of 3.2 beer, baskets of curly french fries, burgers, and big whopping bowls of chips with jalapeño dip. Then Hal Neustaedter, the owner, announced Josh White. The room hushed when Josh stepped onto the stage, all eyes watching him through the silvery cigarette smoke and drifting wisps from the candles that burned on each table. He was an established star, and the audience was already in awe of him.

Josh would start his show with a big, resounding chord on his guitar and launch into "St. James Infirmary." With another ringing chord he would take us into the morgue, show us the hovering figures, the long white table, the body under a sheet, "so cold, so still, so dead." I was totally mesmerized.

More than twice my age, Josh had lived a rich life, filled with controversy. He had been blacklisted during the fifties and for many years had had a hard time getting work, but he was now recording for Elektra Records and experiencing a real resurgence of popularity. I knew his recordings well, but nothing prepared me for his live performances.

He was tall, powerful, and impressive, and a natural storyteller; then Josh took you with him into "One Meatball," a song from the Depression. His songs came alive in his one-man theater performance. By the third song he would be drenched with sweat, an unlit cigarette behind his ear or a lit one stuck onto the end of one of his guitar strings at the neck of his guitar—a trick I would immediately copy. His shirtfront would be open to the third button (which I did not copy).

Later I would hear Billie Holiday's famous version of "Strange Fruit," and I would hear Odetta sing it, but it was Josh who introduced me to this powerful song, there at the Exodus. The song tells the story of a lynching, and Josh, a black man born and raised in Greenville, South Carolina, in the Jim Crow South, would sing it with the power of someone who had been there and probably seen it happen.

Southern trees bear a strange fruit,
Blood on the leaves and blood at the root.

Josh had been a confidant of Franklin D. Roosevelt, and the Roosevelts were godparents to his son, Josh junior. White sang at Roosevelt's inauguration and was the first African American to sing command performances at the White House. The Roosevelts often invited him to their home in Hyde Park, New York, and FDR appointed him a goodwill ambassador. Eleanor Roosevelt took Josh to Sweden with her for an international conference after World War II. The Swedes asked Josh to sing "Strange Fruit," but he declined, saying that he did not want to talk about the racism in America while he was a guest outside his country.

Josh tried to teach me what he could about singing, about the life that I would lead if I continued down this road. We would drink together between shows. I told him, probably the first time I told anyone, that I was afraid of my drinking.

"The travel," he used to say, "will probably kill you before the whiskey does!" He seemed so sure.

When Josh broke a string, he would put the guitar behind his back and play "Summertime" on it backward, while he put on a new string. He'd finish with a flourish, the guitar, new string and all, suddenly in front of him. You knew you had seen something wonderful if you were lucky enough to witness one of these impromptu repairs. The thing is, he would do that at each show, and I never did figure out how he managed to get that string to break night after night!

From that time on, Josh took me under his wing, telling promoters about me, getting me on shows he was doing around the country. I owe Josh so much, and won't be able to pay him back, except by trying to do the same for some other artist.

*E*VERYWHERE I worked, I listened, watched, and learned from other artists, honing my own performances. I also learned how to put on a good show after I'd been drinking all night; I learned just when to stop, because when I drank too much I couldn't sing. I had started having depressions again and thoughts of suicide after Clark was born, and for a long time I thought the drinking relieved them. It would be years before I realized the drinking deepened them.

But work always seemed to save me, and now I was making my bones, learning my craft, becoming steady on my feet as a performer, and starting to hold my own.

In January 1960 I got an offer to sing at the Limelight, a music and supper club in Aspen, Colorado, for a month, working with the Smothers Brothers. Peter drove me up, helped me get settled into the gingerbread house on Main Street where the owners would be putting me up, then turned around and drove back down to Boulder. It was my first real time away from my marriage, and I would miss Peter and Clark. I took our dog, Kolya, a husky, who loved the snow and would walk me to the club every night and wait outside, sleeping in a snow circle and greeting everyone who came to the door of the club. I got to know Dick and Tommy Smothers well over those weeks and would often work with them in the future.

The Smothers Brothers had been born on Governor's Island, off Manhattan, two years apart, Tom in 1937, Dick in 1939, the year I was born. Their comedy act consisted of milking each other's weaknesses and strengths, on and off the stage. That first night I met them at the Limelight I was nervous about working with these new strangers, but I loved them from the start. Standing at the back of the club near the bar as they did their turn, I giggled and guffawed at their antics while Quinn, the club's bartender and sometime cook, who once chased Tommy with a cleaver through the kitchen in a drunken rage, smiled and shook up the martinis and the Black Russians, which I used to take the chill off the cold nights in the mountains. Tom and Dick made gentle fun of me from the stage, me with my engineer's boots and with my husky who followed me to work every night. They mocked my seemingly endless songs with, as Tom would tell me later, "every verse that was ever written, boring the bejesus out of the worn-out skiers!" They twinkled with fun at their own humor, and seemed on and off the stage to have the same semi-taunting relationship. They were young, funny, and easy to be with, and I always thought of them with affection. Once Tom was driving back from Denver when he ran into a deer on the highway; they hauled back the carcass, which

Quinn butchered, and we shared fresh sautéed venison liver. I took off my boots and dug in, loving every bite.

AFTER a month, I returned to Boulder, to my life with my husband, who had been pulling double duty as dad and student. On a ski trip in February I took a bad fall and had to have surgery for a double spiral fracture, spending a week in the hospital. Back at home I hobbled around on crutches, but took more weeks of work at the Exodus and at Michael's Pub. Peter and I managed the duties of child care, physical therapy, and breadwinning together.

I always knew Peter was brilliant. After all, it was he who'd suggested I get a job singing! If it hadn't been for Peter, I might still be filing papers at the University of Colorado. So I was not surprised when in May 1960, graduating with his B.A., he was awarded a teaching fellowship at the University of Connecticut. That same week, I received an offer to work for six weeks during the summer at the Gate of Horn in Chicago, and we were offered the fire watch at Twin Sisters, a pair of peaks in Rocky Mountain National Park. A plethora of opportunities! Our heads were spinning.

We had a lot to think about. We packed a lunch and drove out to one of our favorite spots in the mountains, a green meadow overlooking Genesee Park outside of Denver. I was still in the heavy cast I would be wearing for the next three months and hobbled over the rough terrain to the picnic table. From there, we looked out at an entire range of glorious mountains in front of us as we ate lunch, Clark crawling at our feet. We talked about what we might do about our futures.

I remember crimson paintbrush and blue and lavender columbine swaying among the mountain grasses, and it felt as if these familiar friends were saying goodbye to us. The truth was, we were headed out of this world of mountains and majesty. We both knew we could not really take the fire watch at Twin Sisters; if there was a fire or any other emergency at the Twin Sisters site, with my leg in a cast I might be more of a burden than a help, and hinder our chances of getting to safety with our baby. And while I wanted to stay in Colorado, I also wanted to sing at the Gate of Horn. We said nothing for a while, and then finished our lunches and made our way back to Boulder to start packing. He would go to Storrs, for Peter's job, and on the way spend the summer in Chicago, where I would continue my metamorphosis into a folksinger.

Today, on my trips to Colorado, going up to Vail from Denver, or back to Berthoud or Estes Park, I pass that park often. As you drive over a rise in the highway, suddenly the mountains appear in front of you. Often you can see a herd of buffalo a little farther down the hill, and then there are the picnic tables. I always look, and I always wonder how our lives would have turned out if we had stayed in those glorious mountains where my heart still yearns to be.

But by then, the circus had begun and there would be no turning back.

Chapter Eight

Gates of Horn and Ivory

And the ship, the black freighter
Turns around in the harbor
Shooting guns from her bow.

—Kurt Weill and Bertolt Brecht
(translated by Marc Blitzstein), "Pirate Jenny"

Summer in Chicago, 1960. A big, sprawling apartment on the lake, on the South Side, a sublet from friends of the owners of the Gate of Horn. When Peter and I walked into this place our eyes nearly popped out. It was huge, luxurious, on the lake, and near the University of Chicago. It was only a few miles from downtown Chicago and the club where I would be working.

The Windy City was hot as hell in the summer but even warmer with appreciation for artists and musicians, a real center of art, music, and culture. Chicago had harbored this richness going back more than a half century, when the World's Fair of 1893 had brought together artists, architects, and visionaries of every kind. The city became a magnet for talent and boasted world-class theaters and a distinguished opera house. The lakefront, chosen for the site of the fair by Frederick Law Olmsted, offered a gleaming vista of white sails, green parks, and public gardens, with the Art Institute of Chicago and Louis Sullivan buildings strung along a winding boulevard of fine shops. There could hardly have been a better place to have a folk club where the music could flourish.

Albert Grossman and Alan Ribback, both Chicago natives, founded the Gate of Horn in 1956. I would get to know both men well over those first years of working at the club, and I liked them both enormously. The club was a true gathering place for musical greatness and represented the tastes of the two owners.

Alan and Albert told me that the name of the club came from the musings of Penelope in *The Odyssey*, who has a dream that she relates to a stranger:

> ". . . I dreamed of two gates, a gate of horn and a gate of ivory. I was told that dreams which make it through the gate of horn are the dreams that can come true."

The Gate would help many of my dreams come true.

My first night at the Gate, I was still in a cast, and swung through the entrance on my crutches. Alan's skeptical frown greeted me. After my first show, however, his face lit up with a smile.

"You can sing here in a cast anytime," he told me, "as long as you sing 'The Great Selchie'!" It was his favorite song, and for many seasons he would insist I include it in my shows.

Afterward, Alan and I shook hands on my salary: $125 a week. The following year he had me back at the Gate for $250 a week. He was honest, and a handshake was all it took.

Alan knew what he liked and was generous to a fault. He had a limp from a childhood bout of polio. He introduced me to his Chicago friends, among them the actor Severn Darden from Second City; Michael Flanders and Donald Swann, the English comedy duo, who came through Chicago to perform; Nelson Algren, who wrote *The Man with the Golden Arm*; Barbara Siegel, who owned Barbara's Bookstore and became a friend; and other club owners. The journalist Studs Terkel became a friend when he first interviewed me during an appearance at the Gate; Norm Pellegrini at WFMT put me on his radio show often when I worked at the club; Roy Leonard made sure folk music got on the airwaves in the Windy City; Ken Ehrlich produced a television program with the Canadian folksinger Leonard Cohen and me and would take the knowledge he gained from *Midnight Special* and *Soundstage* in Chicago all the way to the Grammys, which he has produced for decades.

Alan regaled me with his intelligence and passion—for the music as well as the politics of the times. I learned a great deal from Alan, and through him I met and worked with some wonderful artists, from Theo Bikel and Sonny Terry to Cynthia Gooding, Odetta, and the South African singer Miriam Makeba. These were experiences that would help my life as well as my career in the folk music community into which I was being initiated, where I began to find my musical place.

Albert Grossman appeared only from time to time at the Gate. He was the traveling partner, flying even then between New York, L.A., and Chicago, looking for artists to hire and, sometimes, to manage. I always liked Grossman and appreciated having a drink with him on his visits to Chicago, sharing his quiet, subtle humor. Some nights after my shows we would walk the windy streets of the Near North Side, talking or harmonizing on old sea chanties. I sometimes glanced over at Grossman as he spoke about all the artists he was looking to manage and all the groups he wanted to start, and he seemed to me like a barracuda waiting to pounce. (Bob Dylan, who first met Grossman at Gerde's Folk City in New York and would become one of his first management clients, said Grossman looked like Sydney Greenstreet in *The Maltese Falcon*.)

It was at the Gate of Horn, in that little club in the center of

Chicago, that I began to drink in a brew of diverse musical sources and genres and appreciate musical stories from different times and cultures.

*T*HAT first gig, I opened for Will Holt and his wife, Dolly Jonah. Will was always dressed to the nines in a tailored suit, a tie, and a crisp white shirt, and he wore his close-cropped hair neatly combed. He would pull out my chair for me, or hand me the crutch I was still using. I thought he was daring and amazing. Will and Dolly's repertoire was wide-ranging. In the same set they might sing a Kurt Weill song, perhaps "Pirate Jenny," and then "Lemon Tree," a song that Will had written and Peter, Paul and Mary would make a standard. "Raspberries, Strawberries" was another of his compositions, which had been a hit for the Kingston Trio. Then he might sing "Streets of Laredo," and Dolly might do a heart-wrenching version of "Surabaya Johnny" from Kurt Weill's *Happy End*. I loved to hear Dolly sing this song. The lights framed her heart-shaped face in white while the rest of her body disappeared into the cigarette smoke and soft lighting. She staggered on her high black heels at the end, teetering toward the barstool that served as a chair on the stage behind her. She would kind of collapse and reach for her drink as the applause rose, and then toss back the contents of her glass and take a bow. It was all very startling and dramatic. Will would let her cool her heels, finishing the set with "The Golden Apples of the Sun," a song based on a William Butler Yeats poem, "The Song of Wandering Aengus."

Dolly would say, as I spun out the tenth or twentieth verse to a seemingly endless ballad, "When are you going to find some up-tempo material? The audience is dying here!" I thought they were merely mesmerized! But I did start, when I was working with Dolly and Will, to take some of the advice that Bob Gibson had already given me to lighten up a little. Still, Dolly would have to sit through a lot more long, sorrowful songs about drowned maidens and silver daggers.

Will had begun his career in the 1950s, and by the time I worked with him he had made a couple of records for Stinson—*The Will Holt Concert* and *Pills to Purge Melancholy*, the latter a collection of happy-go-lucky mood-changing songs about therapy and self-help. Will had studied at Exeter and also at the School for American Minstrels in Aspen, Colorado. The school was started by the English countertenor Richard Dyer-Bennett, who recorded beautiful folk songs in a clear, vibratoless voice—and had I known, I would have tried to get over Independence Pass from Denver to study with him in Aspen.

Will and Dolly became my friends. One of the things I learned from Will was that you could protest and be a force of change while looking dapper, being elegant, and having manners. You could cut like steel, sting like a wasp, go for the jugular with language, style, wit, and music while wearing a suit and tie.

That first summer at the Gate of Horn reinforced the importance of my life with my son and my husband. The years to come would be harder, as I began to travel on my own, sleeping in strange hotels, traveling all over the country, making my nights and my days as tolerable as I could, with one-night stands and fair-weather friends.

But in the summer of 1960, in the thrill of my fourth truly grown-up, professional engagement, I went home to my husband and my baby every night, and it was heavenly—a loving and settled time. Sometimes Peter and I could find a babysitter and he would come to the Gate to watch me work. If we had been able to continue sharing our worries and our pleasures, our marriage might have stood the test of time.

Chapter Nine

Gerde's, the Village Gate, and the Folk Blitz: Joan, Mary, Bob, Carolyn, and Richard

Here's to you, my ramblin' boy
May all your ramblin' bring you joy

—Tom Paxton, "Ramblin' Boy"

By 1960, I was a regular on the folk circuit. The Exodus, the Gate of Horn, Michael's Pub, and the Gilded Garter had put me on the folk music map. I could earn a decent living, and Peter and I were both on upward paths in our careers.

In August we traveled to Westchester, New York, for Peter's brother Gary's wedding to Minky (Mary Anne) Goodman. My most vivid memory (I was still in a cast from toes to hip) was meeting Ed Sullivan at the reception. We danced in the enormous, rose-strewn tent behind the Goodman mansion in Westchester. I drank a good deal, and when I fell into the pool, soaking my cast, it was Ed Sullivan who bent over gallantly and pulled me out.

After the wedding, Peter, Clark, and I headed to the University of Connecticut. Our happy little family settled quickly into the lush, rolling hills forty minutes east of Hartford.

Clark was walking, talking, beginning to name the birds and to sing a little bit. I would set my guitar in his lap and watch him giggle as he ran his hands over the strings, singing.

"I like to sing Mommy songs," he would say. Clark knew a lot of the words to songs like "O Daddy Be Gay" and "The Gypsy Rover." He could hum along on most of them. I knew from the time he was two that he could sing. He had the family gene!

While Peter taught at the university, I would leave Storrs to go out on the road, to Denver, Chicago, Boston, Washington, D.C., St. Louis, and Canada. We made friends in Storrs—some students, teachers, some couples—and really had a very good life there, though I was traveling much of the time.

I knew, as I crossed the country, that I was one of the very few women singing folk music professionally at that time. Judy Henske, Carolyn Hester, Jo Mapes, and Cynthia Gooding were making recordings and singing in the clubs as well.

And now it seemed that everywhere I went I heard about Joan Baez. Joan's was a heart-wrenching, glorious voice. She chose mostly traditional songs. The photograph on the cover of her first album captured the essence of the gleaming, dark-haired queen of the folk movement. There was that hurt in her eyes, and her voice soared like saints rising.

Bob Gibson was the first person to tell me about Joan. He had heard her in Boston, where she had begun singing, and described her to me: "Joan Baez is bare feet, three chords, and a terrified attitude!" In 1959 Bob called Albert Grossman, who along with George Wein, Pete Seeger, and Theo Bikel was creating what would become the Newport Folk Festival. Bob told Grossman that Joan would be perfect for the new venue. Robert Shelton of the *New York Times* was at first unconvinced that a big folk festival would go down well with the public. But that summer in Rhode Island, Grossman told Shelton, "The American public is like Sleeping Beauty, waiting to be kissed awake by the prince of folk music."

Joan's appearance at Newport caused a huge sensation. She sang "The Four Marys" as well as an a cappella version of "We Shall Overcome." Her performance was otherworldly, startling, unlike anything folk music fans had known. Grossman promptly took Joan under his wing, escorting her to Columbia Records to see John Hammond, the legendary producer who had discovered Billie Holiday and Benny Goodman, among many others. Joan found the company (and, she said, John Hammond) too slick for her. Then Albert introduced Joan to Maynard Solomon at Vanguard. Joan felt Maynard, and the label, were more akin to her style. Vanguard released Joan's album that year and couldn't press enough vinyl to fill the orders. Her name was on the lips of every promoter in the business. I was playing the same circuit, but making a record had never crossed my mind. To me, records were for learning songs.

Like most Americans who had read about Joan Baez in *Time* magazine, I knew a great deal about her personal life and her politics before I ever met her. I knew that Joan had been born on January 9, 1941. Her mom, whom all of us who are her friends still call "Big Joan," is Scot, and her father, Al, a physicist, was of Mexican descent. The family moved from New York to California, where Joan was raised with her two sisters, Pauline and Mimi. The family became Quakers when Joan was in her teens. I listened to her record, fainting with admiration.

My little book of income shows that during the year 1961 I worked at the Gate of Horn from January 2 to January 29 and made $600. I worked through my mother's birthday, through my brother Denver's birthday. I stayed at the Cass Hotel, where I slept half the day and worked half the night.

Odetta was a big part of the folk revival; her voice, her presence, those muumuus in silks and satins, in shades of blue and green and fuchsia that seemed to illuminate her ebony face, a face full of light and beauty. She had a smile that took in the entire room, and she seemed to embrace the entire world. I saw in her the promise of a better world for women, for singers, for blacks, for children, for everyone. She seemed, in her choice of songs and in her life, to be someone you could follow anywhere and she would never, never disappoint you. The 1960s, and the folk movement in its entirety, would have been less than what they were without Odetta. I believe that if we had a leader, a clarion call to arms, in the service of humanity, it was in the voice of this amazing woman.

The first time I saw her, she was on the bill at the Gate of Horn the week before I opened, but I got to Chicago in time to see her show. Her performance swept me away. She walked onto the stage dressed in green silk, and I could smell the fragrance of whatever she was wearing, some exotic perfume. She took over every corner of the room with her energy and that powerful voice. She sang big, completely embracing songs, including "He's Got the Whole World in His Hands," "The Midnight Special," "We Shall Overcome," a terrifying song called "Gallows Tree," and "All the Pretty Little Horses." I listened that night as she, too, sang "Strange Fruit," and I wept when I heard it.

Odetta had recorded many of these songs for her 1957 *Gate of Horn* album. She was a favorite of Alan Ribback and in fact of the whole city of Chicago. I drew inspiration from her every time I saw her perform. Martin Luther King Jr. had called Odetta the "queen of folk music" (though he was also a good friend of the other queen, Joan Baez).

IN my gig that January at the Gate of Horn that I would work again with the Tarriers, who had made a change in personnel. Bob Carey was out and Marshall Brickman was in. Eric Weissberg was still in the group, he on whom I had developed a terrible crush when we worked together at the Exodus. It went nowhere then, but always made seeing him a sweet experience. He is a fantastic musician, a guitarist and banjo player, with a thick head of hair (still!) and a solid, reassuring demeanor. He has a smile that is usually slow in coming but is worth waiting for. There was always something held back about Eric; he never made advances or said things that led you to believe he was sexually predatory, and a girl can tell, believe me. I have always found him attractive, and often ask him if all the girls were as wild about him as I was. He just smiles without divulging a thing, but I think that he is flattered by the suggestion, and that I am not so far off the mark.

Marshall Brickman was a tall, good-looking, and musically impressive twenty-three-year-old who played beautiful banjo alongside Eric. He was Eric's oldest friend from New York and had a sweet, deep baritone voice. I liked his silences as well as his quick and facile wit. Marshall never bought a laugh at your expense. He would go on to play banjo with John Phillips in the New Journeymen (before John started the Mamas and the Papas) and then write for television on shows that included *Candid Camera*, *The Tonight Show*, and *The Dick Cavett Show*. He then spent many years writing Woody Allen movies. More recently he wrote the books for *Jersey Boys* as well as *The Addams Family* on Broadway. Marshall, Eric, and I have remained friends for more than fifty years.

Every day I look at a color photograph of Eric Weissberg and Marshall Brickman, both playing the banjo. It's a cover of an Elektra album they made later in the sixties called *New Dimensions in Banjo and Bluegrass*. Standing beside them under a spreading chestnut tree in Central Park is my son, Clark, then about seven years old and looking up at these amazing musicians with wonder in his eyes. He loved their music, and loved being with them while they played.

HOME to Connecticut after my four weeks in Chicago, I settled in with Peter and my baby. We were now in our farmhouse in Storrs, Connecticut, and after a couple of weeks of solace and silence I headed back down to New York to work for two weeks at Gerde's Folk City, the center of the folk music boom in Greenwich Village.

The club originally had been a pizza joint at West Fourth and Bleecker streets, near New York University. Just like Michael Bisesi at Michael's Pub, where I'd had my start two years before, Mike Porco, the owner, had served pizza, pasta, and booze and had no entertainment—until Charlie Rothschild and Izzy Young convinced him to start hiring folksingers to perform. Charlie took over the folk music bookings at Gerde's in 1961, and it was Charlie who got Porco to hire Bob Dylan for his first gig at the club.

I would have a long relationship with Charlie over the years. He looked a little like a walrus, with his bright eyes, round face, and handlebar mustache. He had a big smile, a bigger heart, and great taste in music. He had an ability to spot talent and take care of it. As my road manager and agent for a few years, it was Charlie who drove me to the dates, settled the finances, took care of transportation, and at times made me crazy, as any good road manager will do to almost any artist from time to time. He had a quality that I always felt needed protecting, in spite of his gruff manner. Once, on his birthday, one of the musicians in our group shoved a cream pie in Charlie's face as a joke. Charlie took it like a champ; I fired the guy who threw the pie the next day.

It seems to me that *everyone* was at Gerde's when I got there in February 1961: Joan Baez; Cisco Houston, a great singer and a friend of Pete Seeger's and Woody Guthrie's who had been on the New York folk scene and played with the Almanacs (Cisco would be dead of cancer within a month of our meeting); thirteen-year-old Arlo Guthrie; and Eric Weissberg.

The first night at Gerde's I met Ramblin' Jack Elliott. He and I were sharing the bill. He sported a cowboy hat and rough-out Justin boots, and he wore his hair long and curly. His Stetson came down over his eyes, and around his neck was a little flowered cotton scarf. He stuck out his hand when we met and said "Howdy," like some hand on a Colorado ranch. But something in his voice gave away his origins in Brooklyn, New York. Born Elliott Charles Adnopoz, he was the son of a New York doctor who would have liked his son to be a doctor, too. There was a sweetness and gentleness about him.

I watched from the bar as Jack wound that audience at Gerde's around his little finger with charm and talent. He sang "Talking Merchant Marine," a Woody Guthrie song about a merchant sailor who goes into the navy during World War II, and then he did a few more songs. He bowed deeply before he came back to the bar to join me. He doffed his hat, flashed a beautiful smile, shook out his curly hair, and settled down to drink me under the table. I liked him immediately. He was friendly, and boy, could he hold his booze. He also noticed that I could not, and was gentleman enough not to mention it.

Ramblin' Jack could finger-pick like mad. He was a master of "Travis picking," the style named after Merle Travis, who invented the rolling thumb-and-forefinger technique now used by many strummers. Jack and Dylan met in Minnesota and Jack seemed to loom as large in Dylan's life as Woody Guthrie had in Jack's own (in fact, Jack was at Woody's side for a few years at the end of his life, even taking care of him at the hospital when Woody was dying of Huntington's disease). Some people even referred to Dylan as "Jack Elliott's kid," because he sang the same Guthrie blues Jack performed. But soon Dylan began to produce earth-shattering songs, making it clear that he was not just Ramblin' Jack's kid but a force in his own right—a true original.

I also met Peter Yarrow at Gerde's. I would see him around clubs in the Village, guitar under his arm, a singular, thin man with a sweet voice, searching, serious, and earnest. One night when I couldn't drive home—because of the weather or being too drunk, I don't recall—he took me under his wing.

"Come home with me," he said, "it will thrill my mother, she loves you!" Peter drove me to the apartment where he lived with his parents and I slept soundly in the guest room. A few nights later his mother sent my pajamas down to Gerde's in a little package. It caused a bit of talk, which Peter and I still have a chuckle over.

TALL, willow-thin, with straight blond hair falling around her face, Mary Travers was often at Gerde's, shining like a light among the other ragged folkies who were dressed, it seemed, in wrinkled clothes of indeterminate origin (except Dylan, who seemed to have calculated the impact of his outfits). Mary would join all of us as we talked about the war, the politics of the day, the candidates, the problems in the country. Occasionally she would sing along with a guitar picker. She was striking, with a totally unique, off-balance beauty, and she seemed to dance when she walked. I remember singing harmony with her behind Ramblin' Jack one night, with Cisco Houston and Carolyn Hester chiming in. Mary was a harmonic dream, finding all the right notes and making us sound better than we might have otherwise.

In the late spring of 1961, Albert Grossman had chosen Mary as the ideal person to fill out the trio he was assembling with Noel "Paul" Stookey and Peter Yarrow. The chemistry was immediate, and the album *Peter, Paul and Mary* appeared in stores in no time, it seemed. By 1962, "Lemon Tree" and "If I Had a Hammer" were playing on the radio and the trio was a worldwide phenomenon.

I saw Mary often over the fifty years we knew each other— at concerts, at festivals, and in our homes. Sometimes we would talk on the telephone or in person, and we had rambling discussions about life and love and work, the books we were reading, the books we were writing or intending to write. I met her daughters, Erika and Alicia, and visited with her and Ethan, her fourth husband, in New York and at her home in Connecticut. The rooms in Mary's homes were always lined from floor to ceiling with books,

books, books. She usually had a book in her hand—politics, biography, poetry, economics, history, Keynes, Schlesinger, Marx, Dostoevsky, Byron, Yeats. She usually had a particular issue on her mind, some axe to grind.

Mary grew up in Greenwich Village with parents who were journalists and organizers for the Newspaper Guild trade union. She sat at the feet of Pete Seeger and Woody Guthrie, attended the Little Red School House, and left school when she was in eleventh grade to sing backup for Pete on an album called *Talking Union* on the Folkways label. Mary had yearnings for the theater. She had the looks for it and the passion. She was intense, outspoken—never shy.

She and I told each other war stories about traveling, about promoters, managers, record executives. We laughed a lot, and sometimes cried together.

Mary once expressed to me her rage at one of the most famous folk stars of the day—"Miss Thing," as she called the diva—by whom she said she had been upstaged at a Newport Folk Festival finale. Miss Thing stepped in front of Mary during the encore, elbowing her way to the front for the cameras and the television audience.

"I would never do that," Mary snapped a few days after the show. "Who does she think she is? She stepped right in my face, as though she didn't know I was there."

It would have been very hard to miss Mary Travers anywhere, even with Miss Thing around.

Mary had a profound influence on the music of the times. Peter, Paul and Mary recorded many songs that were musical bellwethers, from "Blowin' in the Wind" to "The Times They Are A-Changin'" to "If I Had a Hammer." On November 22, 1963, the day JFK was assassinated, there were three of their albums on the charts. Their popularity was overwhelming, and in the face of her fame, Mary was not afraid to travel around the world in support of her favorite political causes. She stayed involved with the peace movement, the civil rights movement, and Cesar Chavez's farmworkers movement.

In 1961 Bill Cosby was just getting started in the tiny "pass-the-basket" clubs in Greenwich Village, making about $69 a week, when he saw Mary in the park. She grabbed his arm as they strode through Washington Square, turning heads, the tall willowy blonde and Cosby.

"You know what people are saying?" Cosby asked her as he struggled to keep up with Mary's wild rhythm.

"What?" she asked.

"They are saying, 'There goes May Britt and Sammy Davis Jr.'!"

*I*t was in those two weeks at Gerde's that I met Bob Dylan for the first time. At least I thought it was the first time, but Bob told a different story.

One night I had just finished my set and was sitting at the bar, sipping Pernod, the drink that turns foggy yellow before hitting you in the solar plexus, which had become my drink of choice. I was wearing a Romanian blouse that tied in front, a long denim skirt, and a leather vest. I had straight hair, brown and a bit unruly, with a part in the middle. I wore dangling silver earrings and a couple of silver rings, one with the onyx that Angelo Di Benedetto had made for me in that seemingly distant past in Central City. I was smoking my favorites, Gauloises—strong, fragrant French cigarettes.

Bob Dylan strolled across the dingy, smoke-filled room toward the bar. He was wearing rumpled clothes, a battered-looking pair of boots, and Levi's. He had some kind of ragged scarf around his neck, like his hero, Ramblin' Jack Elliott. His hair was indescribable, unkempt but soft like a child's. The curls framed his face, a sweet face but one full of contradiction, a combination of innocence and arrogance.

He stuck out his hand and told me my set had been great. We

both ordered drinks and began to get a bit tipsy together. I offered him a Gauloise. He took the cigarette, made from Turkish and Syrian tobaccos, and rolled it between his fingers before I offered him a light.

I said it was nice to meet him, but he shook his head, as he inhaled the strong, distinctive aroma.

"Don't you remember?" he said, squinting through the smoke from our cigarettes.

"Remember what?" I said.

"I sat at your feet." Bob smiled shyly under his stained hat and described how he had come to hear me when I was first singing in Central City. He told me he had been singing at a little bar in Cripple Creek, just up the highway, when he was still Bob Zimmerman. I nodded, but didn't have a clue.

Behind the bar the bottles of booze shimmered in reds and yellows, blues and greens. I was a little drunk, and so, it appeared, was he. I heard him sing his set then, a few songs, mostly Woody Guthrie. He had an okay voice and was a good storyteller, but there was not much to look at. (Much later, after their affair had begun, Joan Baez would admit that when she first heard him singing Woody's songs she thought Dylan looked like a toad!)

I would see Bob around in the Village, at Izzy Young's Folklore Center, sometimes hanging out by the fountain in Washington Square on a weekend, where the guitar players drifted from one side of the park to the other, and the smell of pot washed over the scene. In July, at a folk festival at Riverside Church, Dylan met Suze Rotolo, the long-haired, pixie-faced, bright-eyed seventeen-year-old from Queens with whom he would spend the next four years. Their relationship would become a part of the lore of the 1960s, a well-known chapter in the seemingly magical life story of Bob Dylan.

But no one really knew what that story was, or even where Dylan came from. He tended to be vague, at best, about his roots, and often deliberately misled people about them. He was known over the years by different names at different times: Elston Gunn, Blind Boy Grunt, Lucky Wilbury, Elmer Johnson, Sergei Petrov, Jack Frost. Sometimes he had grown up in a junkyard, was born in Kansas in a snowstorm, had been in the circus, or worked as a fruit picker for most of his teenage life in rural California with migrant workers. You get the idea—it was anything to get you off the scent of a relatively typical upbringing in Hibbing, Minnesota.

Oscar Brand, who has had a folk music show on New York's WNYC-FM on and off since 1945, told me that Dylan came on his show pretending to be someone from the Dust Bowl.

"He just plain lied. He was a nervous wreck. I guess he didn't like his own story much; it was never the same. He was very interested in where everyone came from, what their stories were. I think he was all nerves." Brand smiled at the recollection.

Dylan offers a more credible tale in his wonderful book *Chronicles: Volume One*. He came to New York, he says, with no money, but he got to know people who were willing to lend him a pad for varying lengths of time. He spent his days reading the books on their bookshelves. He says his education really began during those weeks and months in 1960 and 1961 when he read voraciously, everything from Plato and Sophocles to Salinger and Shakespeare.

The songs were incubating. We would have to wait just a little while longer.

WHEN I was on the road, it was rare that I was able to go to clubs and concerts to see other artists perform. I was usually singing six nights a week, two or three shows a night. So I was fortunate to hear Barbra Streisand sing in St. Louis in 1961 at the Crystal Palace. I was working with the Smothers Brothers at the Laughing Buddha, across the street from the Palace, in the Gaslight district. The club was a thriving musical mecca. Tommy Smothers took me to meet Barbra, who was then an up-and-coming diva but not yet well known.

After we listened to Streisand, we went backstage. Barbra shook hands coolly and moved to her dressing room, elegant but aloof.

"So, what do you think?" Tom asked me after we had met "the voice." She would, of course, go on to have the career every girl from Brooklyn dreamed of. "They say she is going to be a big star."

"Well," I replied, "I liked her, but I could think of some other material she might do." Barbra was singing "A Sleepin' Bee," a song by Harold Arlen, and other chestnuts from the Great American Songbook that I considered passé at the time. I don't remember what I suggested, but it was probably some Pete Seeger songs and perhaps an old Irish ballad. She made *The Barbra Streisand Album* two years later, with "A Sleepin' Bee" on it. It won her three Grammy Awards, including Album of the Year. Always glad to be of service!

On April 27, 1961, a day off from that four-week engagement, I flew from St. Louis to New York's La Guardia Airport and took the bus to Greenwich Village in the rain. Spring was starting with a blast of wet weather. Guitar in hand, I trudged down the now-famous stairs to the basement of the Village Gate. I had been invited to appear on a television show to be filmed there with Josh White, Lynn Gold, the Irish folk group the Clancy Brothers and Tommy Makem, and Theo Bikel.

Chip Monck, the Village Gate's lighting magician, was setting up for the show that night. Chip always wore jumpsuits in psychedelic colors with pockets and zippers everywhere. Bill Graham once gave Chip an oversized zipper because he said Chip had zippers on his zippers. Blond, handsome, quick with a smile, Chip could indeed make us all light up beautifully with his craft.

I sang "Anathea" and "Golden Apples of the Sun," and when

I exited the stage, a tall, good-looking man wearing glasses greeted me. He offered his hand.

"My name is Jac Holzman," he introduced himself, saying he was president of Elektra Records. "And you are ready to make a record!" he said.

I looked up as he leaned in over me as though we were the only people in the room, as though we were a couple. He wore a jacket over a dress shirt open at the neck, and his hair was cropped short. He had a firm handshake and looked more like a college professor than a record mogul, from what I knew of record moguls, which was not much. He was scholarly-looking, and there was a glint in his eye that told you here was a man who knew his own mind, a man you didn't argue with.

When I met Jac, Elektra was ten years old. Jac had started the label in 1950 from his dorm at St. John's College in Annapolis. His first recording was a group of lieder pieces, which included *Songs of the Auvergne*. The label's co-founder was Paul Rickolt, Jac's pal from St. John's. Each man put up $300. Soon Jac bought out his partner and began to haunt the clubs in New York and the folk festivals. He decided that folk music was the way to go.

The year I met Jac and he signed me to Elektra, the folk music world was abuzz with Joan Baez. Jac told Mark Abramson, his main producer at Elektra, that not having a "Maid of Orleans" rankled him.

"We'll find our own" was Mark's response. Mark, the man who would produce many of my albums in years to come, would later tell me that I looked like a skier—"blond, athletic, strong forearms." He must have been thinking of my brother Dave. I was certainly not a blonde, at least then! And what was that about those forearms?

"Judy . . . looked like definitely a product of the West," Mark said in *Follow the Music,* Jac's book about the Elektra years, "and there was a certain fresh-air feeling to her, which was not really too much in evidence at Elektra, with people like Dirty Ed McCurdy." McCurdy could become rather vociferous when he had a few drinks, and a little bawdy, some might add. He was also a wonderful songwriter from Canada who wrote "Last Night I Had the Strangest Dream."

Mark later told me that I was really the first person who was seen as someone to get Elektra on the map. "We were looking for our star!"

It is funny to think that Jac and Mark were calculating, at that time, that anyone could be a star, let alone a (blond?) skier type with strong forearms. Jac would later say he had lucked out.

"I hadn't found my Joan Baez; I had found my Judy Collins."

In June 1961, I signed my Elektra contract. I felt like I was on top of the world. I went to perform at the Indian Neck Folk Festival, at the rambling old Montowese House, a hotel in Branford, Connecticut.

It was pouring that night. The rain slanted down through the pine trees and flooded the stage, which had to be mopped up after every act. Everyone was scrambling to keep his or her guitar dry. After I sang, I listened to Dylan give the first of many performances that would be recorded and archived for posterity. He sang three Woody Guthrie songs, "Talking Columbia," "Hang Knot (Slip Knot)," and "Talking Fish Blues." He left the stage with no particular fanfare, although the audience seemed to like him. At some point on that rainy weekend, Dylan and I both met Bob Neuwirth, who became Dylan's close friend and road manager.

Neuwirth emerged as a kind of folk icon himself over the years, a painter, singer, rogue about town, and protector of all things Dylan. For many years Bob took Bob under his wing, or vice versa, emphasis on the vice. I remember catching my first glimpse of Neuwirth and thinking, "Bad boy, long hair, dangerous to fall in love with, would love to get to know him but I dare not!" For a long time I kept my distance, sensing I could not have handled all that charm. Bob and I are good friends now, and I have always had a soft spot in my heart for the handsome devil with the angelic smile.

After hearing Dylan that afternoon, I went to the food tent, looking for tea to warm me from the rain. I then poked my head under the eaves of the hotel, where I ran into Carolyn Hester, coming back from the stage. She, too, was on a tea search.

Carolyn was strikingly beautiful, with shining brown eyes and a chiseled, delicate face. She could have been a movie star. She had a high, sweet voice, a soprano with a kind of quiver that touched your heart when she sang those heart-wrenching songs that I loved; "The Praties They Grow Small," "Brave Wolfe," "Simple Gifts," and "Cuckoo."

The Cuckoo is a pretty bird, and she sings as she flies
And she never hollers cuckoo till the fourth day of July.

She also had a kind of kinetic energy you could feel. Even as she stood there on a muddy path at an obscure music festival—rain-spattered, her hair limp from the humidity—Carolyn was a knockout.

She had made her first record in 1957, the year I graduated from high school. It was called *Scarlet Ribbons*, on the Coral label in Texas. Born in Waco in 1937, Carolyn was known as the "Texas Songbird." I picked up a copy of the album at the Denver Folklore Center and listened over and over to her sweet, lilting voice.

As we walked and sipped our tea and heard the bluegrass players warming up onstage, I told her I had fallen in love with her version of "She Moved Through the Fair."

Don Heckman, of the *Los Angeles Times,* described Carolyn as "one of a small but determined gang of ragtag, early-'60s folk singers who cruised the coffee shops and campuses, from Harvard Yard to Bleecker Street, convinced that their music could help change the world." John Hammond signed Carolyn to Columbia in 1959. She had also caught the eye of Al Grossman, and said that Grossman had wanted to put her in a trio—first with Bob Gibson, then with Peter Yarrow and Noel Stookey.

Carolyn was on a fast track to stardom by now. Like some of the other "ragtag" folk girls, she focused primarily on traditional music and other songwriters' songs, but she also wrote her own contemporary compositions. She turned down Albert's offer to trio with Noel and Peter, leaving the door open for the fierce Mary Travers. (By 1964 Carolyn would even be on the cover of the *Saturday Evening Post*. Her lilting voice was compared to Joan's and sometimes, later on, to mine.)

She had met Dylan only a few months before, when Dylan talked the owners of a club she was playing in Boston into letting him open for her. The two bonded over their shared love of Buddy Holly and spoke of performing together more, and even about the possibility of Dylan playing harmonica on one of Carolyn's albums. (Dylan would play on her Columbia album in September of that year.) I remembered seeing a picture of Carolyn in *Life* magazine, with Bruce Langhorne and Bill Lee, Spike's father, who also played bass for me on many occasions; Dylan was in that picture as well, and Carolyn shone like a diamond in a patch of autumn grass.

"I just got married," she said that day in Connecticut, lifting her hand and wiggling her ring finger, where a small diamond sparkled in a gold setting. As she spoke about her new husband, she exuded happiness. In real sixties fashion, she had impetuously married a man she had known for only eighteen days.

"I want you to meet Richard!" She took me by the hand and led me to her room, where her new husband, the mysterious and handsome Dick Fariña, was lying on the bed playing the guitar, candles burning all around him.

With his dashing good looks and magnetic charm, Dick Fariña was undeniably seductive, sure to capture your heart as quickly as he caught your eye. He had dark hair and sparkling eyes that seemed to fathom you as he held your gaze. Dick's sense of humor and his appreciation of life's absurdities appealed to me, and we were destined to become friends. In the years we knew each other, I never laughed so hard with anyone else, or felt so close to either madness or sanity. He brought out my giddiness and made me feel young and vulnerable. I adored him.

He had flown into Carolyn's life, seeming to arrive out of nowhere, the same way he floated into all our lives—like some powerful visitor from another, very romantic world. By the time he and Carolyn met, Dick had heard Jean Ritchie play a dulcimer at a party in New York, and he'd adopted the instrument himself. He played in a very nontraditional way, sometimes turning the delicate dulcimer into a rhythm instrument. As a wedding present, Carolyn gave him a beautiful handmade Emerson dulcimer.

Richard climbed quickly aboard Carolyn's rising star, riding it as far, some people said, as it would take him.

"Where did you two meet?" I asked as I lay between them on the velvet coverlet of their double bed. The light of several candles glowed around us. Carolyn smiled at Dick.

"At the White Horse Tavern," she said, referring to the legendary bar in the West Village where Dylan Thomas finished drinking himself to death a couple of years before I arrived in New York. "Tommy Makem introduced us, and this beautiful boy seduced me," she said.

Fariña, like Dylan, told some tall tales about where he was from and what he had done, and some of his stories were as exotic as Dick appeared to be, involving things like fighting in Cuba, meeting Hemingway, and running with the bulls in Pamplona. Some were actually true, and others were pure fiction. Although he really had gone to Cuba as he claimed, Fariña was born and raised in

Brooklyn and attended Brooklyn Tech. Dick wanted to be an engineer but then got a scholarship to Cornell and eventually majored
in English. He got to know Peter Yarrow and Thomas Pynchon at
Cornell, and he published articles for a few national magazines, including the *Transatlantic Review* and *Mademoiselle,* before finding his
way to New York.

Carolyn sang "She Moved Through the Fair" for me that
night, her dark hair shimmering in the candlelight. The song was
gorgeous and so was she. She and Richard sang some oddly touching new songs of his as well.

Dick met Bob Dylan that weekend, triggering a sort of
high-powered duel between the two men for primacy among
philosopher-poets of the counterculture. Although it seemed very
real at the time, I think the duel played itself out mostly in Fariña's
fertile and gifted mind.

Two years later, Dick and Carolyn would divorce, and Fariña
would marry another singer with a rising star in the family—Mimi,
the younger sister of Joan Baez.

Chapter Ten

The Lark in the Morning

The lark in the morning
She rises off her nest
She goes home in the evening
With the dew on her breast.

—Traditional, "The Lark"

I*n* 1961 I began to make my first album.

Maid of Constant Sorrow captured the collection of songs I had honed on the road and sung all over the country. Jac set up the recording at Fine Sound on West 57th Street. He was a stickler for the right song sequence and to this day has never lost that instinct for what goes with what, to best serve the musical journey you want your listener to take. Jac brought on Fred Hellerman, from the Weavers, and Erik Darling, who founded the Tarriers and was also in the Weavers at that time.

The songs on that first album were the foundation of my early repertoire. Each one spoke to me in its unique way at that moment in my life. But what amazes me is how those songs have continued to resonate with me through the years. I believe that this album defines my love of people, politics, and life itself. There are songs about war and our addiction to it; about passions that leap out from our ancient, primitive beliefs and hopes; songs about the agony of young men dying, all over the world, for all time; and about miracles as well.

Other songs on the album remind me of my father. "Bold Fenian Men" and "The Rising of the Moon" both honor the Irish who stood up to free their land from the brutal English yoke. I was drawn to the passionate imagery and lyricism of these songs as well as to their politics. My love affair with "The Rising of the Moon" is deep and enduring. Even now I can hear the powerful lyrics, the sound of the river singing beside the marching Irish men at night.

"Wars of Germany" is about the tragedy of war as seen through the eyes of those who stay behind, while "Tim Evans" takes on another form of barbarism: capital punishment. By the great Scot writer Ewan MacColl and his wife, Peggy Seeger, Pete's half sister, it tells the haunting tale of a man hanged for a murder he did not commit.

There were songs, too, about the trials and triumphs of love. "The Prickilie Bush" is the story of every girl who was ever brought down by her passion and her curiosity, the lover of her choosing—perhaps a carefree wanderer, a gigolo, a rogue—leaving her when she needs him the most. "Sailor's Life" describes how often lovers are parted by work, sometimes for years.

"Wild Mountain Thyme" is a haunting song that combines a deep connection with nature and a yearning for love that will not fade. I learned it from the McPeake family of Belfast.

FROM the beginning of my life as a singer I knew immediately whether a song was meant for me. There are songs I will never sing because they have a phrase I would never speak. Language is so very intimate and vital, and I choose only those songs that reflect the way I might say things. I am sure I learned this in the womb, from the panoply of long-forgotten ancestors who sang all kinds of music, as well as from the talented choices my father made in his years on the radio. This is a continuation of a family business, and I believe it started long before I knew my own name.

When *Maid of Constant Sorrow* was finished, I felt as though I had just graduated from the kiddie pool, where everyone screamed and splashed water everywhere, and was finally being allowed into the grown-ups' pool, where you could drown. I wasn't going to drown. I couldn't swim yet, but I knew I would learn. I would stay close to Jac, and to safety.

I was a professional now, with a record, work, a family to support. We celebrated when we were finished recording, but as exciting as this first recording experience was, I recognized that it also came with a tremendous responsibility to myself, to my family, and to the music.

Maid had taken only a few days to record. I was back in Storrs when the completed album arrived in the mail at the end of summer in 1961 with Lida Moser's lovely photo of me on the cover, that dark shot she took in the ruins of an old church in Greenwich Village. August in Connecticut was sweet and homey. The fireflies were out in the evenings and the water was cool in our secret swimming hole, sheltered by the woods. We grilled sausages and corn and chicken outside, walked in the woods, played with Clark, sang songs, and spent time with our friends from the university. The satisfaction of having my own record out was sweeter still, and I felt completed in a way that I'd never felt before. I was going to do this—be a singer, someone who had a calling, a profession, and a direction.

I had a record. I had arrived.

Chapter Eleven

Golden Apples and the Beginning of the Affair

Tell me who I'll marry
Tell me who he'll be.

—Traditional, "Tell Me Who I'll Marry"

JAC Holzman told me it was now time I had a manager for real. I said I had already met one, through Marshall Brickman of the Tarriers. Jack Rollins was a good-looking, polished, and sophisticated man who managed Woody Allen. I had been very excited about our meeting, but Rollins told me that although he liked my work, he was waiting for Jo Mapes to make up her mind as to whether or not she wanted to be a star, and if she decided to go for it he had to be available for her.

Jo had a promising career. She performed in all the best clubs, and in the early 1960s she sang in the Rooftop Singers, with Erik Darling, Bill Svanoe, and Lynne Taylor. They had a hit with "Walk Right In," which reached number one on the *Billboard* charts. So Jac was holding out for Jo; another woman singer would take up too much of his time.

It was a good line; it may even have been true.

Holzman then set up an appointment for me to meet with Harold Leventhal in Harold's office at 250 West 57th Street, near Carnegie Hall. Inside, the walls were lined with photos of Woody Guthrie and Pete Seeger, posters of Carnegie Hall concerts, framed flyers from union rallies where Pete or Woody or the Weavers were singing, and pictures of Lee Hays, Freddy Hellerman, and Ronnie Gilbert, the other members of the Weavers. Of course I was nervous as a cat, and hoped yet another manager would not turn me down.

Harold was a stocky, bespectacled man with a cigar that was, I would learn, always clenched between his teeth. He was forty-two when we first met, and his hair was already thinning. His checkered suit was slightly rumpled, and as he waved his cigar across the table, aiming for the ashtray and missing, his mouth turned up in a wonderful smile.

Harold told me that he had been a song plugger for Irving Berlin and had left the family lingerie business to manage Pete Seeger and the Weavers. He was one of the most down-to-earth people I ever knew, with a gentle, low-key sense of humor. He was managing Alan Arkin, Theo Bikel, and a few other artists at the time we met. People spoke highly of him, and he of them, he might have said. He was already producing many of the major acts in the musical world, including Jacques Brel, the great French singer/songwriter, and Nana Mouskouri, the Greek singing star.

"You're just a kid, aren't you?" Harold said. I smiled at that, thinking that I *was* just a kid. I had a child and a husband and a career, but I was twenty-two and it seemed I had just stepped out of my high school graduating class. Harold put me immediately at ease.

"I can work with a kid," he said. "A kid is a good thing. You probably don't have too many bad habits I'm going to have to change!"

As we left his office, I noticed a figure stretched out behind the couch in the outer room, a man who was snoring softly.

"Don't mind him, he's sleeping," Harold said. The figure had a banjo by his side and was lying prone on the floor. He had a handsome, clean-shaven face and was dressed in a checkered shirt, long pants, and the kind of boots a logger might wear. He wore no watch and no coat. His face, turned to the side in repose, seemed to be smiling up at me.

"That's Pete," Harold said. I had no doubt who this was, even though it was the first time I had seen the great Seeger in person, the man who had written "Where Have All the Flowers Gone" and "Turn! Turn! Turn!" I knew he had been called in 1955 to testify before the House Un-American Activities Committee, Joseph McCarthy's Red-baiting engine that had ruined careers in theater, film, music, and politics. I knew he was riding out the storm after having refused to name names; he'd been blacklisted but was still singing, making records, writing songs, speaking out, appearing at union gatherings, and generally doing what he always has done—making a difference. Even with him stretched out on the floor, I felt his force and was awed by his presence.

"Shhhhhh, let's not wake him," Harold said, stepping around the sleeping troubadour. "He has to rest up. He has three concerts tomorrow, each in a different city, and I have to get him to all of them and then home again." He took his cigar out of his mouth and tapped it in an ashtray shaped like a banjo as we headed for the door.

"I hope you aren't going to do things like this to me. I can only take one Pete Seeger," he added. I promised I wouldn't, and knew Harold had just agreed to be my manager.

Harold started negotiating my contracts with Jac and Elektra, as well as helping me to plan the concerts in New York. He took over my work life and my benefit life—there were many benefits for good causes. Marjorie Guthrie, Woody's wife, was at Harold's often, working on Woody's archives and history now that he was so ill. Harold's wife, Natalie, spent as much time there as he did. Every time I called that office—Judson 6-6553—over the next forty-five years, either Harold or Natalie, or often Marjorie Guthrie, would answer the phone.

I met extraordinary people through Harold: Millard Lampell, who wrote songs with Woody and Pete and was one of the original members of the Almanac Singers; Lee Hays of the Weavers; and Pete Seeger, either asleep behind the couch or leaning over from his height to listen to the much shorter Harold, or maybe just ducking to avoid the smoke from Harold's cigar.

Harold would guide my career from 1961 to 1972. He booked my dates in clubs; he got another of his clients, Theo Bikel, to include me in his Carnegie Hall concert in 1962; he booked my first solo show at Town Hall in 1964, which Elektra recorded for release later that year; and he took care of my recordings. Harold was a mensch, as the saying goes in Yiddish, and he was a workaholic.

I adored Harold. With his gruff manner and ever-present cigar, he always made me feel safe. He was quite tender, actually, and he always knew how to be comforting. I felt that he believed in me.

"How is it going?" he would ask. And even after I left him in 1972 to try to find a way to be more actively involved in my own career, he would still say, "How's business?"

In his later years, after Harold had his arthritic knuckles replaced with titanium, he joked, "Now I could smoke my cigars down to the very end—that is, if I hadn't been forced to quit smoking because of my arthritis!"

*B*y the end of November I had been working at a club called the Buddhi in Oklahoma City for a week with Bud and Travis, an easygoing duo from San Francisco who sang "They Call the Wind

Mariah," "La Bamba," and "The Sloop *John B.*" As cold weather moved in, Bud and Travis headed back to California. In the meantime, Dave Van Ronk arrived in Oklahoma City on the back of one of the biggest storms ever to blanket the Midwest.

I had heard Van Ronk sing at the Gaslight almost as soon as I got to New York the previous spring. He had rumpled hair, muttonchops for sideburns, and a mustache drooping over his lips. He wore thick black-framed glasses, his hair flopped over his forehead, and he was dressed in an army jacket, pilot's trousers, and a pair of engineer's boots. Hunched over his guitar like a mother over her baby, he told stories in a gravelly voice. Then he sang a song called "Hesitation Blues," his guitar sounding like a cross between Mississippi John Hurt and Ramblin' Jack Elliott, but mostly sounding like Van Ronk. "How long do I have to wait?" he sang.

Robert Shelton, the legendary New York rock-and-roll and music critic, described Dave in *No Direction Home,* his book about Bob Dylan: Van Ronk "resembled an unmade bed strewn with books, record jackets, pipes, empty whiskey bottles, lines from obscure poets, finger picks, and broken guitar strings."

One famous night of carousing and drinking at the Chelsea Hotel with Joni Mitchell and Leonard Cohen ended up with Dave's taking authorship of the song found on pieces of paper scattered about the hotel room the following morning. Dave called it "Last Call."

> *And so we've had another night,*
> *of poetry and proses*
>
> *And each man knows he'll be alone*
> *when the sacred gin mill closes*

Dave, who was also known as "Dylan's first New York guru" and the "musical mayor of MacDougal Street," unloaded his bags in the little house around the corner from the Buddhi. The wind was howling and the snow was swirling, and it was freezing-your-tits-off cold; I had no idea how the two of us were going to get along there on the plains.

I needn't have worried. Van Ronk was an angel, come to rescue me from my solitude in Oklahoma. He took the icy upstairs room, giving me the bed downstairs next to the one potbellied stove. Each night I would wait for him to finish his set, listening to him sing the songs that I came to understand were his passion and religion: old Woody Guthrie blues, folk songs, Brecht and Weill, and "The Internationale."

Back at our little house after the shows, we would curl up, me snuggled in the bed beside the fiery stove, and Dave in the chair beside me, his body wrapped in his big New York winter coat and all the extra blankets he could find.

I would burrow down under the covers as the room slowly warmed up, while Dave soothed me to sleep with stories from his life, about serving in the merchant marine or being born and bred a Trotskyite, steeped in political activism. He might recite something from the literature of the Russian Revolution. He would wait until he knew I was almost asleep before he crept upstairs, leaving me to dream of the Decembrists, the Bolsheviks, the songs of passion and union building, and the old, sweet blues he would sing as the fire was dying down and the snow was blowing more softly in the night.

And Dave always left the bottle of good whiskey near my pillow.

"Sweet dreams," he would say as I drifted off and he made his way up the stairs to his freezing-cold room.

In the morning, when we were both staggering out of bed, he brought me coffee. Dave's coffee felt hearty and solid, so unexpectedly delicious, coming out of that tiny little kitchen, as if made of some kind of determination in the face of impossibility. I will always associate Dave with the miraculous appearance of a great cup of coffee in the middle of a biblical storm.

*I*N late February 1962 I started a two-week gig at the Golden Vanity in Boston, a club across from Boston University. Joan Baez ruled the Boston folk scene then, with her long black hair, piercing dark eyes, and beautiful soprano voice. She had some help carrying the Great Folk Scare, as Van Ronk called it, from a leather-jacket-clad, good-looking, Harvard-educated singer named Tom Rush who had played the Golden Vanity just before I got there. *Rolling Stone* magazine credits Tom with ushering in the singer-songwriter era, although one could argue that it had begun two decades earlier with Woody Guthrie and Pete Seeger. Tom would describe his career as that of a singer who sort of muddled along, searching for great songs as though searching for some lost family. He will always have the credit for discovering Joni Mitchell in the mid-1960s and recording her song "Circle Game."

I commuted to Boston from our farmhouse on Browns Road five or six nights a week, driving two hours each way. On the last day of my two-week gig, a great blizzard suddenly slammed into the area. I was about halfway between Storrs and Boston, on the Massachusetts Turnpike. I kept pushing ahead as bravely as I could, but soon I couldn't even see the road. The snowplows and salt trucks were moving up the highway with blinking blue and white lights signaling all traffic to turn back. I turned the Chevy Carryall around and headed back home, stopping at a little grocery store on the way to buy chocolate chips, walnuts, and flour, for the cookies I was going to bake. When you are in a jam, always bake something sweet—that was my motto then. Once back home, as the snow continued to fall, we hibernated like bears. We shared frozen pies and roasts with our landlords, the Scottrons. We ate clam chowder and chicken stew, and we shivered without heat for two days. I was thrilled to be off the road, snowbound in the farmhouse and wrapped in the arms of my husband, Peter, and my little boy.

*H*ow did I keep my sanity on the road? I wrestled constantly with the difficulty of leaving my family behind in order to earn our living. A lot of people I know nowadays take their children with them everywhere, and I wish I could have done that. For one thing, I couldn't have afforded it. For another, Peter was just getting started in his academic career, and needed to stay put to hold on to his position at the college. He liked the stability of looking after our son and our home.

I think the road warriors who travel to sing or do other work all over the world have usually had a hard time juggling responsibilities as both parents and performers. Especially women. There were times I felt torn at being away, but I was learning to leave the pressures of touring at the door.

I knew I would have to leave again, that I had to go where the work was. I still get paid for the travel and for the heartache of being apart from my loved ones.

The music is free.

*S*oon enough, I was on the road again, back in the Village in New York.

Scott McKenzie was singing in the Journeymen with John Phillips and Dick Weissman when we first met. Scott had a dreamy look, a pale creamy complexion, dark curly hair surrounding a Three Musketeers face, and a glint of steel in his glance. He sang in the sweetest voice. It was Scott's voice everyone heard a few years later singing "If you're going to San Francisco, be sure to wear some flowers in your hair" at the Monterey Festival in 1964. He looked at me with dark brown eyes aglow with mischief and promises. I liked him immediately. He felt familiar, like a newly discovered brother.

We were all working at Gerde's, and one night he asked me if I knew anything about New York City beyond the Village. The honest answer was: not much. There was the Fred Braun shop where I bought my leather sandals and the folk music store run by Izzy Young. I knew how to get back on the West Side Highway to drive home to Connecticut. I knew the Broadway Central Hotel, around the corner from Gerde's, where I was staying for $1.50 a night. I knew Harold's office on West 57th Street, and the little studio nearby where I had recorded my first album.

"We have to show you the city," Scott said, and promptly took me down into the subway and whisked me uptown to Tiffany's, where we stood gazing at the dazzling jewels in the big, elegant windows.

"How do you like them diamonds?" he asked.

I said I loved them but only wanted the smallest ones, for my ears. Someday I would have them, but not that day.

Then Scott and I rode back downtown, where he took me to the door of the Broadway Central.

"Do you know about the famous murder that happened here?" Scott asked.

"Murder?" I said. It seemed a pretty calm hotel to me, quiet and very much a hideaway.

He told me the story of Ned Stokes, who had shot Jubilee Jim Fisk in January of 1872 on the grand staircase of the Broadway Central while the men were fighting over a showgirl named Josie Mansfield. The facts of the murder were similar to those of the later 1906 scandal, when Harry Thaw, heir to a fortune and known as the "Prince of Pittsburgh," shot Stanford White, renowned architect of McKim, Mead and White, in a rage over White's previous treatment of Evelyn Nesbit, to whom Thaw was then married.

In both cases, the women involved in the triangles were music hall dancers. Both were stories of scandal and murder, and both men were wealthy and powerful.

I told Scott that such drama was more than I had expected of the Broadway Central, but I knew that it could have been me. I never had an affair with Scott, or even spent the night with him, but the conversation reminded me that I was playing by the rules of the 1960s, where new forms of partnering, including open marriage, were the coming thing. But I was sure my husband had been faithful. Hadn't he? The loosening social and cultural rules and restrictions didn't necessarily mean the end of jealousy and passion. The one-night stands I'd had—although they were few and far between and I didn't think my husband knew about them—could be dangerous. There was no AIDS, and though you might get pregnant, there was no worry about STDs—you could get a shot of penicillin to cure whatever ailed you. Sex was probably not life-threatening in most cases, and the pill had been around since 1960. Still, I knew I should watch myself, I thought as I climbed those same stairs on which Fisk had been murdered.

*J*AC Holzman had a pilot's license and that spring, to celebrate our second album, he took me up in his private plane to show me New York City in a way I'd never seen it before. We buzzed over the Empire State Building, circled Central Park, and streaked across the harbor from the Battery to the Statue of Liberty. You could still do that in 1962, without jets chasing you up the East River or down the Hudson. It was glorious up there, just Jac and me.

Jac would take me to concerts in New York to listen to young musicians and singers. He sent me albums to listen to—which is how I was introduced to Jacques Brel. He played me the recordings of new artists that he was considering signing, who eventually included Jim Morrison and the Doors, Bread, Tim Buckley, Mickey

Newbury, and Aztec Two-Step. He came to every show of mine he could manage to attend, critiquing, pointing out the high spots and the low as well.

I was back in Chicago at the Gate of Horn in early 1962, opening for Bob Gibson and Hamilton (né Bob) Camp. Hamilton looked like an Irish imp, with a small, wiry body and a glorious tenor voice that danced around Gibson's darker baritone. The combination of their harmonies was riveting. You could hear the Irish wit and art in Hamilton, and he was a wonderful addition to Gibson's act. Albert Grossman was managing Gibson at the time and had wanted originally to put Gibson in a duo with Ray Boguslav, a great guitarist as well as a pianist and singer. Somebody recommended Hamilton, who was working at the Associated Press when Albert found him.

One cold night Bob and Hamilton and I had been drinking after the last show, and I was just too drunk to walk home alone through the dark streets to the Cass Hotel in downtown Chicago, where I was staying. It was about four in the morning. Bob offered me a little handgun to protect myself on the way home. I had never touched a gun before, but I slipped it into my pocket as though it were the most natural thing in the world. I kept my fingers wrapped around it as I walked slowly home from the club.

The snow had stopped falling but there were still silver flakes hovering in the light under the lamps. When I got to the Cass, I stepped inside the door of my room. One side of the giant double window was open and the room was cold. I threw my coat on the bed and then held the gun out straight. I thought I should try to take the cartridge out of the gun, as they do in the movies.

The gun went off in my hand, scaring the hell out of me. I dropped it on the bed and rushed to look out the window expecting to see people running, someone shot, the ambulance coming. No one in the street looked up. In fact, there was no one in sight, only those stray, hesitant snowflakes lingering in the air. It was very late, or very early, depending on whether you worked all night or all day.

I'm sure the drinks had blunted my shock. I was free now to sleep it off. When I awoke, somewhat hungover, I found the bullet on the floor at my feet. It had slammed into the steel partition in the window and ricocheted back into the room; I'd been too out of it to realize that it had nearly hit me between the eyes.

I got to the club that night, holding the gun gingerly in my pocket. I handed the weapon to Gibson with a grimace, telling him it had gone off and that it must have malfunctioned. He laughed and told me I didn't know how to handle a gun. As he tried to take out the cartridge, the gun went off again, burying a bullet in one of the doors to the back room at the club.

From then on, I walked back to my hotel alone, early or late, unarmed. And, fortunately, unharmed.

BACK home, Clark was growing up, a little boy with needs and interests and a sweet, curious personality. He seemed to be getting along just fine. I loved him and hated to leave him. I missed out on so much of Clark's early life. I knew I was plying my trade, learning my craft, and bringing home the bacon, but that didn't make it any easier to live with, nor does it make the memory any less painful.

"Mommy, Mommy, what did you bring me?" were the words Clark was learning to say. "Mommy, Mommy, when are you coming home?"

Chapter Twelve

There Is a Season

To everything (turn, turn, turn)
There is a season (turn, turn, turn)

—Pete Seeger, "Turn! Turn! Turn!"

By the spring of 1962, I was keeping my eye on the young singer Bob Dylan, whom I had spent time with at Gerde's Folk City. After I had seen him at the festival in Connecticut, Dylan had written a couple of his own songs to add to the repertoire of Woody Guthrie blues he was performing. John Hammond signed him to a three-album deal for Columbia Records, believing that Bob was the "great white blues hope." Hammond himself was a genius, and could spot genius even before it had proven itself. He had no doubt about Dylan.

Robert Shelton, critic for the *New York Times,* had seen Bob's first proper run at Gerde's Folk City. In September 1961, Shelton served up his take on the young singer: "Mr. Dylan is vague about his antecedents and birthplace, but it matters less where he has been than where he is going, and that would seem to be straight up."

Shelton seemed to understand what would happen before it did. When that review came out, Bob hadn't yet rocked the world with his reach, his imaginative, stunning lyrics, his perfectly conceived melodies. But by May 1962, the guys in the folk music circles, those with great talent and beautiful songs to their credit, sat up and took notice. Dylan, with his new songs, seemed to be in a league by himself. Soon people everywhere were seeing the world through his eyes.

It was in its spring edition that *Sing Out,* the bible of the folk movement, printed the first of Dylan's remarkable compositions, "Blowin' in the Wind." I loved it and learned it, and began to dwell on its elegant structure. The writing stunned me.

Back in Chicago toward the end of 1962, Albert gave me the first tape of original Dylan songs. "What do you think?" he asked. "They say he can't sing."

"Oh yes he can," I replied. "He can sing."

I was traveling across the country, learning new songs, and preparing for my second recording. My marriage was doing fine, I thought. I loved and admired Peter, and I could rationalize the long separations from my son as the price of professional success. I thought I could shake off the terrible emotional hangovers, as I did the physical ones, believing I was somehow above petty self-judgment, and certainly above the judgment of others. After all, weren't we supposed to be moving beyond guilt? We were sixties children.

But during the recording of my second album, *Golden Apples of the Sun,* which I started making in the spring of 1962, I met the man who would be the catalyst for the breakup of my marriage. He was Walter Raim, a talented guitar player and producer whom Mark Abramson had hired to be the album's musical director.

Walter was no stranger in a strange town, but a man, fully present and real, who fell in love with me and who would not take no for an answer.

Walter was Jewish, smart, with an ex-wife, in fact two ex-wives, with whom he was still on speaking terms. He had brown hair, delicate features, and hands that played the guitar tenderly and reached out for me with the same tenderness. He was a gentle soul who played beautifully on my new record and didn't drink or use any drugs. Perhaps he took an occasional toke of something, but he was not an addict, and I would know that, being one myself. I had rarely spent time with anyone who did not drink, and I found Walter irresistible.

We danced around each other at first, while Walter guided the sessions for my second album. Finally, after weeks of flirting and skirting the obvious, I surrendered without even a whimper of protest. What Walter knew about the physical act of love came as a revelation, like fireworks suddenly filling a black sky with brilliant light and electricity. I was simply overwhelmed. Like Madame Bovary, like all the mythic women of romances who had fired my imagination and my creativity, I was swept off my feet. Suddenly I could understand taking that perilous walk on the edge of a cliff that could catapult you, in an instant, into another, sometimes terrible, world. With Walter, I became the heroine in a drama of my own making, a drama that could not end well.

WHILE I was recording the songs for *Golden Apples of the Sun* that spring and summer, I would drive down from Storrs to New York and find a place to park near the studio, where we would work for hours, after which I would go to my hotel. Once Walter and I gave in to our passion, we stayed together more often at his apartment on Hudson Street, not far from the White Horse Tavern. I was experiencing sex in a way I had never imagined possible. It was heavenly and horrible at the same time, because of the guilt I felt. As the affair became more of a presence in my life I grew more and more anxious.

I had never been good at deception, and it was beginning to take a toll on me. I was also falling apart physically—exhausted from travel and drinking too much.

I didn't really pay much attention to it, but I was having trouble breathing. When I breathed in deeply, there was the sound of gurgling in my lungs. I ignored it. I certainly was not going to go to a doctor. We seldom did in our family; we were as close to being Christian Scientists as Methodists could be, and I knew you would not want to take an aspirin unless you wanted to kill yourself!

My weeks out on the road seemed endless, but Walter would sometimes travel to be with me, or I would go to New York for a few precious days with him.

That September, Albert Grossman approached me. "You remember that idea I had for you?" he asked. "I want to put you together with Jo Mapes and Judy Henske. We can call you the Brown-Eyed Girls."

I started to laugh. "Albert, you and your trios!"

"I think it would work," he insisted. "You can get some brown contact lenses!"

By the time our conversation finished, I had agreed, but I was still laughing.

On *Golden Apples of the Sun,* I kept mostly to the path I had begun with my first album. I was gaining a reputation as a singer of traditional folk ballads, although I did take some subtle detours and included an eclectic mix of contemporary and children's songs.

The song "Golden Apples of the Sun" is based on a William Butler Yeats poem, "The Song of Wandering Aengus"; I learned it from Will Holt at the Gate of Horn. "Apples" set the tone for this adventure into another musical world while continuing a relationship with my treasured old friends, the great songs of past centuries. Among the sea chanties, one of my favorite work songs of all, "Bonnie Ship the *Diamond*" played a powerful part in my concerts. I learned it from one of the many albums of sea chanties I loved so much. The story of a whale hunt, it conjures up the beauty and majesty of these magnificent creatures, as well as their terrible deaths.

There was a kind of angry agitation in my singing of the songs that related to what I was doing in my life. I may not have been hauling a sail up a mast, but I was working hard and I identified with people in the world who did the same every day to make a living.

Mystery also played a part in my selection for this early 1960s album. "The Great Selchie of Shule Skerry" had gotten me the job at the Gate of Horn, and there was a kind of sorcery in its strange lyric. A song that originated in the Hebrides, many of whose natives would not eat the meat of seals because they believed them to be bewitched seal-men, this story has a link to the history of magic in traditional ballads. Apples and gold, ships carrying whalers to faraway places, and dreams that haunt the lonely as well as the happy are all on board in my second album, a work full of contrast and, I hope, comfort.

At the end of the summer of 1962, as *Golden Apples of the Sun* was being released, I found I was pregnant. I knew the baby was Walter's. And I knew I couldn't go through with the pregnancy.

I went to Denver for a gig and had two free days afterward. I borrowed my sister-in-law's tiny VW to drive sixteen hours two states north to have an abortion.

In the middle of the night, driving back to Denver, I found myself alone on a moonlit stretch of a Wyoming road. The little

VW motor began missing beats and finally quit on me. I had some car skills, one of which was that I knew this little buggy and was able to put up the hood and file the points in the engine until I got her started again. And again. The moon shone brightly above me, but no one knew where I was. Only Walter knew, and he was in New York.

This was not a safe place and not a place I was happy to be in. I was scared to death, in fact. In those days abortion was illegal. If men had ovaries, I'm sure there would be no question of who has a choice and who doesn't.

I got back to Connecticut, where my marriage, shaky at best, was continuing to crumble. One night Peter and I took magic mushrooms—given to him, I suspect, by a fellow student in his Blake course. Stoned to the eyeballs, we went to the movies outside Storrs. On the way back from seeing *Breakfast at Tiffany's*, with Peter driving our big old Chevy van in the rain, we hit a rabbit running across the road. Truth suddenly spilled out of me—that I was in love with someone else, although I did not say whom. On top of the hallucinogen we had taken, we were both drinking that night, and the alcohol fueled what shortly became an argument. We both said things we would regret, but there was one thing that we both felt we knew: neither of us wanted to end our marriage. After that, our compact with each other seemed firm—I would stop seeing Walter, we would get through this.

But of course I didn't stop seeing Walter. I simply couldn't. The sexual attraction was too strong to resist.

On October 23, 1962, I played Carnegie Hall as the opening act for Theo Bikel. My parents came to New York for the great night, and there was an elegant party for us in the suite at the top floor of the Bergdorf Goodman store, the family business of Minky, Peter's brother's wife. There our marriage seemed to take its last breaths. I drank too much, as I had been doing for months. There were tête-à-têtes between Peter and his brother, and between my sister-in-law Hadley and me. My mother and father toasted their daughter's triumph at Carnegie Hall, perhaps guessing my marriage was disintegrating but hopeful Peter and I would pull through, if only for the sake of our son. They had, after all, faced more challenges than we had ever known. I hadn't the heart to tell them I knew my husband and I were facing problems that we could not solve.

In the midst of my disintegrating marriage, the Cuban missile crisis was in full swing. Everywhere you turned, you saw fright and anxiety on people's faces, and every television set and radio station in the country was carrying the news. President Kennedy himself, that beacon of hope for our times, was troubled, his frown deep, his voice dark, as though he was feeling what everyone else was feeling: terror at what might happen next.

Two days after the Carnegie Hall show, I headed for Tucson, where I had a club date. Clark was in Peter's arms on that windy morning at Bradley International Airport, waving to me as I boarded the plane that would take me far, far away from our life in Connecticut, from the Scottrons' farm where the fireflies floated in the summer fields outside the windows of our red-painted farmhouse, where I cooked and baked and ironed and fed Clark and Peter dinners and listened to tapes of the songs for my next albums. I would look back on that time in our lives and wonder, from distant cities and continents around the world, whether I would ever again find the peace and happiness we once had.

I was very ill when I landed in Tucson, and after I did my first show that night, the two young people who ran the club, Fran and Alice, who had day jobs as medical technicians, insisted I go see a doctor at Tucson General. They picked me up at the hotel the next morning, and on the way to the hospital the radio was playing the Beatles' new release, "Love Me Do," their first single. Fran, Alice, and I bounced to the Beatles on the radio, and I asked them to pull over at a liquor store for a quart of Kahlúa and a six-pack of

Canadian beer. I knew I was sick; I had been having trouble breathing for months, hiding the pain with whatever was handy, and I knew I was lucky with my new friends—like so many strangers who were there when I needed them—who were skilled and saw at once that I needed help. I also knew that I was going to need reinforcements.

Less than thirty minutes later Dr. Schneider had diagnosed tubercular pleurisy. The hospital admitted me and my luggage and my paper shopping bags full of booze with no questions, and I was sent to a remote hospital wing, as far away from the other patients as they could get me. The doctors drained my lungs and put me on drugs for TB. I was to stay there a month.

That first afternoon I found the pay phone in the hall outside my room and phoned Albert Grossman. I knew he was already working on his idea for a trio, networking with Judy Henske and Jo Mapes and God only knew who else. They might not have even agreed to be part of the Brown-Eyed Girls, but his idea had been haunting me.

"I am not going to join the Brown-Eyed Girls," I told him, and explained what had happened.

"Well, I wish you good luck," he said. "And get well soon," he added.

I spent the afternoon being poked and prodded, so that evening, after sleeping pills and liquids, I settled into bed and turned on the little radio, with my stash of booze at the ready. The news broadcasts were still full of the story of James Meredith registering at the University of Mississippi earlier that month, escorted by the federal marshals who had been ordered to protect him by Robert F. Kennedy, the U.S. attorney general. Governor Ross Barnett in Mississippi had called in his thugs, but in spite of them, Meredith became the first black student in American history to be admitted to an all-white school. It was a great moment for the world, and I kicked up my heels again (quietly, painfully, as I was practically unable to stand up from exhaustion and the drugs that had been prescribed) and took a slow turn around my room, celebrating for Meredith and for the country, and toasting him with Kahlúa.

I spent the first few days in Tucson General licking my wounds and getting the attention of Dr. Schneider, who would pull double duty as my unofficial therapist. My isolated room had its advantages. I could gaze out my window at the heartbreaking view of mountains against spectacular sunsets of red and gold as the dry western air soothed my lungs.

As my lungs continued to be drained each day and my doctors ran tests and nodded in agreement over my improvement, a sigh of relief spread through even the isolation wing at the hospital. Doctors and patients alike had been listening to the news of the Cuban missile crisis and reading the papers to find out how close we really were to nuclear war. Outside my windows, in the mountains of Arizona, there were nuclear warheads buried and at the ready, waiting for the signal from JFK to go to red alert. Kennedy and UN secretary-general U Thant reached an agreement with Soviet premier Khrushchev on the missile crisis. A deal was cut with the Russians to end the conflict, and everyone around the country sighed with relief.

I, too, was breathing easier. I was still sick, but my illness, or perhaps fate, had given me the time to think about what was happening in my life. Off the road, stopped in my tracks by something I could not negotiate, I would not be in a plane or spending night after night in a lonely hotel room where the walls or an occasional one-night stand would fill the void. My husband, the child I loved, an often overwhelming career that had swept me into its accompanying chaos—all were on pause. It was a time to reflect, and to face another kind of music. Walter was the catalyst, but I knew my marriage was probably over and that my life was going to change, had to change. The illness would force me to be still, at least for a time.

After five weeks in isolation, I received permission from the hospital to fly to Colorado, where I was admitted to the National Jewish Hospital in Denver. I needed a few more months of hospitalization, and as Theo Bikel served on the board of National Jewish, he was able to get me in as a charity patient. I had no money, and only Theo's goodwill helped me get the treatment I needed to get well. I will never forget Theo's kindness to me then and in years to come.

I was paying keen attention to the news of the war, as usual, and learned from the papers in Denver that Mike Mansfield, the Senate majority leader, had gone to Vietnam to observe its progress. He saw what was happening more clearly than others, and made a historic speech on December 2 in which he spoke out bluntly against the war. He was the first American official to publicly do so.

Jac came to visit me in Denver and brought me the recordings of Jacques Brel, and I listened to "Marieke" and "Chanson des Vieux Amants." I played the guitar and rested, as though I were of the dead, not the living.

In late November Peter flew to Colorado with Clark. Now I would have my son with me. He stayed with my parents and went to a little children's play group. Every afternoon I was allowed out of the hospital and drove to Mom and Dad's house on Marion Street. I played the piano, returning to the Rachmaninoff Piano Concerto No. 2 on my Baldwin grand like a bird to its sanctuary. I played with Clark and fed him his dinner and then made my way back to the hospital.

Peter and I talked and argued and wept on the phone and then in person, when he came to be with me over Christmas while I was still in the hospital, until it was clear that divorce was the next step. On New Year's weekend of 1963, my husband arranged to spirit Clark back to Connecticut, where he could make his legal request for sole custody of our son. His mother, Margaret, and stepfather, Hal, arranged to take Clark for a day and did not bring him back to my parents', but instead took him on a plane to Chicago, where Peter picked him up. I was devastated but helpless. I called the Colorado attorney general and said my husband had kidnapped my son, but I was told there was nothing I could do. I had no separation agreement, and therefore no rights.

I was the one who had broken the rules, who had shattered the peace. I knew I wanted out, and now this was the price I would have to pay. The marriage was finished, but I could not accept losing my son.

I felt paralyzed, but there was nothing I could do except call lawyers and begin to work on a divorce and a plan for regaining custody of Clark. Of course I wanted full custody, but Clark was Peter's son as well. It was not going to be easy. And the custody battle, which began that very day, would seem to take forever.

In the first week of January 1963, I filed for divorce. The proceedings would take two years, and at the same time I would be fighting for custody of my son, a battle that would continue after the divorce.

But finally I was beginning to regain my health. The doctors released me from the hospital, so I could go back to—what? I would not be returning to Connecticut. I would not be going home. Instead, I would go to New York, where Walter lived. Where the music was being created, where the folk revival was at its most exciting.

To a new life.

TOP: *M*y father, Chuck, at his typewriter and Braille writer, preparing for his radio show.

ABOVE, LEFT: *M*e, age four, Seattle. RIGHT: *M*y mother, Marjorie, Seattle, Washington, 1939.

ABOVE: *M*e, age six;
my father, Chuck;
and my brother, Mike,
age two, Los Angeles.

LEFT: *J*unior high school,
Denver, Colorado,
1954.

*M*e and Peter Taylor,
Denver, 1956.

*W*ith my son, Clark, age seven.

*C*lark, age twenty, New York.

ABOVE: *M*y mother, David, Denver
John, me, Holly Ann, and Mike on the
way to a reunion at Fern Lake Lodge—
Fern Lake Trail, Colorado, 1978.

RIGHT: *I*n Colorado with Holly Ann,
1978 (top) and Denver John Collins,
1979 (bottom).

BELOW: *C*lark and his daughter,
Hollis, St. Paul, Minnesota, 1989.

OPPOSITE:
*L*ouis Nelson, my beloved
husband, and me after our
wedding, New York, 1996.
"Uncle Louis in the rain forest
with a girl," said Rowen Kahn,
Holly Ann's three-year-old.

LEFT: *H*arold Leventhal, my manager from 1961 to 1972 and friend for life.

BELOW: *J*ac Holzman, president of Elektra Records, and me, upon release of *Colors of the Day,* 1969.

Onstage with
Kris Kristofferson.

RICHARD GORDON

LEFT: With Rosa Parks.

BELOW: Joan Baez
and me singing
"Diamonds and Rust"
in the rain, Newport
Festival, 2009.

Fritz Richmond, Joni Mitchell,
me, John Cooke (Cookie),
Nancy Carlen, and Joan Baez at
Big Sur Folk Festival, 1968.

Dorchester Hotel,
London, 2009.

Chapter Thirteen

Wild Rippling Water

As I was a-walking and a-rambling one day
I spied a fair couple a-making their way
One was a cowboy, and a brave one was he
And the other was a lady, and a fair one was she.

—Traditional, "Wild Rippling Water"

ONCE the doctors at National Jewish Hospital released me in February 1963, I collected my guitar and packed a tiny bag with a dress, some makeup, an extra pair of shoes, and the TB drugs I would have to take for another year and a half, and I headed for Washington, D.C. I was bound for New York, but first I had been invited to join a group of singers in a special performance for President Kennedy, to be televised to the nation. My mother and father took me to the airport, where we said an emotional goodbye. My mom was still angry about Peter having taken Clark back to the East Coast.

I was not worried about my voice or my guitar playing. I had been singing every day in the hospital and playing the guitar; I knew I could carry on. I had learned some new songs, particularly ones I hoped to record—a couple from Tom Paxton and Pete

Seeger, including his wonderful "Turn! Turn! Turn!" I had been brought low by illness, but in a way it was a peaceful valley amid the mountains of chaos that had become my life. For nearly five months I had been sheltered, taken care of, healed. And separated from Peter.

I walked out of the doors of that hospital with no place to go but forward and nothing to do but sing. It was, in many ways, a path to the unknown. But I was ready, and I was filled with a kind of wild faith that everything was as it should be.

THE preparations for *Dinner with the President* were already in gear when I arrived at Washington's Sheraton Hotel. Television cameras were filming; I was late, having been delayed by an early spring snow that had slowed everything in D.C. to a crawl. Harold greeted me, and then someone rushed me to the stage, past the tables covered in white linen and ornate floral centerpieces. I joined the rehearsal and we ran through our songs as waiters hurried about with trays of glasses, cups, and dinner plates.

Robert Ryan, the actor, was onstage already, and his presence dominated the room even though at that moment it was filled only with waiters and performers. Ryan was an impressive man, tall and handsome, with dark hair that fell over eyes that seemed to single me out, looking directly into mine. I knew Robert from New York, where Harold had introduced us. He was fifty-four then, but already his face was familiar from his acting in *The Longest Day*— about the D-Day invasion—which I had seen on its release in 1962. I had the feeling that Ryan couldn't have cared less if the crowds had not yet arrived. He was the same in public as in private. His looks and demeanor set him apart as a star, but his smile was warm and welcoming and his politics (he was an early opponent of the war in Vietnam) were as friendly to my own as his smile. He put his arms around me in a welcoming embrace, and I felt I belonged;

he was someone who made you feel that way always, whether he was in the limelight or you were, or neither of you were. It is a rare quality.

Ryan was the emcee for the night, and he took control of the show while men in dark suits with wires in their ears—the president's Secret Service detail—paced the hotel lobby and roamed the ballroom. President Kennedy and his brother Robert were to be seated directly in front of the stage. We would be looking right at them when we sang.

Upstairs in the big suite where refreshments were being served (food and lots of bottles of whiskey and bourbon), Josh, Lynn Gold, the Clancy Brothers and Tommy Makem, Odetta, Robert, Will Holt, and everyone else who was in the show welcomed me and peppered me with questions. They all wanted to know how I was feeling. Had the hospital been terrible? Was I able to smoke, to sing, to work, to go on the road? I was happy to tell them that the doctors had given me a clean bill of health, and I truly believed everything would be all right. Singing for the president was a great way to come back to performing.

It really began to feel like a reunion of old friends. Will told me that if I had been diagnosed with TB in an earlier era, I would have spent a year or more at a sanatorium in the mountains somewhere. Now, with the drugs that were available, I'd be able to get on with my life, my divorce, my music, and my next album.

But now I began to feel the sadness, the heartbreak, of leaving Peter, and it would come and go, painful and sorrowful, for years.

The Clancy Brothers and Tommy Makem had been making records for decades. They had toured extensively through the States after arriving from Ireland. I had known them since the television show at the Village Gate on the night that Jac Holzman signed me to Elektra. I admired and respected them, and we had a great time whenever we were together. They were in their standard uniform that night—white fisherman sweaters. Tom, who was also an actor, always flirted with me. I enjoyed their attention, very masculine but sweet and innocent. They were all married, mostly happily, and I knew from experience that some of them didn't drink. Tommy Makem never touched a drop, having taken the "pledge" as a teenager in Ireland.

Just before we went downstairs to begin the performance, they held out their hands for me to take an Irish friendship vow with all of them. I felt embraced and appreciated; it was the nicest thing they could have done for me at that moment.

Robert proposed a toast, wishing us all well in the show—and expressing the hope that the poetry and music of the evening would help convince Kennedy to reconsider the war in Indochina. The show proved to be a great success, from what we could tell. Kennedy was smiling, nodding, clapping, and enjoying himself. I watched him when I was not singing. I had voted for him and celebrated his glorious triumph over Nixon, thrilled that this vibrant newcomer had found his way to the White House, signaling a new generation of leadership, empowering the youth of the country to make a difference. We were all enchanted with Kennedy's personal charisma and ready to follow him toward the brighter world he promised. He said he would see that we got to the moon, and we believed him. The whole nation had watched him bring us safely through the Cuban missile crisis, making decisions that would protect the world from a nuclear holocaust.

When the show was over, the performers all passed through a long reception line to shake the president's hand. He was handsome beyond his photos. The cameras continued to roll as JFK touched my hand and looked into my eyes; I felt the electricity that comes from certain people. It felt as though he could do anything, answer any question, and solve any problem. He was *the man*, and you would do anything he asked.

Afterward, I headed to New York, where I would be starting over.

Chapter Fourteen

The Kettle of Fish

The fishermen are pitching pennies
In the sand beside the sea
The Sunrise hits their oilskin boots
and their painted boats and me.

—JUDY COLLINS, "Fisherman's Song"

$\mathcal{A}$T the end of March 1963, I spent a few days with Walter on Hudson Street. Finally free to be together, we found we didn't get along as well. It was as though the fire had burned bright when we had to hide our relationship, but now the ice formed around my heart.

Soon I found my own place in Greenwich Village. The rent was $135 a month. I had not worked for months, and there was no money. Jac had advanced me a little against royalties, but I could afford the apartment only because I shared the space with Vera Hertenstein, Jac's secretary at Elektra.

My new home, not far from Walter's, was on the corner of West 10th Street and Hudson, in the heart of Greenwich Village. I felt somewhat lost, having left my home in Connecticut and my marriage. At the same time, I knew I had finally come home at last. Everything I needed was in New York, except my son, Clark. He would visit me on weekends and during vacations. Soon began the long and drawn-out custody fight to keep him with me permanently.

For now, I lived in the center of the folk music revival. I was a couple of blocks from the Kettle of Fish and a few more from Cafe Fiorello's, the Village Gate, Gerde's Folk City on West 4th, and the Gaslight on MacDougal. I could wander at night over to the clubs to hear music and have a meal.

The key people then at Elektra were Jac, who was president; Mark Abramson, who engineered and produced albums; Vera, Jac's secretary; and Bill Harvey, who did the covers. By the time we started working together, Mark had been with Elektra for a couple of years. In addition to the artists he worked with, Mark had recorded the sound archives Elektra released in the late fifties and early sixties, in which trains whistled, dogs barked, motorbikes revved up, men snored, wind chimes sang. In those days you could find ambient sounds (for films or TV, mostly) only if you went out with a microphone and recorded them.

Jac and Mark were both obsessive. Each had the ability to concentrate on the work at hand, which over nearly two decades came to benefit me when it came to recording. Mark was as totally focused on getting the best possible album out of me as he was on his train whistles. I liked him from the start.

Jac, who knew him well, said of Mark, "He always struck me as a person who wouldn't be surprised by any oddity of human nature, a friend with whom you could confide your most agonizing personal secrets. He was amused by the human condition but took it seriously in a light way."

Mark was twenty-five, two years older than I was when we began working together in 1962. To me, he always seemed so much older and wiser. His dark good looks reminded everyone who knew him of a young Jean-Paul Belmondo, and he kept his body fit by running and working out, even though exercise was not yet in vogue. He was an intellectual who could often be found reading Henry Miller or Jean Genet, and his soft and gentle manner concealed steely determination. He was smart and at times very funny. Mark was in love with his college sweetheart, Janis Young. I knew Janis, and we sometimes even went out together, the three of us, or with Jac or others from the Elektra family.

Mark did not drink or smoke, though I think he might have liked a little marijuana now and then, and maybe acid. Like many of us, he was searching for a spiritual path to follow that offered something more than the faith in which he'd been raised.

Mark was imaginative, supportive, and always an enthusiastic companion on the long days and nights of mixing, looking for songs, haunting the thriving clubs in Greenwich Village. He challenged me to take greater artistic risks. The music we shared was a life-changing love affair, and if I had a constant, enduring relationship with a man in those years, balancing out my search for love and the people I might take hostage for a few weeks or a few years, it was with Mark, my musical soul mate.

There is great intimacy in making music with other musicians, producers, and engineers. You spend interminable hours in the studio, and you think and talk about work and finding material. Mark and I searched and listened to what were mostly newly written songs by Woody Guthrie, Pete Seeger, and Tom Paxton. We sat with Jac, getting his take on our choices, exchanging ideas about what we would record. We were already breaking the rules—the folk music police, especially the bible of the times, *Sing Out*, would not approve the new songs that we were mixing in with the traditional folk repertoire—but Mark and I had discovered that doing the unexpected was what we liked best. The challenge was to do it as artistically as possible.

Mark spread the word that we were looking for new songs.

Between us, we knew just about everyone in Greenwich Village, and the songs started rolling in.

I would run into singers on the streets and in the clubs at night: Phil Ochs, Dave Van Ronk, the deliciously cute David Blue. David, one of the old-guard Village singer-songwriters on Bleecker Street, was talented and good-looking, a folksinger with curly dark hair, an angelic face, and a sweet voice. I had a very brief affair with him. One night? Two weeks? A month? Truly an example of "if you remember the sixties, you weren't there!" David had an antique single bed in which we struggled to find room for our passions, and for his boots, which I finally got him to remove. In the few mornings we spent together we would get cups of coffee and wander through Washington Square Park below the tiny apartment where he lived, listening to the banjo and guitar players, and he would sing me his songs in a seductive voice.

I would meet up with Tom Paxton on my strolls through the Village. He always had a twinkle in his blue eyes. Two years older than me, Tom was a hell of a good writer who played guitar and had a sweet, unaffected voice. Over a cappuccino at Cafe Fiorello's we would talk about our lives. He said he had been born in Illinois and partly raised in Oklahoma, where Burl Ives had inspired him. He became enchanted with folk music, listening to the recordings of Woody and Pete. He had been in the army typing school at Fort Dix in New Jersey, and would spend his weekends in Greenwich Village, hanging out in the clubs listening to music and learning. After his discharge, he came to the city and auditioned for the Chad Mitchell Trio. When he sang one of his own songs, "The Marvelous Toy," for Milt Okun of Cherry Lane Music, Tom became Milt's very first client. Tom went on to write many great and enduring songs.

Whenever Tom ran into me on Bleecker Street he would want to sing me a song right there. If it was raining, he would pull me into a storefront and start singing "Rambling Boy," "The Last Thing on My Mind," or "Bottle of Wine," which had particular resonance for me.

> *Bottle of wine, fruit on the vine*
> *When you gonna let me get sober?*

Many of the artists I would meet and get to know, like Tom, were already on Elektra. It was a small but happy family in the Village. I could wander over to Izzy Young's Folklore Center on MacDougal Street and buy guitar strings and copies of *Sing Out*. The magazine had established itself as the voice of the folk movement, with Irwin Silber's editorials (Irwin would be the one to write the blistering slam of Dylan's electric transformation at Newport in 1965) and songs by new writers, as well as articles on their music and their lives. I could get the skinny on where everyone was playing.

From time to time I would make my way down Hudson Street to see Walter, but our lovemaking had grown practical and mechanical. It still comforted me, but now it also made me a little wistful; I remembered how passionate it had felt at the start. Walter had become a security blanket for me, and I wasn't quite ready to give that up.

As soon as I was settled in my new digs, I would go to pick up Clark for a couple of weeks' visit to my new home in New York. Peter would drive down to the midway point on the Merritt Parkway—some sterile and desolate Howard Johnson's—where we would meet to exchange scowls and Clark, though my heart would sometimes ache for my lost marriage.

My apartment mate, Vera, had become a friend over the two years I had been recording for Elektra. She was single, slim, and good company. Thankfully, she was also a hell of a cook; her spaetzle was one of our regular accompaniments to roasted veal shank. I had been a pretty good cook once—baking bread and pies on a woodstove, managing the kidney pies, tacos and enchiladas, meat loaves, and great big pots of spaghetti sauce—but all of that was a distant memory now. I was on my own, sharing the living room and my spacious bedroom (but not my bed) with Vera.

I had been settled in my Village digs only a few weeks when a court-appointed social worker from Connecticut came to visit me and evaluate my fitness as a mother. The divorce was moving forward, and Peter and I had started the battle for custody of Clark. The social worker sat in my one little rocking chair, under the window that looked out over the White Horse Tavern.

The woman from the agency strode into my apartment with a frown on her face, clearly neither amused nor impressed by my rocking chair, my imploring looks, my roommate, my cheap apartment in the Village, or my profession. She was in alien territory, coming from the clean streets of the Connecticut suburbs, and looked extremely uncomfortable, as I am sure I did as well. The meeting was tense and her disapproval was obvious. But as she searched through my apartment, full of Clark's toys and his books—Dr. Seuss, whose *Green Eggs and Ham* we read over and over together, and *Curious George*—she seemed to soften. Still, she made no promises. When she left I fell into a deep depression. If I had to rely on this woman to plead my case, I might as well give up, I thought.

My law firm, famous for their success in custody agreements, told me there was no way I could lose custody of Clark. Mothers did not lose custody, they assured me.

In April I asked Jac to find me a lawyer to write the new Elektra contract, as we were approaching my third album, and he suggested David Braun. David was busy setting up the legal relationships between record companies and their clients and represented a lot of my peers at the time. David, gentle, smart, and kind, would become my lawyer and lifetime friend. And he did right by me, as well as by Elektra.

ON April 12, 1963, Jac and I went to see Bob Dylan in concert at New York's Town Hall. Dylan was singing new songs, songs that made me sit up and listen in a completely different way. Jac kept poking me in the ribs—"That one," he would say, or "That one would be perfect for you!" I wrote down some of my impressions from that night in my journal:

> It was quite an experience; suffice to say that this boy is not by any stretch of the imagination an entertainer, but he sings songs that he has written, with almost no voice, playing the simplest of chords, not looking so great in his dusty jeans and leather shirt, with a rig on his neck to hold the harmonicas he plays, and all the while looking something like a dancing bear . . . and I feel that this was the most important concert I, personally, have ever been to. His material is so unfettered by any attempt at entertaining . . . that it makes everyone else working in the field look a little pale by comparison. I heard Pete Seeger three nights later sing one of Bob's songs at the Bitter End, and there is nothing like the material he [Dylan] writes anywhere around.

Bob Dylan had arrived. I always felt the explosion of Dylan's going electric at Newport two years later paled in comparison to the impact of the first songs that night at Town Hall. "Blowin' in the Wind" shot out like a bright star in the firmament as if it had been divinely inspired.

After hearing Bob at Town Hall, I decided to record "The Lonesome Death of Hattie Carroll," which I performed at Town

Hall in 1964, and "Masters of War," which I sang on my third album.

Pete Seeger had a show that week at the Bitter End, and sang that new song of Bob's. Pete and Toshi, his wife, Harold Leventhal, Mark Abramson, and I all had drinks after Pete's show. We talked about the war—when and where the next rally would be held, and who would be singing. Pete was so young, so vital, and such a singer! Toshi was a powerful Japanese woman who seemed to be a great force in Pete's life. Pete said he had known the minute he met Toshi, in 1943, that they would spend their lives together.

That night I decided I was going to record "Turn! Turn! Turn!"

Walter got me paid singing gigs on whatever he was producing. I did film recordings, commercial jingles, and some singing for the score of the television production of *Birth of a Nation*, by Millard Lampell. The dollars began to float into my purse and then my bank account. Having a roommate helped, and I started to get on my feet financially.

When Clark visited we wandered the city, combed the Village for toy shops, went uptown to stare at the dinosaurs at the American Museum of Natural History. We ate burgers, fries, and sundaes at Rumplemeyer's on Central Park South, and sang songs together while I played the guitar. Sometimes we would meet friends for an iced orange drink on Sheridan Square and tool around 8th Street and the West Village.

Although I was thrilled to be living in the Village, and glad to have Harold helping me get my recording career moving with Elektra, I could also see that all these external trappings of stability and success couldn't make me whole. I was still Judy, still troubled, on the road or in New York, having affairs or not. I began to see that the inner demons were still eating away at whatever serenity I momentarily achieved.

By the summer of 1963 I had fallen into a deep depression

again. My drinking worried me more and more. I could never count on waking up with a clear head. Efforts I made to moderate my intake of alcohol were pathetic and, finally, useless.

I remember one day in particular. The sun was pouring through the windows that looked out onto Hudson Street, where the trucks rolled downtown. The Hudson River gleamed and danced between the buildings on the West Side. I felt like hell, hideously hungover and extremely anxious. Although the social worker didn't know about my drinking, and I would say even now that the drinking did not interfere with my relationship with my son, I was worried. Harold and my new agents had set up enough dates to keep me busy in the coming weeks, but that particular day was quiet; everything looked bleak. I wouldn't see Clark for another couple of weeks, and I was lonely.

My anxiety attacks had begun to reappear when I moved to New York, and I had called a doctor (recommended by Harold), who prescribed Miltown, a fashionable drug in those years. Sometimes it worked, but more often it didn't and for the next twenty years I would keep that, along with Dexamyl and the various other uppers and downers I would acquire from this and other doctors in New York, in my purse along with my keys, my money, my makeup, the notebook where I wrote the lyrics to new songs I was learning, and my address book. I used these drugs sparingly, thank God. I was afraid they would interfere with my drinking!

But from time to time I would simply spin out of control, regardless of whatever mixture of medications the doctors had provided. I used alcohol to medicate anxiety, but that, too, was becoming unmanageable. And I began to struggle with food, dieting and bingeing and starving myself, the first signs that there was another addiction beginning to rule my life.

One week I tried to stop drinking for a few days, but somehow it only made the situation worse, and I began drinking more than ever. I was trying to lose weight and had started to exercise, bending and stretching and eventually making the Royal Canadian Air Force exercises a regular part of my routine.

I remember one summer afternoon wearing a white cotton Mexican wedding dress, weeping, and talking to my new doctor, Dr. Marchand, on the phone. I told him I thought I was being poisoned. He prescribed some more pills for my anxiety, and then he said I should try to find a therapist.

I knew Walter had a therapist. It was one of the first things I had learned about him. I talked to Walter about the depression I was feeling one day when we were in a taxi. My anxiety was such that I had forgotten where we were going, or why.

"Why don't you go see Ralph Klein?" Walter suggested, referring to a therapist he knew. "Ralph has helped Bob [a singer we both knew] with his drinking. Maybe he can help you."

Bob was a big man, and kind of a famous drunk. I had sung on jingles with him and knew he could be obnoxious and unpleasant, missing lines when he was drinking and giving the other singers a hard time. He had had a bitter battle with booze, but lately he was looking thinner and drinking only beer.

I got Ralph's number and trekked uptown from the Village to my first session at his apartment on the Upper West Side. I don't know what I expected, but Ralph would prove to be just what I needed at that moment.

I needed to talk about my depressions, and about the suicide attempt that I had made when I was in my teens, and about my father. Most of all, I needed just to talk.

I told Ralph in our first session that I knew I was an alcoholic. I had known before I was twenty. By now I was rather proud that I could drink grown men under the table and drive better when I was plastered. Ralph said he felt that when we got to the bottom of my emotional problems—why I had tried to kill myself, and why I was depressed—my drinking would become manageable. He even suggested it might stop. I realize today he had not one single clue about alcoholism. I did not drink because of my problems. I had problems because I drank. It would take me twenty-three years to figure that out.

But I could talk to Ralph about everything. I hadn't even realized how badly I missed that in my life, really being able to confide in someone. I had always been able to talk to Peter—until our lives began to fall apart. I would see Ralph professionally for seven of my many years of therapy. From the first session I began feeling better, and looking better.

I experienced classic symptoms of transference with Ralph, having visions of him throwing me across the couch and having his way with me. Although he invited me out to his house in Amagansett that winter, I found myself sleeping alone in his guest room. Ralph and I had great conversations, but the sex never materialized. I was crushed, but he helped me get over it, talking to me about my overzealous expectations.

Ralph and a number of like-minded therapists were in a group that called themselves Sullivanians, after Harry Stack Sullivan, the psychoanalyst. Their leader was Saul Newton, who with his wife, Jane Pearce, wrote *The Conditions of Human Growth*, a book this group essentially adopted as their bible and made required reading for all of their patients. Newton and Pearce had worked at the William Alanson White Institute, which had been co-founded by Sullivan, but after Sullivan's death they broke with the institute to pursue their own practice. Saul had some radical ideas about the relationship with the traditional family; he said the family was itself a contributing factor to mental illness. He and his group encouraged individuals to let go of custody of their children, to practice a communal and sexually promiscuous lifestyle, and to drink alcohol as a treatment for anxiety and "nerves."

In the beginning of my sessions with Ralph, all I knew was

that I was getting help. The extent of the group's philosophy was not clear. Only later, after I had left them, did I realize I had fallen under the spell of a cult.

After Ralph I moved on to Julie, another therapist in the group, for five years; my son had counseling with Mildred Antonelli; and later I was in treatment both with Saul Newton and briefly with his wife, Jane Pearce.

Ralph referred me to Saul (whom the group called "Father") for occasional sessions when Clark was beginning to show signs of (untreated and undiagnosed) drug addiction. I found Saul Newton to be a tyrant, the star of his own soap opera. He was very good-looking and charming. We talked politics as much as we had therapy. He had fought with the Abraham Lincoln Brigade in the Spanish Civil War, had been a union organizer, and was bright, cultured, and ambitious.

I did not adhere to some of the Sullivanians' concepts. I did not live in their commune, and I followed my own path in most areas of my life. I was closer to my family than my shrink might have liked. But I sure got a lot of mileage out of the Sullivanian belief that alcohol was good for anxiety and that having multiple sex partners was a political statement and a healthy lifestyle.

Married couples were told they must live apart for the mental health of their children, so the kids were likely to be raised by nannies or babysitters; parental visits were limited to one hour a day and one evening a week. When you look at it now, these rules sound very much like the habits of the elite from another century! Saul was a little overbearing, and frankly, anyone who tried to tell me what to do was going to run into a wall.

But certain revolutionary ideas Saul Newton and Jane Pearce practiced were attractive to an already liberal girl working her way into a career in the arena of music and social justice. At the time, everyone in my peer group was espousing free love. Communal living, group parenting, and sharing the wealth were sixties ideas, too.

But the Sullivanians went too far and in the 1970s were accused of kidnapping children to get them out of the clutches of their parents. In later years Newton would face legal battles and professional condemnation from his peers.

Having said that, and in spite of their pushy social beliefs and knowing that they enabled my alcoholism, I am still grateful to the Sullivanians for the way they helped hone my creative process. They encouraged a set of habits that had begun in my family and tied my work and my studies—singing, piano, cello (short-lived!), even making pottery—to my dreams and my values. That was essential to my growth as an artist, a performer, and a person. They helped make it possible for me to earn, with only one year of college under my belt, what amounted to a Ph.D. in my profession.

Sex continued to be a pleasure I sought out, and I talked to Ralph about all of it. There was plenty of it to talk about, more so now that those little white pills took pregnancy out of the equation. I believed I was doing nothing more than any of my peers were doing. I explored sex with the same curiosity and enthusiasm that I explored everything else in life.

There were a few women with whom I had more than friendly relationships. One friend told me that if she were a lesbian, I would be the woman she would choose to be with. Another woman with whom I had a yearlong sexual relationship reminded me that I was not up to intimacy with a person of the same sex after dawn or while sober. Exploration was fine, but falling in love never seemed to happen. And I was probably too square myself to engage enthusiastically in an affair with a woman that would entail any kind of commitment. In fact, any real emotional commitment seemed impossible for me, regardless of the other person's gender.

My explorations with women did confirm that I was really attracted to men. Men made me more comfortable. But the drinking and the sex were inextricably connected. Sex was, for me, a political statement as well as a personal one, and according to the

Sullivanians, having a free attitude about sex was also about being artistically free as well.

But the truth is that I often blacked out by the time the act itself occurred.

My drinking increased, and now I seemed to have less control than ever. I told myself that the booze blurred the pain, but really the booze caused the pain and sustained it. I was often nursing an awful hangover, but I did not think anything of it; I never felt any guilt. Should I have? I was certainly taking advantage of most sexual opportunities that came my way.

Ralph Klein made one very interesting observation: he called my father's confiding in me about his affairs a kind of incest. I insisted on calling it a kind of trust; I said that my father needed to talk to someone about everything, and that I was all right with it having been me.

I still feel that way.

As therapy continued and I began to settle into my New York life, my career seemed to be shifting into a higher gear. I had more work than ever before, my records were selling well, and I was making a little money. I missed my son but grew optimistic, even enthusiastic, about the outcome of the custody case.

Every other weekend, as the judge had agreed, I tried to have Clark come to the city. I would often pick him up at our meeting place at Howard Johnson's. The exchanges with Peter were painful and tense. Clark must have felt it, that boy whose eyes were just like mine, whose face was freckled by the summer sun. His life was torn into two pieces, and the poor boy became lost somewhere between his father's life in Storrs and his mother's in the city. He would ask me why he couldn't stay with me, but I had no answer. I had to wait for the court in Connecticut to decide our fate. The lawyers continued to reassure me that no mother loses her child in a court of law.

But the odds against me were getting higher each day. I, who was my own worst enemy, needed a best friend. I thought booze was my friend. I did not know I was in a fight—not just with my lawyers, not just with my husband, but also with my disease. I didn't know I could not win this one on my own, that it would take years, and a change of mind and heart, to win the battle with an opponent I could not even see.

Now, like my father before me, I would have to find the radar to make my way through the darkness around me.

Chapter Fifteen

Judy Collins 3

It ain't the leavin'
That's a-grievin' me
But my true love who's bound to stay behind.

—Bob Dylan, "Farewell"

My new life in New York took on every appearance of flourishing even as I spiraled deeper into the abyss. I was surrounded by exciting people, and there seemed to be a stream of new opportunities. In late 1963, I began hosting a radio show on WBAI. Artists would come by for an hour, I would put a bottle of whiskey on the table, the engineer would turn the dials, and we would be off to the races.

Some of the guests included Tom Paxton, Pete Stanley, the Freedom Voices, and the band Koerner, Ray and Glover. We would talk music and often politics, as the two seemed to always go hand in hand in those days. The McPeake Family also came to do the show. Pete Seeger had "discovered" them and suggested they tour the States, which they would do in 1965.

I kept in touch with the McPeakes after they sang on my radio show. A few years after I recorded their beautiful song "Wild Mountain Thyme," I made a trip to Belfast, where I was singing in concert. The whole family came to see me, and then I visited their home. The patriarch of the McPeakes was in his eighties by then. Everyone called him "Da," and he had helped bring the Irish harp back into fashion. He was a lovely, gentle Irishman who was not getting around very well at his age, and sat in his rocker on an early winter's night.

From their little house in Belfast, two of the brothers and I walked to the neighborhood bar, where they stood me to something called a Black Velvet. I think it was Irish magic mist, some concoction of dark beer and powerful whiskey. I have never had one since, but I will never forget it. My eyes were crossed as we walked back to their house, where we all sang "Wild Mountain Thyme" in glorious harmony. They had to see me to my hotel.

I was exposed to all kinds of new issues and new ways of thinking. One night I would meet the playwright Lorraine Hansberry at her home in the Village, where she was holding a fundraising luncheon for SNCC, the Student Nonviolent Coordinating Committee, which was becoming a major voice in the civil rights movement. Lorraine was also a big supporter of SCLC, the Southern Christian Leadership Conference.

I would run into Suze Rotolo at Izzy Young's Folklore Center, Dylan following like a mangy puppy dog. I remember seeing them as they appeared in Don Hunstein's photograph on the cover of *The Freewheelin' Bob Dylan*, with Bob in those rough-out boots of his, his hair tousled, his shirt still wrinkled, his smile crooked and charming. Suze's warm and open smile is one we would all come to know well. The fact that they were in love shows everywhere in that picture. Arms entwined, their faces full of the carefree innocence of two young people, the photograph captures a precious moment before all the electricity and power of fame paradoxically drained some of that miraculous energy. He was twenty; she was just seventeen. It is a touching photograph, and timeless.

That summer, Jac and Elektra had begun to branch out, and there, too, I was along for the ride, in the company of so many new musicians and writers. The label moved uptown to Broadway and West 61st Street, and Jac attracted all kinds of musicians and groups. In the coming years, Phil Ochs, The Incredible String Band, Paul Butterfield, and eventually Harry Chapin, Carly Simon, and the Cars all came to the label.

Jac was open to all kinds of music, relying on his impeccable taste and an ear for unique, gifted artists. He was a one-man think tank about talent and how to find it. Many times he was simply in the right place at the right time, as he had been with me.

THINGS would change quickly in popular music as the 1960s rolled in. The timeless moon-June-spoon lyrics of Rodgers and Hart standards would be joined on the radio, in clubs, and on records by the words of the newly minted singers and writers who poured out their passions, both personal and political, in song. Inspired by artists such as Woody Guthrie, Pete Seeger, Ramblin' Jack Elliott, Tom Paxton, and Bob Dylan, they ushered in a new musical era. The opinionated, the determined, the angry, the oppressed, the ones with the searing, searching points of view, took center stage.

I think of Bob Dylan, who was writing those breathtaking songs, sifting through the embers of earlier fires, making new images, creating fresh visions in his lyrics. All around us there was an awakening social consciousness—against the war in Vietnam, against segregation, about labor concerns, about the union-busting that had been a problem for decades, and about immigration—as well as a desire to speak of personal issues. These concerns inspired artistic expression and political engagement. The Beatles gave a heart-lifting backbeat to the changing times, and Dylan put the fire in our bellies. The music we loved and sang in those smoky little clubs all over the country was becoming the pop music of an entire generation.

The times, they certainly were a-changin'.

I WAS fortunate to have found Elektra, or rather, to have had Jac Holzman find me. The right record label meant the world to a recording artist, and sometimes represented the difference between success and obscurity. Joan Baez, Joni Mitchell, and I benefited from the owners of Vanguard, Asylum, and Elektra, who had reputations for making a commitment to each of their artists. They put promotional muscle behind each new release, and they had the heart to stay with an artist through the ups and downs of a recording career. In that era, before so many record labels were gobbled up by huge media conglomerates, each label had a distinct personality and direction.

Long-term relationships in the record business, however, were still rare. I couldn't have seen ahead to the nearly fifty years during which I would remain with Elektra and Rhino, Elektra's distributor of my back catalogue. But I did know that I was in a safe place, with people who believed in what I was doing. And now I would begin my third album for the label.

Walter—no longer my lover but still my musical director—took me on a quick plane trip out to Las Vegas in the summer of 1963 to hear Bobby Darin at the Flamingo Hotel. Walter wanted me to meet Jim McGuinn, a young guitar player and singer who was working with Darin, to see if he might be a good match for the new album.

We got dressed up for dinner and were shown to a table next

to the stage, where we ordered drinks and settled back to watch a master perform. I had not been to a club like this since going to see Tempest Storm, and I felt very out of my depth. The folk clubs I was playing did not have waiters in black tie and drinks in frosted glasses, but I soon settled in with a martini of the right size—extra large—and got comfortable.

I was unprepared for Darin's sophistication, his down-to-earth humor, and his wonderful voice. He came onstage, dark haired, slender, almost like a boy, and showered us with gentle banter between songs and a light touch in his manner. He was dressed in a shirt and trousers, no jacket, and his manner was very personal and direct. He acknowledged Walter with a nod before breaking into his first song, with a kick-ass band behind him. Walter pointed out Jim McGuinn, who sat prominently near the front of the band, dressed in clean-lined black pants, shirt, bare-headed, his banjos and guitars at the ready.

Walter had known Darin for years; they were both New York boys, musical, intelligent, and articulate. Darin had become an overnight success after working his ass off, both personally and professionally, all his life. When he began to make records, he made intriguing choices: "The Rock Island Line," a song performed by Huddie Ledbetter (Leadbelly to the folk world), which indicated what my father would have called gumption; "Splish Splash," which got the little girls screaming à la Buddy Holly and the Beatles; Brecht and Weill's "Mack the Knife," from *The Threepenny Opera,* which became number one on the *Billboard* charts; Charles Trenet's "La Mer," which Darin called "Beyond the Sea"; and a beautiful and still haunting version of Tim Hardin's "If I Were a Carpenter." Hearing Bobby today, I am moved and amazed at the range of his musical choices. They are brilliant, and totally Bobby Darin. Or totally Walden Robert Cassotto, which is the name he was given at birth.

Now, up there on the stage at the Flamingo, he had a young

folkie in tow, the guy who had come out of the Chicago and New York folk scenes, and was accompanying Darin on banjo and twelve-string guitar.

Jim McGuinn was a dreamy guy with a lean and hungry look, almost gaunt. He wore his dark hair long. He was dressed in a sharp suit and had thick lashes and bedroom eyes. He sang occasional harmony with Darin in a sweet, twangy voice, half country and half crooner.

Walter told me over the applause that Jim was a kid from Chicago who had gone to the Old Town School of Folk Music to learn the banjo, and been a fan of Elvis Presley. He had already had success playing backup for the Chad Mitchell Trio and been a sideman with the Limelighters. Darin was supported well by McGuinn on his hits, and I was impressed with Jim's musicality and his timing.

When McGuinn did a fifteen-minute solo turn, he was very appealing and sexy, singing songs like "John Riley" and a few sea chanties.

After the show, we met both Darin and McGuinn backstage. I liked Jim's friendly, easy manner on and off stage, and by the time Walter and I left that night I had hired McGuinn to be part of my new album. He said he'd come east as soon as he finished his gig with Darin at the end of July. We would rehearse in Lenox, Massachusetts, where I had found a rental for a couple of weeks.

During those sessions, each of us fighting a demon (Jim with his bad teeth, always going to the dentist, and I always trying not to drink too much), we cemented a friendship that has continued since. Jim wove his shimmering twelve-string guitar into our new arrangements as if he were sewing jewels into the fabric of the music. His playing contributed a great sound to this album, and pushed it into what I now see was a more contemporary feel. "Turn! Turn! Turn!" accompanied by Jim on the twelve-string was to become one of my first songs played on the radio.

In the coming years, McGuinn would form the Byrds (along

with David Crosby, Gene Clark, Chris Hillman, and Michael Clarke). One of the first songs they recorded was "Turn! Turn! Turn!" and it became their first radio hit as well. Jim made a tremendous and important mark on the music industry, leading it more and more toward a synthesis of rock and folk music. He plunged that twelve-string sound into the depth of pop music, where it has lived ever since. In 1967, as a follower of the Indonesian spiritual practice Subud, Jim would change his name to Roger.

Judy Collins 3 included the great Woody Guthrie social commentary on immigration, "Deportees," and songs about work, such as the rollicking sea chantey "Bullgine Run"; there were songs by Shel Silverstein and Freddy Hellerman of the Weavers, and songs about love. "In the Hills of Shiloh," another song by Shel Silverstein and Jim Friedman, is a song about a woman wandering in a daze looking for her lover, who was lost in the Battle of Shiloh forty years earlier. "Farewell" typifies the sweet, uncomplicated melodies of early Dylan songs. It is simply one of the prettiest songs I know. I listen to my Travis-picking on this track with a certain amount of wistfulness, knowing my fingers aren't quite up to it anymore. In contrast, "Masters of War," also on the album, is Dylan at his complicated and uncompromising best.

These new songs were the product of a growing musical and social consciousness of the times. I was finding a new world, exploring the singer-songwriters of Greenwich Village. I took these songs into my heart, sang them in concert, recorded them, and made them part of my life and the lives of my audiences.

I WAS slated to play the Newport Folk Festival that year at the end of July, as was Joan Baez. Joan gave an electrifying performance that riveted the audience and the world. I can see her dark hair shining in the lights of the stage, the awed audience bending to her every note or phrase. Her voice soared over the water as if calling to ships at sea. Every girl and woman in the audience wanted to be like her, and every man wanted to be with her, yet her heart had been won by the guy she had referred to as a toad.

Dylan was there only for Joan, who shot into Bob's life that year like a bolt of lightning. Joan's thing with Bob seemed somehow to be about so much more than just two people in love. Joan needed to sing the songs of Dylan. She needed to introduce him to the world, onstage next to her. The thousands of fans who came to see Joan would be swept away by this paler star who suddenly shone so brilliantly in the spotlight. They were surreal together, entwined in the lights and the searing soul of the sixties. Some said they *were* that searing soul.

Joan and Bob had first met at Gerde's "hoot night" on April 10, 1961, the night before Bob's first "real" gig there. At Newport two years later, all of us were together, talking about what to sing for the encore. Mary Travers, Peter Yarrow, and Noel Stookey, and of course my friend John Cooke (Cookie), who was appearing with the Charles River Valley Boys. By then Cookie was a splendid photographer and took many pictures of Joan, her sister Mimi, and Dylan. All fell under the spell of Joan in an instant, or so it seemed.

In Murray Lerner's film about Newport, Dylan seems an innocent child of nature in spite of the engineer boots and wild hair and eyes that darted about. Murray later told me Dylan was intrigued by Joan's fame, how she handled the crowd, the press, and her electric connection with the audience. I think we all were. She would open her mouth and sing and people would practically faint away. *Festival*, the black-and-white documentary about the Newport Folk Festivals of 1963, 1964, and 1965, captures singular moments in time when we were the young and mostly (except for Joan) unknown ragtag folksingers out by the ocean, happy in our own world, yet hell-bent on changing the rest of the world.

Joan's appearances with Dylan, the new kid on the block, her hair flying, the two of them singing together with all their fireworks and drama, startled her audience both on and off stage.

When Joan and Dylan went to London the following year with Bob Neuwirth, Al Grossman, D. A. Pennebaker, and the film crew for *Don't Look Back*, Dylan had huge shows at the Royal Albert Hall in London. But not once did he invite Baez to share the stage with him. That lapse would be costly for Dylan as well as for their love affair, and it was chronicled in Joan's beautiful 1975 song "Diamonds and Rust."

Joan, Bob, the Preservation Hall Singers, Mississippi John Hurt, and Son House were all at Newport that weekend in 1963. So, too, were the Stanley Brothers and the Staple Singers, seasoned musicians with established audiences, the Stanley Brothers in country, the Staples for their gospel-based music. Even in 1963, Ralph Stanley was considered the true royalty of southern folk music; dressed in their best clothes for the show, Ralph Stanley and the Clinch Mountain Boys added a touch of class, in contrast to the kids in wrecked Levi's wearing peace signs. But no one cared about what others wore; we could finally dress the way we wanted and not feel strange.

And when Ralph Stanley finally sang "O Death" a cappella late on Saturday night as the moon rose from behind the trees and everyone was a bit high from booze and grass, you could feel the power of the music in your bones and you knew you had heard something you would never forget.

Pops Staples, black as Ralph Stanley was white, had greatness in him, too. Under Pops' guidance, the Staples family and their name became synonymous with the melding of spirituals and gospel with popular music. Pops and his daughters, Cleotha, Pervis, Yvonne, and Mavis, fired up the evening concerts with rock-and-roll religion as well as Dylan songs. The girls wore silk tops, their hair done to a T with sparkle and shine to match their clothes. This was deep-dish soul served to the kids who were yearning, I thought, for something to replace the religions most of them had abandoned. The night was full of shouts of "amen" and "hallelujah," rock and soul. Pops and his daughters won an audience new to the beat of the Christian drum, and in future years the Staples would make records that reached Top 40 eight times, including Dylan's "A Hard Rain's A-Gonna Fall" and Stephen Stills' "For What It's Worth."

The integrated scenes we yearned to see, blacks and whites united in common purpose, were rare in America outside of New York in 1963, but they were part of the culture of the Newport Festival. This was still the time of segregation; the Voting Rights Act was an unrealized dream. In most parts of the country you could not register in a white hotel if you were black, or be seen comfortably with a black man if you were a white woman. In sixteen states, the law still prohibited intermarriage. The community of folk music seemed to be one of the only places it was common to be in mixed company.

George Wein, who started the Newport Jazz Festival in 1954, attracted many artists, among them Duke Ellington and Miles Davis. His wife, Joyce, a beloved, vital, energetic, and attractive African American who was deeply involved in every aspect of the jazz as well as the folk festival that was launched in 1959, had a lot to do with the trust that arose at the festival among black artists. With George, a Jew from New York, Joyce presented the image of an integrated couple making a historic contribution to equality. Newport was certainly a great contributor to the civil rights legislation that was passed in 1964. Fighting racism, it turned out, like fighting for peace, was part of the musical as well as the political struggle.

Among the mansions of Newport, bastion of the old moneyed

East Coast, we could be together more comfortably than in many other places we knew. It was one of the great joys of being part of the festival.

I adored Mavis Staples, a beautiful woman whose smile could light up the room and whose voice could sound like a thousand gospel choirs. I followed her around like a puppy dog in my long blue print dress. She was two months younger than me and had already had a radio hit with "Crying in the Chapel" on Stax Records.

"Bob Dylan asked me to marry him," Mavis told me with a disbelieving smile after he had sung his set on the last night. "He is such a rogue!" Dylan didn't look like the marrying kind to me, and Mavis knew he was having her on. He had once famously said that romance was like hitchhiking, and I had begun to agree. And anyway, Dylan's humor always seemed to have a bite at the end of it, a bite usually taken out of whoever he was talking to or about. Everyone got to laugh with Mavis, whether it was at her own foibles, or at the twists of fate, or at pain. Dylan's brand of funny could make you cringe even then, but Mavis' jokes always warmed you.

At the end of August 1963, my new album, *Judy Collins 3,* was finished. Jim Marshall took the photograph for the cover, and then we had to sit back and wait for the release. The traditional songs I had sung on my first two albums were now gently moved aside and I switched into the gear that would become my standard mode for decades: songs by contemporary writers who were collectively sketching out a new musical landscape.

*T*HEN, on November 22, 1963, the stars seemed to fall out of our sky with the assassination of President John F. Kennedy. I had been scheduled to sing at the Shadows, a popular folk music club in Georgetown, where I had often shared the bill with John Phillips and Scott McKenzie in their Journeymen days, and with Donny Hathaway before he recorded with Roberta Flack.

I heard the news about the shooting as I was boarding a flight to Washington, D.C., on that terrible Friday. My first hope was that Kennedy would live; the second was a prayer that the shooter had not been black (there had been race riots and violence in cities around the country). When I got off the plane, I learned that our president was dead.

I had just been with him, touched his hand, a few months before. His was a thrilling presence, and I could not imagine the force of his personality and charisma gone, like smoke, in an instant.

I would not be singing at the Shadows, and in the days immediately after the assassination, all performances, all shows—all joy, it seemed—were canceled.

There would be only the sound of the black carriage wheels and the trumpet playing "Taps" while JFK's flag-draped coffin was drawn behind high-stepping horses. Among the multitudes who wept and watched, a handful of figures walked behind the coffin; in their midst was an elegant woman in a black veil. Later, as the casket was carried down the steps of St. Matthew's Cathedral, a blond girl of nearly six and a boy of three stood squinting against the sunlight beside the woman in the veil, the boy's small hand lifted in a salute to the president, his father.

Chapter Sixteen

Blacklist

Out under the winter sky
Stars come trembling to my eye

—Billy Edd Wheeler, "Winter Sky"

By the end of 1963, the Bitter End, a wonderful new club, had opened in Greenwich Village. I met the owner, Fred Weintraub, when I was doing one of my many gigs at Gerde's.

"I am up to my eyeballs in folksingers," Fred Weintraub said. "But I'd love you to come and play my club!" Of course I said yes, and the Bitter End quickly became one of my regular venues.

I always liked the good-looking Weintraub, a complicated but sweet guy who had a true passion for music and performers. Like some of the other club owners who were featuring folk music in the major cities of the country, he loved what he was doing and knew there was a huge audience for it.

Gerald Nachman referred to Weintraub as a "misfit" and a "maverick." In San Francisco, where he had lived for a few years, Fred was in the thick of the California scene, and kept Lenny Bruce company on the way to jail when Bruce was arrested for obscenity at the Hungry i. Fred came back to the East Coast in 1961 and bought the Cock and Bull, a run-down joint with paint peeling off the walls that served shrimp cocktails and martinis and sported a rotting neon sign that hung out on Bleecker Street. Fred cleaned up the building, in the process leaving one brick wall exposed in the club, a look that would become synonymous with the Village. Then he began to hire folksingers.

Fred would always take the time to talk to me, to ask how I was doing. He was like that with everyone, and also shared freely of himself. Fred had studied business and earned his fortune, he told me, making baby carriages, but had walked away from that life.

"I threw it all over," he told me once over drinks after my show. "The wife, the business, everything! To play piano in a whorehouse in Havana and fight Batista." I told him it all sounded very romantic.

"Romantic, bullshit!" he said. "I nearly got myself killed!" We had been talking about Richard Fariña and Carolyn Hester's divorce, which had happened quickly in 1962 after only a year of marriage, and whether Richard and his new girlfriend, Mimi Baez, might come to the club to play now that they were writing songs and performing together.

"That's where I met Richard, in Cuba," Fred told me, "in Havana on a dark night before the revolution. Richard almost got killed, too!" He would say that Cuba was their Spanish Civil War. "We had to fight somewhere, and Cuba was the only revolution that would have us!"

Fred was truly in his element and soon had the most successful club for folk music other than the Village Gate, Art D'Lugoff's club, across the street. The Gate showcased folksingers as well as comedy, but it was fundamentally a jazz club. Every folksinger in the business worked at Fred's club, and some of the comics, too. Arlo Guthrie, Carly Simon, Frank Zappa, Harry Chapin, Linda Ronstadt, Joni Mitchell, and Lily Tomlin all played at the brick-walled club with a hundred seats and a tiny stage.

"I love to see those babies packed in as tight as ticks!" Fred would say. Fred soon started a "hootenanny" every Tuesday, an open-mic night so that new singers and others who just wanted to try out material could come and be heard. One night I watched Bill Cosby and Alan Arkin, both at the beginning of their careers, pile all the chairs in the little room onto the stage and then take them all off again, getting the few of us who were in the room (it was about one in the morning) first to stand up and then become hysterical as the chairs proceeded to make their voyages around the room with these two very funny guys wisecracking as they slung chairs to each other. It looked to me like something out of the Second City in Chicago—impromptu and hilarious.

There was usually a sort of female cabal sitting on the church pews in the back of the club—Carly Simon, Lucy Simon, Bette Midler, and Mama Cass—dishing the talent, cadging drinks, and generally putting out the philosophy of the age: end the war, make love.

In 1963, Fred sold ABC on a concept for a new television show that he would produce. *Hootenanny* was a natural evolution of Weintraub's Tuesday night showcase of singers and became an instant success—a televised version of what Freddy had been doing since the Bitter End's opening months.

One of Fred's goals in producing *Hootenanny* was to get Pete Seeger on network television. Pete was in a down period at that moment, feeling neglected by Columbia Records. He was upset, and Harold, who had managed him for years, would say Pete believed he had been used by Columbia to get some of the newer folk artists on the label—Dylan, for one.

"We'll get you on *Hootenanny*!" Fred told Pete when he made the deal with ABC. He was excited and told many of his friends, including me, that the show was a go and that we would all, including Seeger, be on it. Before long, however, a rumor began to circulate around the Village that Pete's appearance had been scratched. People in the know believed that there had been pressure from advertisers and local stations outside of New York to remove him from the hootenanny schedule because of his politics. Nat Hentoff wrote about the situation in an article titled "That Ole McCarthy Hoot" suggesting that all of us in the folk singing community follow the lead of a group of people—including the Kingston Trio, Joan Baez, and Bob Dylan—and join in a reverse boycott of the program in support of Seeger. Harold, who had already begun talks with the producers about Pete's appearance, was outraged.

From my diary of March 28, 1964:

> If, however, I am not as enthusiastic about *Hootenanny* as I was about two weeks ago, it is because Pete Seeger and the Weavers have been blacklisted from the show. The blacklist is not only in working condition in this country, as it has been for decades . . . there have already been meetings after meetings, with everyone from the Kingston Trio to John Phillips.

Pete had already been excluded, as though by a secret agreement, by all the other networks, including ABC, though Harold had been fighting that fight for years.

The rumble among the troops gained force until it became an angry roar in the wider folk community. While the ABC folk music show would finally bring our music to a wider audience, the blacklist represented a blow not just to Seeger but also to the many singer-songwriters trying to make a living at what they did best.

By now there were anti-ABC protests developing outside concerts, and Harold Leventhal, Jac Holzman, and Pete Seeger called a meeting at Harold's office to discuss the boycott of the boycott. Harold had, of course, managed Pete since the early Weavers days. He had stood by Seeger in every confrontation Pete had faced with HUAC. He knew what they were up against.

"The fate of many artists as well as the health of the growing folk movement has to be considered," Harold said. He represented not only Pete but also many other singers who, like myself, were going to be involved in some way in these decisions about appearing on *Hootenanny*. "If we boycott the show, the entire folk movement may be at stake."

Then Pete Seeger stood up to speak, and told those of us gathered that afternoon that *not* doing the show would hurt the entire folk movement. Pete said the same thing to everyone who was torn about appearing on *Hootenanny*. Pete was always for the singer and the song.

"Doing the show will be good for the music, like nothing else," he said.

The Tarriers, in which my friends Eric Weissberg, Marshall Brickman, and Clarence Cooper played, had appeared on *Hootenanny* in its first season, but in the second season, they were at first booked and then, following the blacklist of Pete, were canceled. The following week, in a surprise move, ABC reversed its position and asked the Tarriers to appear. However, there was a catch: the only time slot the producers said they had open was on the following Saturday, only three days away, and the Tarriers had a gig booked for that night at the Village Gate in New York. Harold called Pete.

"Pete, Pete, I hate to ask you this, but . . ." He filled Pete in on what had happened.

"Of course!" Pete said. And so, while the Tarriers were on the show that he was blacklisted from, Pete Seeger filled in for them at the Village Gate.

Weintraub continued to fight to get Pete on the program, but

ABC would not relent. Seeger, arguably the most important folk artist of the era, never appeared on this pioneering show.

"Pete saved my life," Fred said. "He insisted everyone go on *Hootenanny*. He knew the show would bring the whole world to folk music, as I had known it would."

We spoke of the critical piece Nat Hentoff had written about the "great *Hoot* scare." "Nat was a total bastard to me," Fred said. "He called me names." I said he had done the same to me.

"But Pete knew the truth," Fred continued. "Sometimes the good is the enemy of the best, and Pete gave us the best answer. He said, 'Do the goddammed show—it will be good for everyone!'"

The result was that many protest songs were aired; many groups, both traditional and commercial, had been seen by millions, and the Tarriers had finally broken the racial barrier on TV twice.

Hootenanny was shot at a different college campus each week. From March of 1963 through the following year, hundreds of performers graced college campuses around the country and subsequently appeared on television in *Hootenanny*: Bill Monroe, the Serendipity Singers, the New Christy Minstrels, Eddy Arnold, Pete Fountain, Doc Watson, and the Simon Sisters (Lucy and Carly). Jim (Roger) McGuinn, Theo Bikel, the Chad Mitchell Trio, the Journeymen with John Phillips, and the Big Three with Mama Cass Elliot were on the show, as was David Crosby, who sang with the Modern Folk Quartet. (This appearance preceded his joining the Byrds, which McGuinn would form with Crosby in 1965.) The Limelighters also appeared on *Hootenanny*, as did the Clancy Brothers, Tommy Makem, and Oscar Brand. Glenn Campbell was the staff bass player. I first did the show from Brown University in Providence in May 1963.

By the end of its second season, *Hootenanny* had started making artistic decisions that were not in keeping with any artist's intention: verses were cut from songs, and performances were squeezed into rigid time slots. The show ended in September 1964. Unfortunately, *Hootenanny* is largely lost to history, since most of the tapes of the show were wiped clean long before they could have been transformed into digital boxed sets.

Pete Seeger's position during this time allowed the people and the music he loved to flourish. He had the courage, as he has had all his life, to defy the mob.

Chapter Seventeen

Mississippi Summer

It isn't right to block the doorway
It isn't nice to go to jail.

—Malvina Reynolds, "It Isn't Nice"

Nineteen sixty-four was awash with cultural and political events that would shake up the country. The journalist David Halberstam was openly criticizing the war in the *New York Times*, writing about the lies we were being told, helping to lift the veil of the 1950s, when we automatically believed that those in power told the truth. The country was still swaying with grief over Kennedy's assassination; Lyndon Johnson, who had taken the oath of the presidency on Air Force One on November 22, 1963, after JFK was declared dead, was voted into office a year later by a 61 percent majority. The war in Vietnam was growing more intense. There was hope that Johnson would pull back our involvement in Indochina, but now it was becoming apparent that he took the party line on Vietnam.

Young men who were in danger of being drafted were heading north to Canada or finding ways to be exempted. For the first time, mental illness and acute anxiety were being considered as reasons to be rejected by the draft board. Kids, really, were looking closely at their draft numbers—were they high or low?—and deciding, with a new maturity, they were against war. And being against the war became somehow a matter of mental health. Were they crazy to be against war? A therapist could decide. My family worried about our boys: would they have to go off to fight?

Jean-Paul Sartre and Simone de Beauvoir were also in the news. In 1954 de Beauvoir had published *The Second Sex,* a book I'd been assigned in my social studies class, and it had been a bellwether for the coming women's consciousness movement, just beginning to take root in the United States. Like de Beauvoir, Sartre spoke openly against the war in Vietnam. In October 1964 he would receive the Nobel Prize in literature but refuse to accept it on the grounds that it would compromise his ability to be objective. It was a momentous action that caught the eye of the world.

Martin Luther King Jr. received the Nobel Peace Prize and accepted, as was only right. His position on race could never be the subject of a compromise on objectivity.

Earlier that year, in January, Arthur Miller's *After the Fall* opened in New York. I attended the play at a theater in downtown New York with Mark Abramson, sitting so close to the stage that I could feel the heat coming off Jason Robards Jr. and hear the roar of Marilyn's voice in his words. Around the same time *Meet the Beatles* was released in the United States, and the foursome would take the nation by storm with their first American television appearance on *The Ed Sullivan Show.*

*I*n January and February 1964 my destinations were Spokane, St. Louis, Montana, Boston, and Vermont—the same kind of seemingly random scheduling that marks my concert life today. I don't know how I did it then, and I don't know how I do it now.

On February 14, 1964, Jac Holzman gave me his own kind of Valentine's gift—a big press party for my third album, *Judy Collins 3*, at a loft in Soho. Nina Holzman, Jac's wife, had prepared this special party, with mountains of her fabulous, homemade, concoctions. (In L.A. a couple of years later, she would start a catering business called Pure Pleasure. And her food really was pure pleasure, becoming over those years in New York one of the reasons to go to an Elektra listening party for an artist.) Just about everyone I knew in the folk music industry was in attendance: Art D'Lugoff, the owner of the Village Gate; Jack Goddard, who wrote about music for the *Village Voice*; Phil Ochs; Tom Paxton, who was making another record for Elektra; my producer, Mark Abramson; and everyone who had played on the album—Eric Weissberg, Chuck Israels, and the cellist Bob Sylvester. Jim Friedman was there, my friend who wrote songs with Shel Silverstein, as was Oscar Brand. Oscar and I have known each other for fifty years. He, like so many of my friends from that time, has recorded with Elektra: albums of sea chanties, patriotic songs from his native Canada, songs of protest.

Oscar was among the original board members of the Children's Television Workshop, which created PBS's *Sesame Street*, one of whose intentions was to reach inner-city children. Although it has become an American institution, *Sesame Street* initially fell short of its goal in that respect, according to Oscar. Oscar groused about this fact so often, to Jim Henson and anyone else who would listen, that Henson named one of the Muppets Oscar the Grouch.

Ian and Sylvia Tyson and Charlie Rothschild, my road manager, were at the party that night, as was my friend Lucy Simon, whom I had met the year before when I taught her and her sister Carly "Turn! Turn! Turn!" in the funky dressing room at the Bitter End.

In the early 1960s Lucy and Carly formed a duo, and would release their first album, *The Simon Sisters*, on Kapp Records.

"Winkin', Blinkin', and Nod" was a minor hit, and the album was followed by two more, *Cuddlebug* and *The Lobster Quadrille*.

When Carly and I met, she was a few years away from her solo career. She would often tell me shyly that she felt like the odd singer out. She had stage fright and a crippling fear of travel. She had sworn never to fly if she could avoid it. But in just a few years she would dazzle the world with her writing and her sexy, articulate, wondrous songs.

*I*N March 1964 I performed my first solo concert at Town Hall in New York. Harold and Jac suggested that we tape it, and Elektra would release the recording as my fourth album, *The Judy Collins Concert*.

I wore a new green velvet dress. Nina Holzman sent me to Elizabeth Arden—my first time there—for a massage before the performance, to ease my trembling nerves. I was singing new material, and though I was not sick-to-my-stomach nervous—it was more like thrilled-to-the-core nervous—my body was in a knot. But somehow I knew the night was going to be splendid, a one-take concert of new songs for a new album. We were very brave and optimistic, but I knew we could pull it off.

There were songs by Billy Edd Wheeler, a prolific and talented songwriter who would have his songs recorded by Bobby Darin, the Kingston Trio, Johnny Cash, Neil Young, Kenny Rogers, and even Elvis Presley. Billy Edd was relatively unknown when I found three of his songs: the beautiful and evocative "Winter Sky," "Red-Winged Blackbird," and "Coal Tattoo," one of the best work and ecological songs I have ever heard.

> *Traveling down that coal town road,*
> *Listen to my rubber tires whine.*

You can hear those rubber tires whine and the wheels rock in his lyrics about the decimation of the forests in our relentless quest for more coal.

Songs by Fred Neil, John Phillips, and Dick Weissman were also included. Dick, who was in the Journeymen with Scott McKenzie and John Phillips, wrote "Medgar Evers Lullaby," a bedtime story about racial prejudice:

> *Your daddy is dead and he's not coming back*
> *and the reason they killed him was cause he was black.*

There were a couple of traditional songs that tore at the heart, such as "Bonnie Boy Is Young," said to be loosely based on the story of a seventeenth-century arranged marriage.

On "Wild Rippling Water," Eric Weissberg and I play dancing guitars in the story of two lovers in the spring, and there is the Bob Dylan song "The Lonesome Death of Hattie Carroll." The addition of a cello, later played by Robert Sylvester, a classical musician from Manhattan, gave this recording a new and strangely modern feel. George Martin had not yet written the string quartet parts for "Yesterday," the Beatles song that would come out in 1965, but there was a musical feast going on in my own heart and head, and I was happy to break from convention. There had not been a cello on a folk recording yet; or if there was one, I did not know about it. Robert was a wonderful player and added a new dimension to the ensemble of my guitar, the guitar of Steve Mandell, and the classical bass of Chuck Israels, who could be heard regularly playing at the Blue Note with jazz pianist Bill Evans.

$\mathcal{A}$ few weeks after my concert recording was done, Dick Fariña and Mimi Baez came down to the studios of WBAI in lower

Manhattan to be guests on my radio show. Mimi, Joan Baez's younger sister, was strikingly beautiful, with dark eyes and lustrous black hair that grew beyond her shoulders. Her nature was sweet, giving, and openhearted. Mimi's dazzling looks caught at the throat, plunging many men (and even women) into ecstatic claims of love. They were a remarkable couple who had started writing songs as soon as they found each other. That day in the studio, Mimi played her Martin guitar; Dick played his Emerson dulcimer, the gift from his first wife, Carolyn Hester.

I had become close friends with Fariña after we met at Montowese House when he was married to Carolyn Hester in 1961. I visited Carolyn and Dick on Martha's Vineyard, and saw Dick often in New York City, where he had the habit of dropping in to stay at my apartments in the Village and later on the Upper West Side. (There is a quaint picture of Richard and me shopping with Mimi at Zabar's, where we bought exotic cheeses and roamed the aisles while their German shepherd, Lush, waited patiently outside, greeting every customer with a bark and a wag.)

By 1964, Dick had met Mimi Baez and won her heart, and then her hand. Their first meeting was at a picnic in a park near Chartres Cathedral in France. Mimi was just sixteen and still living with her parents. She later told me the story of how she got truly drunk for the first time that day at Chartres and threw up all over Dick. In lighter moments, she would say that had been the key to his heart, which was altogether possible; he was always wonderfully off in the way he interpreted what might be romantic.

Mimi was over the moon about Fariña. Dick wooed her with letters and sometimes poetry—"Young girl, you chose the amber coil of a wish"—using references that occur often in his writing. His poem to me, which he wrote as liner notes to the album on which he and Mimi later played their wonderful songs "Hard Loving Loser" and "Pack Up Your Sorrows," uses a similar scheme to describe the sound of my voice: "If amethysts could sing . . ."

Against her mother's and father's protestations, and in secret, Mimi married her poet/writer/singer in Paris in April 1963. Mimi was only seventeen. A year later, when she turned eighteen, they had a celebration of their wedding in Carmel, California. So in June 1964 I headed out to Carmel to celebrate their marriage.

There were flowers in Mimi's hair, there was music from some local singers, and her sister Joan wrote and sang a song to her sister and her new husband. Dick and Mimi were happy together, and apparently Big Joan had overcome her objections. If she had not come completely around on Dick, at least she had begun to appreciate the joy Mimi took in her husband.

After seeing them in Carmel, and celebrating this romance written in the stars, as Richard would describe it to me, I headed to Colorado to sing at Red Rocks, the outdoor summer venue in Morrison, just west of Denver. In the rugged, open-air amphitheater I sang all the songs I had just recorded, thrilled to be in my Rockies again, even if only for a few days. I saw my mom and my dad, and all my siblings. I had that feeling I always have in the mountains: I felt at peace with myself.

I had Clark with me for most of the summer, in Colorado and in New York. My friend Linda Liebman accompanied us to the 1964 Newport Folk Festival, and someone took a great photo of Clark leaning on one of the fences, looking up at the stage, with Linda at his side. He got to sing and have meals with Pete Seeger and John Cooke, and he simply drank it all in. He loved the music, listening to guitar players, dancing to the banjos.

After the festival, we went to Cape Cod with the Holzmans, where Clark played in the sand with Jaclyn and Adam, the Holzmans' children, and we all ate grilled burgers and hot dogs. Then it was back to Storrs for Clark, and back home for me, to the nerve-wracking reality of the custody case, which was still unsettled.

The Civil Rights Act of 1964 was signed into law by President

Johnson on July 2, 1964. At the same time, the situation in Vietnam was getting hotter with each passing month, with American and Vietnamese deaths piling up; in August, at the Democratic National Convention, Fannie Lou Hamer would present the credentials for the Mississippi Freedom Democratic Party, challenging the all-white Mississippi delegation.

In August Bob Dylan turned the Beatles on to pot for the first time, and in September the Warren Commission released its report on the assassination of JFK, saying a lone gunman, Lee Harvey Oswald, had killed the president. Also in 1964, Lenny Bruce spent four months in jail for obscenity; Michelle Obama and Glenn Beck were born; and it cost 5 cents to send a letter to your congressman or your lover.

But Camelot had lost its king, and a miasma of grief still hung over the nation, while Jackie Kennedy and the rest of the family continued sculpting and burnishing JFK's legacy.

In August I went to Mississippi—a far cry from the quaint villages and idyllic beaches of Cape Cod—to help register African American voters in what would be referred to as Freedom Summer or the Mississippi Summer Project. Workers from the offices of the Council of Federated Organizations (COFO) and the Congress of Racial Equality (CORE), two of the organizations sponsoring groups of volunteers to go South to ensure the enforcement of the Voting Rights Act in racially segregated states, helped organize my travel. I flew into Jackson, Mississippi, where I was met by Barbara Dane, an activist and jazz singer from San Francisco whom I knew.

Barbara had many admirers, including Louis Armstrong, and a solid reputation in the world of jazz. She had opened her own club in San Francisco called Sugar Hill, which featured great jazz and blues artists—Mose Allison, Big Mama Thornton, T-Bone Walker, Sonny Terry, and Brownie McGhee, with whom I had worked in

Chicago at the Gate of Horn in my first few days at the club in 1960. (Barbara later married Irwin Silber, a critic and the founder of *Sing Out*.)

Barbara was thirty-seven when we met in 1964, a big-hearted blonde, outspoken and generous with her knowledge and her insight into what was going on in the civil rights movement in Mississippi. She helped me get settled in with other volunteer artists and lawyers at the Jackson Holiday Inn, introduced me to the people with whom I'd be traveling, and took me to my first voter registration rallies.

The offices of COFO were on Lynch Street in Jackson. A number of workers in the Mississippi Freedom Project had already been beaten up by that time—eighty of them, according to the people I spoke to at the offices of SCLC. During the two weeks I was there, traveling from Ruleville to Greenville to Jackson and back, everyone knew Michael Schwerner, James Cheney, and Michael Goodman had been murdered. They had been abducted, tortured, and killed by the White Knights of the Ku Klux Klan, their bodies buried in a muddy earthen dam. Fear pulsed along the roads and in the towns.

I traveled with the New Gate Singers, a band of three long-haired, sweet-tempered kids from Chicago. We drove in their VW bus through the summer heat of Mississippi, stopping over in black neighborhoods and staying with black families, the only safe places for white rabble-rousers from the North. In the daytime, I would help the organizers I admired so much from CORE and sing for the crowds of people who gathered.

Of the many moving and memorable experiences for me that summer, perhaps none left more of an impression than the few inspiring days I spent traveling with Fannie Lou Hamer. Fannie Lou came from Mound Bayou, Mississippi (home of the murdered Medgar Evers), and was nearly fifty-seven when I met her. She had been an activist most of her life, influenced by Thurgood Marshall,

Mahalia Jackson, and other powerful civil rights leaders and artists. Fannie Lou had been working with SNCC since 1962. She and I talked in the van while I was changing the strings on my guitar, my hands shaking, as we prepared to stop at another site to encourage people to get out and register to vote. I could always feel the violence and hatred looming in the air of the towns we passed through, white faces pressed to windows, white men standing rigid in their yards, staring out from behind their fences, their eyes warning us to go home, telling us we had no business in Mississippi. I asked Fannie Lou if she was afraid.

"Why should I be afraid?" she said. "They can only kill me, and seems to me they been trying to do that since I was a little girl!" Fannie Lou had already seen too much hardship and terror in her life—racism, beatings, and lynchings. In 1961, she had been sterilized without her knowledge or consent while having routine, minor surgery.

"I have my faith," she said. "I am not afraid." I gazed out the window of the van at the cold and hate-filled faces in passing cars. I knew I would have to stay close to Fannie Lou and draw courage from her.

In the heat of a poor black neighborhood in Ruleville or Greenville, where not a soul could be seen on the street, Fannie Lou would plant her feet in the dust in front of a gaggle of run-down houses. Then she'd open her mouth and sing:

"Oh freedom," she would belt. "Oh freedom!"

Sweat would pour down her beautiful black face as she sang. A person or two would peek behind a curtain.

"Oh freedom over me!"

A door or two would open a crack, then another few inches. I stood beside Fannie Lou, starting to hum and harmonize.

"And before I'd be a slave, I'd be buried in my grave!"

Before long, the doors would crack open in house after house, and men and women would shyly start to emerge into the sun, children sheltering between their legs as their mothers wiped hands on aprons, smiles beginning to form in their eyes and hearts.

"And go home to my Lord and be free!" A chorus of a dozen, two dozen, maybe three, then five, would form around Fannie Lou, drawn by her big, round, full notes mingled with my voice. Her singing was like a winding summer vine, corralling their emotions, bringing them out of doors, luring them from their fear. When the yard was crowded with people, Fannie Lou would begin to speak about why she was there.

"I want you to go down to that courthouse and I want you to register your name so that you can vote, put your money where your mouths are, and vote for the people you want to have in your government."

"But we can't do that, they'll kill us," many would shout. Bull Connor was hosing people and bashing heads in Selma and white policemen were harassing and beating black people as well as activists all over the South for the attempts to get blacks out to vote, to eat in public places, to go to school together. People tried to keep their heads down and stay out of the way of the white police, who were armed with nightsticks, and the Klan, which was flourishing in Mississippi at that time. Many had seen crosses burned on their lawns, friends lynched.

Fannie Lou would persist: "You have to do this, you have to use your voices." Those who had not known they had voices would begin to shine in Fannie Lou's light.

For the days I traveled with her, I was a witness to her power. She revived my spirits, too, in that hot humid summer when the trucks passed us on back roads, gun racks visible in their windows, and I didn't know if I should be more worried if the racks were full or if they were empty.

"You got to have faith," she would say to me as we tucked into our borrowed beds in a home one night. I had told her about my divorce and the ongoing custody battle. "You are going to get that boy of yours back, I just know it." Faith was going to have to go a long way, but when Fannie Lou talked to you about faith, you felt certain you could do anything.

I didn't know whether faith would help, but by God I started praying again, all because of Fannie Lou Hamer.

Chapter Eighteen

Pack Up Your Sorrow:
Russian Songs, Broken Hearts, and Max

If somehow you could pack up your sorrows
And give them all to me . . .

—Richard Fariña and Pauline Baez Mardin,
"Pack Up Your Sorrows"

In September 1964 I started looking for a New York apartment big enough for Clark and me. The divorce hearing was scheduled for October 16 and the custody hearing for December 18, after which the judge would decide within a few months whether I would have my son with me. I had been advised by my lawyers to have an apartment in the city that could accommodate us both.

I found a place on West 79th Street near the corner of Amsterdam Avenue on the Upper West Side. I was nearer to my shrink and in a neighborhood of big pre-war apartment buildings, solid and grand—large spaces that were home to artists and all kinds of interesting people, a world somewhat different from the hippies and folkies of Greenwich Village. I was happy to be there but missed the Village. One of my neighbors was Elisabeth Bing, the well-known Lamaze practitioner. Ramblin' Jack Elliott and his wife would come to see Elisabeth and stop by to visit. I had room for Clark and was praying that Fannie Lou was right, that one day he would come to stay for good.

By the end of September I was totally settled into my new home. I even had my piano moved in—an old, great-sounding Steinway on which I have written most of my songs. While the divorce hearing went quickly, the final decision on custody of Clark would not be reached for another five months. Meanwhile, Peter remarried on December 27, to the woman he had been living with since our separation, Sue Tanstall, who worked at the American Friends Service Committee in Boston.

Harold Leventhal, my devoted manager, had been working for a number of months on a trip to the Soviet Union. The Cold War had kept most American performers off of the concert circuit in the USSR, but there was beginning to be a softening between the countries and a newfound taste for negotiation and appeasement in the arts as well as in politics. It was a window that would not be open long, but Harold thought he might be able to arrange a few shows in Poland and then in Moscow and other Soviet cities. He began to make real plans, talking to other artists about joining me. It would, in fact, be groundbreaking.

As soon as I found out about the upcoming tour possibilities for the following year in the USSR, I went to the New School for Social Research in Greenwich Village and signed up for Russian language classes. For such a trip, we would have to plan far ahead. Soon I could write a little Cyrillic and say a few phrases. It would be an exciting time, and I hoped by then that I would have custody of my son. Perhaps he could join me on this amazing journey. He was certainly old enough to come with me now, and would love the travel and the music, the adventure of being in a new and exciting place where few Americans had visited.

I made another trip to Carmel in the fall of 1964 to sing and spend some time with Mimi and Dick in their little cabin near Joan's. I visited with them one magical night in September 1964 and listened to their startling, unique songs, two of which I would record.

Dick wrote "Pack Up Your Sorrows," with help from Mimi's sister Pauline—it seemed the family was falling in love with Richard, giving him the space he needed, embracing him. Dick and Mimi first played this and some of the other new material for me in their enchanted house. The fireplace crackled and its light danced on the walls that night. I can see Mimi's fingers on the guitar and the dulcimer laid across Dick's lap, the quill he used to play it with plucking the strings, as they sang this sweet, simple song. Dick was the dark-haired gypsy with the wickedly handsome smile and all those songs in his heart waiting to be written, waiting to be completed by a woman he loved. Mimi was that woman now, gifted and beautiful, and the song spun out between them like jewels floating in a pond of light.

> *If somehow you could pack up your sorrows*
> *And give them all to me*
> *You would lose them, I know how to use them*
> *Give them all to me.*

I drank wine out of a silver cup, watched the fire, and listened. It was a truly mystical night of music and beauty.

Back in New York one weekend in October 1964, the journalist Al Aronowitz, who had become a friend after he wrote a piece about me for the *New York Post* in his column "The Beat Generation," invited me to Woodstock. We were guests at Albert Grossman's rambling old stone mansion. Aronowitz had recently introduced Dylan to the Beatles. He and Bob were friends, and

Bob, Suze Rotolo, Albert Grossman, and his wife, Sally, were all there. We had a fine evening of laughter, food, and talk of music and art, and I remember going to bed exhausted and happy.

About three in the morning I was awakened by the sound of Dylan's voice—which by then I knew well—drifting up the stone stairs outside my bedroom. I opened my door and, dressed in my best terry-cloth bathrobe, crept down the stairs to listen. I heard Dylan's voice coming from a room at the bottom of the stairs, seducing and captivating as he sang, over and over, the lyrics and newly found melody to "Mr. Tambourine Man."

The walls of Albert's Woodstock retreat and the stairs on which I was perched to listen to Bob were weathered fieldstone. I sat in my robe, shivering a little from the cool air but mostly from the sweet sound of Bob's voice, and those lyrics that struck my heart. In the morning over steaming cups of coffee, I thought about the song and about the genius who had written it. When he came down at noon, rubbing sleep from his eyes and running his hands through his rumpled hair, I told him that I wanted to sing the song I had heard on the stairs. Once back in New York, I would record it for my new album, *Judy Collins Fifth Album*.

*I*N 1965, after I had been living on the Upper West Side for a few months, and as preparations for the USSR trip were taking shape, I suddenly found myself facing an unexpected roadblock: I was having terrible trouble with my voice. I asked around for names of people to whom I could go for help, maybe a voice coach or singing teacher. They said I should seek out Max Margulis. I carried his phone number around on a tattered piece of paper.

One day when I was so hoarse I could barely speak, I called the number I had been given for Max. A man answered, and I introduced myself in my croaking voice and told him he had been recommended to me. He asked for the names of those who had suggested I call him, and I mentioned Irma and Mordecai Bauman, who ran Indian Hill, an arts camp in the Berkshires, where Carly Simon, Arlo Guthrie, and many gifted musicians and artists had gone. Ray Boguslav, who played guitar for Harry Belafonte and was a serious, gifted pianist as well, had also told me that Max was the only game in town if you were looking for a great teacher. Max seemed pleased.

Then Max asked me what kind of music I sang, and I told him.

"Oh, you people are never serious," he said, the graciousness gone from his voice. "I don't want to waste my time."

"But I need help—I'm losing my voice all the time. I don't know what to do." I was truly becoming desperate. "Please, just let me come and talk to you," I begged.

He said no again, but less firmly. His voice softened. Finally he told me, "Well, perhaps we could talk. But only talk, you understand!" Then he gave me his address and went on, "You just ring the bell for 8B."

My mouth dropped open. I said I would be there within two minutes.

Surprised, he said he just might be able to squeeze me in, and asked where I was.

"I live next door to you, in 8A."

I walked out my door on the eighth floor of my building, took two steps past the elevator, and rang his bell. When he opened the door, of course I recognized him, a slight man with glasses—looking very much unlike the ogre I had spoken to on the phone. I could see he was prepared to frown, but a small smile came to his lips, and I sensed playfulness somewhere behind the frown. We had spoken in the elevator a couple of times, exchanging only the briefest of hellos, but our encounters had been pleasant.

Max shook my proffered hand and invited me into the room. There was a blue rug on the floor. The walls were hung with original works of Arshile Gorky and Willem de Kooning, paintings and sketches. A parakeet sang from a small cage in the kitchen, and the scent of roasting chicken filled the room. Max gestured toward the Steinway grand that took over one corner, and we began.

"If you just stay faithful to what we are doing," he told me that day and for all the days that came, "it will change your entire life. Singing and the study of the voice is the most complete therapy there is, because it engages the lungs, the brain, the body, the soul, and the spirit." Throughout my years with Max, he would emphasize two principles: "Clarity and phrasing are the secret."

I endured the fight to get beyond the break in the voice, which all singers have and which the bel canto technique addresses. Bel canto, Max told me, is the Italian vocal style that includes a perfect legato line throughout the range of the voice, from top to bottom, and the use of a shimmering tone in the higher registers but without noticeable vibrato. In bel canto, Max would say, the voice should always be flexible, clear, and unencumbered by shouted phrases or harshness of tone.

Of course, this sounds deceptively simple. Transforming a rough, uneven voice that was "natural" but had great flaws took more than three years. I might get over the break between the upper and lower registers easily one week but at the next lesson be unable to do so. Max would sit at the piano; I would stand, a cup of tea prepared by Max's wife, Helen, in front of me.

Helen was a pianist and cellist with dark hair to her waist who always made me tea and let her parakeet, Papageno, sit on my shoulder. He was named after the character in Mozart's *Magic Flute*. Sometimes toward the end of a lesson Helen would come stand in the archway to the kitchen and listen.

"That was a wonderful sound you were making there," she would say. "That was so clear." They had been married for years. She was from Texas. Max would tell me he never went to Texas after the first time because of the chiggers.

Max's father had been an opera singer in Chicago, and Max

himself was an accomplished violinist. He had been friends with Gorky and de Kooning when the painters first came to New York—de Kooning as a stowaway—in the late 1920s. The trio shared a cold-water flat in lower Manhattan and one winter coat, which they passed between them when a trip to the freezing outdoors was required. Max had observed (aloud, no doubt, since they were very forthright with one another) that de Kooning seemed unable to paint hands accurately, and de Kooning responded by painting a picture of Max with hands not exactly perfectly formed and giving the painting to Max. It was this painting that Max got permission from de Kooning to sell—it eventually wound up in the Boston Museum of Fine Arts—so that Max could buy the rare Guarneri violin he had coveted all his life.

In the 1960s, Max taught singing to Italian tenors and basses and French sopranos who left a scent of exotic colognes in the hallway and the elevator. He taught Laurence Olivier to sing for the movie *The Entertainer*. He wrote for *The New Masses,* one of the left-wing papers of the time. He loved Frank Sinatra, Luciano Pavarotti, and Ella Fitzgerald. He seldom ventured out to see anyone in anything, but when he did go out, you knew it was going to be something worthwhile.

Singing and speaking, Max believed, come from the same instrument, so singers and actors alike found his teaching valuable. Stacy Keach was his student for a time, as were Harris Yulin and Sigourney Weaver (who says her friends laugh when she says she studied with Judy Collins' singing teacher).

He would sing "Vissi d'arte" or "The Last Rose of Summer." His voice was no voice at all, but I got the idea. I would repeat the phrase. He would nod. I would repeat the phrase again, this time thinking of the clarity, of the smooth transition, the long line, thinking through to the end of the phrase, as he would remind me to do. I would start an "ah," the vowel clouded, trying to get from low to high or from high to low, past the break. Max would sing it clearly. I would try again. I would rest, just looking out the window, thinking, "This is mad. This man is crazy, maybe. What am I doing here? I should be at Max's Kansas City, getting drunk with Paul Butterfield, not here in this apartment, staring at an Arshile Gorky painting. I am a folkie." But I spent a few hours a week for the next thirty-two years of my life in Max's living room, learning from an eccentric, enormously intelligent man who would teach me everything about singing with the whole voice. I went in with a voice that was breaking up, hoarse on a regular basis, full of dark tones and compromised clarity. And then one day a few years after I first walked in that door, just like that, I sang the "oh" and the "ah" in a seamless ribbon of tone from top to bottom, no break, no cloud, and no clutter. Just music.

"Clear as a bell," he said, and smiled, a rare thing for Max.

CLARK continued his visits to New York at least a couple of times a month for weekends and holidays. He had already made his bedroom in my new apartment into his own. Peter was not an unreasonable person, and since we had practically an amicable divorce, there was no need to legislate my visits while I was trying to get full custody of my son. The judge had instructed us to make arrangements between us for Clark's benefit.

At the final custody hearing in late 1964, Ralph's therapist had testified to my fitness as a mother, and encouraged the court to grant me custody. My mother, Marjorie, and Harold Leventhal would both be there to speak on my behalf. My lawyers had been sure that I would not lose my case.

But in May 1965, I learned that I had lost custody of Clark. I remember standing in my new apartment, looking out the window at the passing traffic on 79th Street, weeping. I hurled the telephone across the room and, throwing myself down on the couch—my new couch, next to the piano that I would not be able to play for weeks—I just cried my eyes out. I plummeted into a deep depression, fearing I was going to go under.

My lawyers told me that one of the main reasons I had lost custody was because I was in therapy. Today, you might lose custody because you are *not* in therapy.

I got very, very drunk.

Of course.

I TOLD Harold I just could not go on with the trip we had been planning to the USSR. I imagined getting into bed and never getting up. I contemplated suicide. Again.

"I know this is terrible for you, but you must pull yourself together and do this trip," Harold said in response to my whining. "This is one of those times when you find out just what you are made of. I know you can do this!" Harold could always bring me back to reality. A lot had been done to prepare for this tour by canceling or postponing all my other concerts for the summer. If I didn't go, I also wouldn't have income for months.

"This is a break in the Cold War," Harold said. "It is a historic time. The promoters over there are eager to hear you, not just because you are an American folksinger, but because you are Judy Collins."

Harold was very persuasive. "You must go. It means a lot to those who have not seen or heard much Western music in decades." He had been able to get our visas, no mean feat in those days. The Tarriers would also be on the trip, another reason Harold told me I must not cancel. He would go with us as far as France, where we would have dinner one night with Big Joan Baez in Paris, where Al was working for UNESCO. From there we would go on to Poland with Arlene Cunningham, who worked for Harold and would be our road manager on the trip at last. I surrendered.

I called my ex-husband and asked him if I could have Clark for the month of August, after I got back from the USSR. Peter was strangely agreeable, and I was thrilled. That meant that I would be able to take a house out on Long Island, where we had friends, and Clark and I would have a good long stretch together in late summer. I told Harold I could manage it—just. I would go.

I would be with my old friend Eric Weissberg, who had played guitar and banjo on many of my albums. Clarence Cooper, a rail-thin man with a sweet, wood-smoky voice and heart problems, would also be part of our group on guitar. I adored Clarence, a shy and gentle man from Virginia. Clarence recorded the blues and gospel record *Going' Down the Road,* for Elektra in 1954. I had known Coop since he replaced Alan Arkin and Bob Carey in the Tarriers, and had worked with him in Chicago. He appeared frail, and by the following year he had retired from the Tarriers. George Wein would ask Clarence's help in putting together the blues and gospel shows for the Newport Folk Festival.

Also with us was Al Dana, who had replaced Marshall Brickman in the Tarriers. Our technical manager, John Gibbs, had a light heart and a light touch, and I knew he would make the music sound right and the hotels as comfortable as possible.

I had grown up reading Dostoevsky and Tolstoy and Pasternak— *Crime and Punishment, The Double, The Brothers Karamazov, War and Peace, Dr. Zhivago.* I felt a closeness to Russians from reading all those books in the night, reading until I could not keep my eyes open. In my classes at the New School I had learned to say *hello, goodbye,* and *thank you* in Russian; from Ethel Raim, Walter's ex, who made records with a group called the Pennywhistlers. I had even learned, over the course of the first six months of the year, to sing a song in Russian.

I called my mother and asked her if it would be all right if I took my sister, Holly, with me. I thought if I could just have my beloved sister along, I could make it. Holly was eleven and was thrilled at the prospect. She and I were very close, but in some ways, she felt more like my child than my sister, being only six years older than Clark. Mother agreed that Holly should join me for this trip, and I really don't think I could have done it without her. She was articulate and great company even at eleven. She loved Clark; we talked about him all the time, filling the gap left by his absence. I was grateful for her presence in my life, and for the knowledge that the three of us would be together at the end of the summer.

After Paris, we flew to Warsaw, where we landed in the airport in Krakow, sang a concert that night, and then boarded a bus. In the morning we drove through the beautiful countryside, past houses with roofs of grass, chickens pecking among the flowers, women in their patterned aprons waving, men in work clothes, horses nodding as they pulled plows, children everywhere. Through-out Poland, our concerts were advertised as "Judy Collins and Her All-Negro Band." Clarence, tall and dignified, was followed around in the towns by a gaggle of little blond boys and girls who had never seen a black man before. In Rzeszow, Poland, we had to delay our show for the night, postponing it till the next day, be-cause the town needed the electricity that would have run the lights at the concert in order to operate the coal mine, its single source of income. At our stops along the way, when we needed a drink or a rest, we found what my sister Holly called "memory water," a cold, bottled drink that was thirst- and sorrow-quenching.

About halfway through our travels into the lush, green Polish countryside, our bus passed a sign on the highway that read "Oswiecim"—Auschwitz. I knew we had to stop to pay our re-spects to those who had suffered unspeakable atrocities beyond those arches.

The man behind the wheel of the bus made gestures that in-dicated he had no idea what we wanted. Our translator inter-vened. A skull and crossbones greeted us with "Halt! Stol!" Barbed wire clung to the walls of dark buildings; rooms were piled high with shoes and eyeglasses, teeth and clothes; a sign spelled out

"Krematorium." We saw the open doors of ovens where bodies had been burned, and then peered into the shower rooms where the victims had been gassed after giving over their few precious belongings, murdered while the butterflies bobbed gently among the Queen Anne's lace in the yard.

In stunned silence, we made our way to the only bright spot in this place of horror, a low-slung brick building where the children had painted brilliant colors, clouds, happy faces, and rainbows on the walls before they, too, perished.

Holly and I were weeping by the time we climbed back onto the bus, our eyes down, our minds numbed. Our driver said he was sorry we had stopped, but we disagreed, knowing it was important to have borne witness, to grieve, and to honor in some small way the victims of the Holocaust.

I was glad Arlene Cunningham had come on the trip. She worked for Harold and was a true professional and totally discreet— so much so that I would not know until much later that she had been an assistant and friend to the actor Montgomery Clift for many years, up until his death. She is a truly brilliant woman who later married my friend Dan Kramer, photographer and famous for the cover of the Dylan album *Bringing It All Back Home,* as well as many other iconic photos of the 1960s.

We flew to Moscow, and from there to the seaside cities in Russia. I taught Holly the Russian for *tea* and *cheese* and sang my Russian song in all the venues, where the audience would scream with delight, clap, and laugh at my Russian accent. Then they would demand, stomping their feet on the floor, that I sing it again. (When I got back from the trip Pete Seeger asked me to sing on his program *Rainbow Quest.* So I sang "Dorogoy Da." My Russian was better by then.)

In Odessa, in an outdoor arena near the Potemkin Steps, the audience threw apples at me on the stage. This time, we had been advertised in Odessa as "Judy Collins and Her Rock and Roll

Band," and when that didn't pan out, the sailors off the big ships in the Black Sea were not pleased. They wanted to rock and roll, and there we were, singing gentle folk songs. It was the first and, thankfully, the last time—so far—I have had to dodge apples on a stage!

Our translator, the zaftig Nadine, went onstage every night to introduce us in Russian and English. For these brief appearances, Nadine had borrowed a corset from the Bolshoi Ballet costume department. Holly and I cinched her into it before our show, pulling the strings while Nadine held her breath and braced herself against a wall with the two of us at her back, straining like mad dressmakers with their favorite mannequin. I don't believe Nadine ever corrected the misimpression that we were a rock-and-roll band, the Tarriers and I, but she was good company and seemed to like our music. But she only ever gave us three choices in the restaurants, and since my Russian was not yet so hot, we never ate anything but beef Stroganoff, chicken Kiev, and lamb (shashlik).

I loved the Russian audiences. They were wildly enthusiastic and gave us standing ovations that sometimes lasted ten or fifteen minutes. People showed up with flowers, pictures of themselves and their families, and books about the cities we visited for us to take home to show our American friends. In one city on the Black Sea the audience stood in a pouring rain with umbrellas raised over their heads—umbrellas of every color—while we sang and sang, even after the main show was over, doing encore after encore. Sopping wet, they then gathered, a thousand or so of them, to greet us as we left the stage and went back onto our bus. The crowd swarmed over our bus, clapping and shouting, "We love you!" We were wet and happy. It took half the night to get back to our hotel.

I remember standing in line for hours in Moscow's Red Square, staring at the ancient minarets and waiting to see Lenin's tomb. I would drink to the revolution! I suppose I would actually drink to anything in those days. I had brought a bottle of strong dark vodka with me from Poland, and as it soon ran out, I decided I had to get as much booze as I could at the dinners because I was embarrassed to ask our translator to order bottles in the hotels and shops on the road.

We stayed in the Peking Hotel and drank slippery Russian vodka out of shot glasses, hurling the fiery silver down our throats. Finally, someone told us how to say "More vodka, please"—it was one of our Russian promoters, I think—and thank God! I was dying there, going into withdrawal. Clarence and Al Dana and I drank, and Arlene might have put a few away. Neither my sister, of course, nor Eric did any boozing. The Russians, who drank as much as I did, didn't bat an eye. I was drinking half a fifth easily by then, but they couldn't read my mind, and I was finally going to have to say "More, much more!"

In Moscow we sang at the Moscow Opera House, a white building adorned with curlicues, ribbonlike scrolls, and wedding cake filigree. The crowds were enthusiastic, applauding, stamping their feet, hollering, and carrying on until we did a number of encores in this great hall, where so many artists have performed, including Van Cliburn and Byron Janis, pianists who were often able to bridge the cultural gaps between the USSR and the United States. Our reviews, read to us by our translator, were ecstatic.

On our last day in Moscow Nadine and the reporter who'd traveled with us left us at the door of the American embassy. We were to be given a big party to celebrate the end of our trip, and we begged them to come, but they told us they could not because if they did, they would be accused of spying. The Cold War, we learned, had not thawed as much as we had been led to believe.

The party was at Spaso House, the residence of the U.S. ambassador to the USSR, Foy D. Kohler. He was from Ohio and was our host that night. When we told him we were upset that our translator and the journalist could not join us at the embassy, he just laughed and remarked that the countries had come a long way but still had far to go. He, too, told us that if our Russian friends appeared at the U.S. embassy, they might be accused of spying, but also they might lose their membership in the Communist Party, and that would be very bad for them, since the Party was the only means of advancement and acceptance in the USSR.

We had a fine time at the embassy that last night in Moscow. The Americans and Russians who were there really knew how to drink. There was vodka aplenty! I was poured onto the plane home the next day, trying to look my best.

It had been a bittersweet trip, but by the time I was through, I was glad Harold had insisted I go. My sister, Holly Ann, had been such a lovely and enthusiastic presence. Her beauty, wonderful mind, and spirit helped me with the pain I was feeling about losing custody of Clark. She brought me smiles and kept me company all throughout the trip.

We visited great and fascinating countries whose histories were filled with shadow and light and whose people had welcomed me with their flowers, their cheers, and open arms. Someday, I promised myself, I would return.

But for now, I couldn't wait to get home again to noisy, dirty, fabulous New York City—and to my son.

Chapter Nineteen

The Coming of the Roads

Now that our mountain is growing
With people hungry for wealth . . .

—Billy Edd Wheeler, "The Coming of the Roads"

August on Long Island was blissful. We spent time with friends and enjoyed fish dinners, lobster, and white wine at Gosman's in Montauk. Clark loved holding the chickadees in his hands when they came to the bird feeder. We had long lunches in the sun at Amagansett, as well as visits with my therapist, Ralph, and his son Josh, who was Clark's friend. Holly and I were still talking about our Russian trip and had brought back beautiful old enameled Russian boxes for everyone.

At the end of the summer I returned Clark to Peter in Connecticut and eased back into the rhythms of life in the city.

I resumed my lessons with Max next door. Though I was living uptown, I remained as involved as ever in the vibrant Greenwich Village folk music scene. At the Village Gate, the Village Vanguard, or the Gaslight, I might drink the night away with

Steve Katz, Jim Morrison, Dave Van Ronk, and Dave's wife, Terry. There is a photograph of me, Mimi Fariña, Joan Baez, Dave and Terry Van Ronk, and my friend Linda Liebman. Dan Kramer shot this picture in the Van Ronks' apartment early in 1966, around the time I was getting the songs together for my sixth album. Mimi and Dick were living in Carmel, but remained closely connected to the New York scene. They were recording for Maynard Solomon at Vanguard and would stay with me when they were in town.

I was also getting to know Phil Ochs better. He was a Texas kid, from El Paso. A good friend of Al Kooper, he and I would sit down at some bar in the Village to listen to the band, or get together at my place, where he would sing me his songs.

Phil called himself a topical and protest singer. He performed at everything from antiwar rallies to Carnegie Hall. He was a good-looking fellow, very social and fun to be with. He always had a smile on this face in those days, and an urgent energy that seemed to burst out in every direction. I loved being with him because he had a ferocious sense of humor. We laughed a lot at the world and how our lives had become so focused on the war, Mississippi, and social justice. We had to laugh, for sometimes these things seemed difficult. Phil was a critic but also an optimist, he would say. He would write and sing about anything that moved him, which was one of the reasons I liked him so much.

He and I often shared a pint—more than a pint in my case, but he kept up. He was outspoken in his writing, and his 1964 album for Elektra, *All the News That's Fit to Sing,* had brought him more attention. Phil knew I was planning on recording his great song about the race riots, "In the Heat of the Summer," on my new album. He came by my apartment to sing it for me, throwing back his beautiful head of hair. His voice was somewhat ragged, both moving and dynamic.

So wrong, so wrong
But we've been down too long,
And we had to make somebody listen.

It was a fine song, one of his very best, and painted a picture of pain and hope in vivid detail. That was one of Phil's great gifts. His story songs are still as fresh and engaging as they were that morning when I listened to his urgent and optimistic voice. I knew his songs made a difference in the world and told him so.

Phil was in that cluster of singer-songwriters who congregated around Dylan. The aura of fame and the drama of Dylan's work washed over all these men, each of whom was, in his own right, an extraordinary writer: Phil, Van Ronk, Tom Paxton, Richie Havens, David Blue, Eric Andersen, Al Kooper, Tim Buckley, Len Chandler, and John Winn. Eventually, even some women found their way into that circle of light—Joni Mitchell, Laura Nyro, Joan Baez, and me, although neither Joan nor I was writing songs yet.

Sam Hood, who ran the Gaslight, would lock the club down, shutting out all but the anointed on the nights when Dylan deigned to appear, slouching through the door. Bob and Joan were doing a lot of touring now. Joan was putting Bob in her shows, introducing him to the sometimes ten-thousand-strong audiences coming to hear her. Suze Rotolo said she was getting fed up with the situation but deeply wanted to hold on to her friendship with Bob, even if they were no longer living together. Every now and then, when Bob would show up at these clubs, Suze would again be on his arm.

Back in New York, I spent as much time as possible in the clubs downtown, listening to songs, learning new ones, looking for the next writer. Between shows at the Gaslight, songwriters might congregate at the Kettle of Fish, drinking coffee with shots of Irish whiskey ("to sober up," a lot of them would say) and talking, talking, talking. They rubbed elbows and egos, honing their personas, all the while praying for inspiration, and probably for courage. Life wasn't that easy for most folkies—living and writing in sometimes dingy hotel rooms or traveling on planes and cars and trains. But the Village was like home, a safe place to come to roost for a time, to get rested and refreshed.

By the end of the summer I was ready to go back into the studio again, and that meant that Mark Abramson would again become a daily fixture in my life. Mark, of course, had been my producer on all of my albums, but the first time we slept together was late in that autumn of 1965, after I had come back from the USSR. There were times during the fall when I thought he might be the right one, the answer to my dreams as we began to plan and work on the fifth album. After all, he was already the answer to my artistic aspirations.

Mark and I were not in love, certainly, and yet we had a loving and successful working relationship that had as much sex in it as I think I could tolerate at that time. And perhaps as much intimacy as well.

He was exactly what I needed, falling into my lap and later into my bed. But the bed was not our best thing going. From the very first album we made together, Mark and I were deeply committed to the business of my records, to creating the best records we could—not just a string of songs but albums that had heft and meaning and would last forever. That was the way we thought.

The people who played on the album were mostly friends—Richard Fariña on dulcimer, Bill Takas on bass, and Bill Lee also on bass, for starters. Eric Weissberg played guitar and sang background vocals, Danny Kalb played guitar, and Chuck Israels doubled on bass and cello. A special guest was John Sebastian, playing harmonica on "Thirsty Boots."

Judy Collins Fifth Album stuck fairly closely to the model that had worked so well on the previous records, combining my favorite traditional songs with the works of contemporary singer-songwriters. Many of the new songs had the feel of classic folk songs but seemed destined to become folk standards. Dylan made an appearance on my *Fifth Album,* with "Mr. Tambourine Man," "Tomorrow Is a Long Time," and "I'll Keep It with Mine," which Bob said he wrote for me.

During this recording there was an argument on the phone between my lawyer, Bob, and Joan Baez, who swore Dylan had told her he wrote the song for her. I think Bob had just forgotten whom he wrote it for, or perhaps he wanted to make Joanie mad. They had been an on-again, off-again thing for a while. I won, if you want to call it that, but I always wondered if, in fact, he had told me the truth.

Years later, when I was recording an all-Dylan album, I found that Bob had written extensive liner notes, in which he clearly acknowledged writing "I'll Keep It with Mine" for me. I was, of course, honored. Who wouldn't be?

Dylan would record "I'll Keep It with Mine" twelve times over the course of his career, in live concerts and on studio albums. My recording was the first, and was followed by recordings by Nico and Dusty Springfield. I only released "I'll Keep It with Mine" on a single; it never appeared on an album. And Joan Baez never did record it.

The difficulty with Dylan was that very quickly after the success of those first records with all his powerful songs, he became somehow larger than life. Sometimes he seemed to take up all the air in the room, leaving little for the cluster of great writers around him. Suze Rotolo would say about her longtime beau that after the floods of fame had come, he had somehow felt entitled to do or say whatever he wanted. While she would describe Bob as charismatic and like a beacon, she would also compare him to a black hole.

And sometimes people acted as if they believed Dylan could walk on water, while the rest of us could barely swim. In the early days of that meteor-like fame, Dylan didn't exactly try to disabuse anybody of that notion.

He does remain a unique and complicated man.

And of course, a genius.

*F*ROM Phil Ochs, as planned, came "In the Heat of the Summer." He also contributed in a very personal way to another of the songs on *Judy Collins Fifth Album*, "Thirsty Boots." In the spring of 1965 he had told Eric Andersen that I was looking for new material. They both arrived at my place, and as soon as Eric walked through the door he asked if he could use the bathroom. That was where he finished writing the last verse of "Thirsty Boots." He sang the song for me right then and there, and I said, "Great, I'll record it tomorrow."

Traditional music is the foundation of what the folk music revival was about—songs of unknown authorship handed down through the generations. I keep returning to these old, classic songs, often bringing them back to find new meaning and fresh interpretations. "Danny Boy," "The Lark in the Morning," "Barbara Allen," "So Early, Early in the Spring," and "The Gypsy Rover" have lasted for years and will endure for years more. They touch your heart, and for anyone trying to write new and original songs, they stand as an unspoken challenge: make something as good and as timeless as this and you will have won the heart of your listener. You also will have added something to the story of humankind.

Traditional songs didn't just spring from the earth, of course. Somebody somewhere came up with a melody through which to tell a story, and that story-song got passed along. These songs survive in the memory of a culture because they tell stories of universal emotion and experience—of love, heartbreak, mourning, abandonment, victory, and defeat—and because they are so very adaptable to so many times, to so many people. One person would add a verse; another would change a melody a bit. This is what we call the "folk process," borrowing to fit the time, the person, the incident.

I have sung many traditional songs but always thought "So Early, Early in the Spring" to be one of the best, and I included it on this album. Eric Weissberg and I played the two dancing guitars in a way I can't quite replicate anymore.

I KEPT very busy in the fall of 1965, running in a dozen different directions. In September, I did Studs Terkel's radio show in Chicago. Studs and I had met after I made my first album, *Maid of Constant Sorrow*, and began a years-long friendship. Studs was intrigued by "The Great Selchie of Skule Skerry," which he heard me sing live at the Gate of Horn and on my second album. He found it curious that my father was blind, and felt that his influence— especially his reading to us at night with the lights out—and his remarkable life might explain my passion for mysterious songs such as this ballad. Studs was always a great interviewer, going beyond the mundane and giving you something to get your teeth into. We always had a fine time. His stocky figure, trademark cigars—until doctors made him give them up—his tender feelings for his wife, and his truly brilliant thoughts about people were attractive and engaging.

In New York, my WBAI radio show was still on the air, and I did shows with Guy Carawan, an oft-recorded singer who was active in the movement for racial equality as well as the peace movement. He had made many albums for Folkways and practiced the art of the hammered dulcimer. Koerner, Ray and Glover, a Minnesota blues band, was a guest on the show as well. "Spider" John Koerner, Dave "Snaker" Ray, and Tony "Little Sun" Glover—young and vibrant—recorded for Elektra and sang "white blues," inspired by artists such as Son House and Mississippi John Hurt. I had met them at the Newport and Philadelphia folk festivals, and I had a brief romantic interlude that fall with the handsome and talented Koerner, who was slim and tall and gentle, and I needed gentle.

Jac was continuing to sign artists to Elektra that were eclectic. He brought me a recording by a new band that he wanted me to hear, and I encountered Jim Morrison's amazing voice and songs for the first time. Jac has since told me that he was very nervous about my opinion of the group.

"They were so different, and by that time, you had every right to know where the record label you were with was going next," he said. My response to the Doors was nothing but positive, and I could see that, in addition to signing Paul Butterfield, whom I adored, Jac had made another very important contribution to the label.

Jac signed the Doors that year after watching them play at the Ritz in L.A. They were raw, dropped by their first label, and the other labels were not lining up in droves to sign them. But Jac heard something in Ray Manzarek's bottom keyboard line from "Light My Fire"—for Jac, that was what he would often call the "Rosetta stone," the tipping point in Jac's decision to sign any group or individual. Ray Manzarek of the Doors described his first impressions of Holzman: "He was the only person who was interested. He was an intellectual, the cowboy from New York. He was like Gary Cooper riding into town."

*I*N 1965 I made my first trip to Australia and New Zealand. I was to tour with the Limelighters, and they introduced me to Tina Date, who became a friend. She belonged to a cluster of free-loving and free-drinking artists and musicians in Sydney, living in group houses and sharing wives, husbands, lovers, children. Tina introduced me to many of them, and they reminded me of the crowd who clustered around my therapists in New York. They made me comfortable in the thriving, exciting city of Sydney.

After I returned from Australia, my schedule didn't let up. In late 1965 I attended a meeting of the Newport Folk Festival board. I had been asked to join the group, which already included Pete Seeger, Harold Leventhal, Peter Yarrow, Ronnie Gilbert (of the Weavers), and George Wein. Theo Bikel was on the board as well. Of all of us, I was probably the least obsessed with keeping the folk tradition pure at the festival. I saw that the new writers—not least of all Pete—were building something new out of the very tradition they were steeped in.

That November I was on tour in California, and performed around Carmel, where Joan Baez was living. We made a date to see each other on that trip. Over the years our friendship grew in fits and starts; Joan invited me to concerts when she was playing in New York City, and I invited her to come to the shows I did in the San Francisco area. We have always been closer than meets the eye.

In addition to her beauty as a singer, Joan brought more than bare feet to the folk fashion table. She looked fabulous in everything, and often wore a white silk blouse before any of the rest of us even had a clue that silk was not polished cotton. I don't think Joan ever wore a pair of Levi's unless she was cleaning out the barn. I have a sweet memory of hanging out one night at her hotel in New York after her Carnegie Hall concert. She, Mimi, Big Joan, and I were celebrating with flowers and glasses of Moët et Chandon champagne. Joan had on a silk blouse (of course) and Mimi was letting loose her delicious giggle over the fact that Joanie had gotten through the concert without throwing up. Joan always said that her nerves were often a-jangle before going onstage, but she performed beautifully that night.

Like everyone who heard Joan in those years, I was moved by her voice and by the intelligence and dedication behind her singing.

Soon, as we both were making records and going on the road, there began a sort of gentle competition between us, fueled by the media, by our audiences, and by our place in the culture. My friendship with Mimi may have been a factor, but I don't think so; Mimi and I had a relationship very different from the one I had with Joan. Joan and I both know the price it takes to do what we do, to be where we need to be, so I never felt that competitiveness was helpful or warranted. We were very different people, different singers, and the durability of both our careers was not dependent on a contest between us. But if she was Ceres, the goddess upon whom the entire existence of Roman society was dependent, I was Diana, the goddess of transition, a huntress. And the forest is a big, thriving place, chock-full of gods and goddesses. Both of us would have to make our mark, and each of us faced far more serious challenges than competition from a woman we respected. The question would come down to whether, with all that chatter in the woods, we could become friends.

That would be a race worth betting on.

While promoting *Fifth Album*, I went to Carmel. I had already heard the rumors that Joanie had walked into a Jaguar showroom in her bare feet, told the dealer she had to have a Jaguar because she lived up a hill, put down five thousand dollars in cash, and driven off. Indeed, Joan picked me up in her Jaguar XKE roadster and drove me out to her Spanish-style villa near the sea. It was quiet in the house except for music and our voices. As we told our stories and shared our secrets over a single candle, I remember looking at Joan and thinking that no diet was going to ever make *me* that thin! And of course Joan's beauty put me in awe, as it always has. She made me laugh, imitating my lisp. It was so like her. I smiled as she begged my pardon, and forgave her.

Joan had prepared some supper—cheese and olives and baklava, served on southwestern plates with paintings of churches and seascapes that mesmerized me. We played guitar and sang songs for most of the night. The candle flickered and the wind blew outside the door, and then she floated up to bed in her silk skirt and blouse, leaving me to sleep in a wrought-iron bed in the guest room. I lay awake for a long while and thought about how much Joan wanted me to see her as strong, and about how profoundly vulnerable she really was.

In 1965, Joan had started the School for Nonviolence in Carmel with her mentor, the activist and Gandhi scholar Ira Sandperl. The next morning we visited the secluded spot under the eucalyptus trees where Ira was teaching a class on nonviolent protest to a number of young people.

"Here's where I really belong," she said to me. "The music is just what I do to support this school, right, Ira?" Ira was also under the sway of the Maid of Orleans, as were all of the young people who joined Joan and Ira's school. The smell of the trees, the dusty hillside, and the faces of those eager youngsters—their hair long like Joan's, their faces filled with adoration—made an indelible impression on me.

"See, they love nonviolence, just like we all do," she said, her hand holding mine. I could have stayed there forever, I thought.

Joan and I have fought similar demons. We both found therapy early in our careers, at early ages. In the early 1960s, Joan saw Eric Berne, the psychologist who popularized the concept of transactional analysis in his book *Games People Play*. I was deep into my own therapy with the Sullivanians.

In a letter to me dated July 13, 1964, Dick Fariña wrote:

The private terrors you speak of, Judy, stalk us all. I can think of no one in our limited acquaintance who has not been tempted to cup his fingers over his ears and run moaning into the night. [But] when you've walked a

little with death, you learn to court it, play with it, defy
it if you choose.

Friend to us both, Dick might have been writing to Joan as
well.

One way or another, it seems, Joan and I both managed to find
ways to weather the storm, to battle those doubts.

*B*ACK in New York that year I was dating Dick Lukins, a native
New Yorker with a wicked sense of humor and a great laugh. I
needed the laughter. After we stopped seeing each other (Dick
soon met and married Sheila Block, who as Sheila Lukins started
a world-famous catering and food emporium called the Silver Pal-
ate), he introduced me to David Levine, a medical intern studying
psychiatry. David and I went to a few movies together, had a few
meals, and enjoyed a brief romance. I was drifting romantically, but
I liked David a lot. He was smart and charming, and I realized I
wanted him in my life in some way. He was a keeper, not my lover
but certainly my good friend. I would make every effort to hold
him close.

There was a march on Washington to end the war in Vietnam
on November 27, 1965, and I joined thousands of Americans on the
National Mall. Soon after that march I attended the first of Jacques
Brel's concerts at Carnegie Hall. He was a dazzling performer, and
though he spoke no English and my French was limited, I was able
to tell him through his translator how much I loved his work when
I began recording it on my sixth album, *In My Life*, beginning with
"La Colombe."

On Christmas Day I did my first Carnegie Hall solo concert,
which Harold produced. At the party following that Carnegie
Hall concert, I introduced my friend Lucy Simon to David Levine.

They went home together that night, married, now have two children, and began producing music together. In the early 1980s they received Grammys for *In Harmony: A Sesame Street Record* and *In Harmony 2*.

ᴀᴛ the end of December, Peter informed me that he had taken a job teaching English literature at the University of British Columbia in Vancouver. He would be moving out west in a short time, putting an entire continent between our beautiful redheaded son and me. As usual, I made every effort to be there for Clark, traveling to Canada or bringing him to see me whenever I could.

I was in the beginning period of a thriving, satisfying, exhausting career. My love life was going nowhere, but I was working hard at therapy, still drinking, rushing around the world, and trying to forget what I had lost.

And to appreciate what I had been given.

Chapter Twenty

Blue Strangers and Blue Friends: Dick Fariña, Mimi Baez Fariña, Joni Mitchell, and Leonard Cohen

The ponies run
The girls are young
The odds are there to beat

—Leonard Cohen, "A Thousand Kisses Deep"

On New Year's Day 1966, Simon and Garfunkel's single "The Sound of Silence" reached number one on the music charts. The haunting words of the opening verse—"Hello darkness, my old friend, I've come to talk with you again"—had been written, I knew from talking with Simon's friend, Al Gorgoni, as a sort of adagio for our lost president, JFK. It poured from every little bodega on the Upper West Side, every cab I took, every record store I visited, and every party I went to.

The song moved me deeply as Johnson roared further into the darkness of Vietnam. It seemed a fitting way to start a new year. I hoped it could fuel the peace movement in a new way. In some ways it was the catalyst for my involvement in co-producing an album to raise money for Women Strike for Peace, a powerful antiwar group in New York. Ethel Raim, one of Walter's ex-wives, and I put the album together, gathering our friends to create *Save the Children—Songs from the Hearts of Women*. The list of women participating is impressive, even today: Odetta, Buffy Sainte-Marie, Mimi and Joan Baez, and Janis Ian, among others.

Save the Children was my answer, for that moment, to the question the war always raised: what could I do?

ON my trip to Australia during 1965 I told my new friend Tina Date that she could stay at my New York apartment when she came to visit at the beginning of 1966, as I would be going to London for a series of shows. She said I should call her old boyfriend, Michael Thomas; They had split up, she said, but he was a good friend and I would like him. I should have known she was still carrying a torch.

In February, Tina arrived in New York as I headed to London. I called Michael out of good manners, really. I expected nothing, and invited him to the party Elektra was putting on for me to celebrate my latest album. He was very good-looking. We talked for a couple of hours as the party swirled around us, and then found ourselves hand in hand, walking to the Strand Hotel, where I was staying. By morning, we were sleeping together in the spoon position while Tina was taking care of my cats and watering my plants back home.

I had a magical interlude with Michael in London: trips to Portobello Road where he bought me a tie-dyed skirt; visits to the National Portrait Gallery and the Tate; seeing the changing of the guard at Buckingham Palace; eating lemon curd on toast at his little apartment off King's Road; walks along the river near Westminster Abbey; and plenty of wild sex. At the end of my trip Michael took me to the airport and said he would see me soon, and as wonderful as our time had been, I assumed our mad fling would never amount to more than an enchanting memory.

But a few days later, Michael arrived on the doorstep of my Upper West Side apartment in New York, bearing books and typewriter, clothes for a year, jars of lemon curd, presents from Harrod's, and a big, loving smile. His arms opened wide, and like the song says, he took me inside. He was there to stay.

Tina was still in my apartment, and we all wound up sleeping in the same bed that night; although I would have some exotic sexual experiences in the future, there was no sharing that night. By the next day, Tina had moved out and Michael had moved in.

Michael and I settled into our lives in New York like a young married couple. He met my mother and father in Colorado and received their approval; got drunk many a time with my brothers and my dad; went horseback riding with us and learned the secrets of the family. In July, John Lennon of the Beatles famously declared, "We're more popular than Jesus now," and Michael, in his intense English way, decided he had to go home to see how England was dealing with the band's newfound status that trumped, as he put it, the Holy Lamb of God. Doing research for his new book, he then continued around the world, searching for answers. He visited the rock critic and my friend Lillian Roxon, who was back in Australia. He went to see Maharishi Mahesh Yogi in India and brought me back a sitar, the quintessential gift of love in 1966. We smiled as the first thing our cat, Moby, did was to make himself comfortable in the sitar case.

We got along well and continued to have a great sex life, enlivened by reading *The Story of O*. Although it was a time of open marriage and open relationships, Michael was devoted to me, and I was as devoted to him as I had ever been to anyone. I trusted him.

I never doubted Michael's love for me or my son, Clark, and we had something wonderful together for a long time. But I never seemed to know when I was in the right place until it was over, and by then I was always someplace else.

I ADORED Dick Fariña. Mimi later said she thought that there was something else going on with us, since we fell over laughing and took walks and talked together about everything. But she was wrong. My friendship with Dick was like my friendship with my old pal John Gilbert in high school—purely platonic.

Dick was one of the funniest, most intelligent people I have ever known. His mind was quick, his humor was effervescent, and I always felt he saw the bright side of things rather than drifting into intellectual despair about the world. I always felt loved and appreciated by Dick and was never sexually attracted to him. With Dick there was an intellectual connection, one that soared during the five years we knew each other. I craved the buoyancy he brought when he entered a room, the whiff of adventure in his stories, the feeling that all of life was coming at him and he couldn't wait to meet up with it.

When Dick and Mimi lived in Boston I would stay over at their place and take morning runs along the Charles River with Dick and their German shepherd Lush. Dick thought I should assume custody of Clark, keeping him with me the next time he came to visit. He knew it would cause legal problems, but Dick felt it would be worth it; I should just let the chips fall where they may. He said he and Mimi would help me, and I was sorely tempted. But I know now it would have destroyed my relationship with my son.

In the spring of 1966, Dick had finally finished his long-awaited novel, *Been Down So Long It Looks Like Up to Me.* Mimi's twenty-first birthday coincided with the publication of his book, and he and Mimi and a crowd of friends were having a triumphant party in Carmel to celebrate. I had been invited but had a show in Colorado that night, so had to say no.

Later in the evening, with everyone well lubricated, Dick jumped onto the back of a friend's motorcycle. Before the two of them drove off, Dick, with that wild smile on his face, handed Mimi the keys to their car, which she had never driven. The crowd remaining at the party heard him shouting with pleasure as they peeled off on the dirt road, heading toward Carmel. He never came back. The bike flew around a corner on the dirt road, spun out, and threw Dick fifty feet into a fence post. The blow to his head killed him instantly.

When Nina Holzman called and gave me the terrible news, I simply couldn't accept it. I was in Denver with my family and flew to San Francisco in a daze, driving down the coast to Carmel, where I met up with Mimi, who greeted me with tears in her beautiful eyes. Nancy Carlin, who was a close friend of the Baez family, was there, as was Pauline, Mimi's older sister. All of us spent three days in Carmel after the accident. We huddled together, rehashing every moment of Dick's last days. We would become hysterical, then sober, then despairing again. Joan was in Europe with her mother, doing a concert tour. Mimi, Pauline, Nancy, and I took Lush for runs on the beach, and we gave Mimi's hair an inexpert trim; we did anything that would get us through the next minute and the next hour.

At the ceremony for Dick we threw roses onto his grave while someone spoke the lyrics to "The Swallow Song," one of Mimi and Dick's beautiful creations—lyrics only, no music, as the earth thudded onto his coffin. Willow trees bent to watch us wander back up the hill.

We were not supposed to cry, Mimi said. But back at the home of the Fariñas' neighbors, somebody played the guitar and then played Mimi and Dick's recordings. All at once we lost it and were in tears. I sang something, too, and cried all the way through the wake and then on the plane back home. It was one of the saddest days. I remember looking back over the ocean from the window of that plane and seeing Dick's grave on the hillside in Carmel.

The end of a friendship, of an era, of a beautiful, promising life. The end of the bright dreams Mimi and Dick had of continuing their soulful writing.

Come wander quietly and listen to the wind
Come near and listen to the sky . . .

LILLIAN Roxon, the legendary rock and folk critic from Australia, was a doll—funny, bouncy, sexy. She was often called the "mother of rock-and-roll journalism." She was ten years older than most of us, the oldest child of a Jewish family who had fled Poland when the Nazis rose to power. After her graduation from the University of Sydney she became involved with the left-leaning, freewheeling "Sydney Push," a sort of avant-garde social and sexually hip group of young artists and writers in that city. Lillian began writing for the *Sydney Morning Herald* and moved to the States in 1959 to become their New York correspondent. She introduced me to her friends Linda McCartney and Helen Reddy and inspired Helen's "I Am Woman." She wrote about the Beatles and the Rolling Stones for *Oz* magazine. We shared a host of New York acquaintances, including my close friend Linda Liebman. I used to go with Lillian to Max's Kansas City in New York when rock was nearing its heyday. Lily Tomlin was a friend of Linda's and Lillian's, and we enjoyed our evenings of music and revelry.

Mary Martin was also in that group. Born in Canada and a powerhouse in the music business, she would convince Bob Dylan to record with the Band, help get Emmylou Harris a record contract with Warner Brothers, and try to persuade Warner to sign

Jimmy Buffett (they passed). Mary was a good friend to all of us, a musical and artistic tastemaker. She worked for Albert Grossman, mogul of moguls. And she introduced me to Leonard Cohen, her Canadian friend. She really just wanted to help him find a way to get his songs to some singers, and he had said he wanted to meet me. When I met Leonard Cohen for the first time, at the end of May 1966, after Dick Fariña's death, Mary had been talking about Leonard for years. I believed her when she told me that Leonard was talented.

"He is a poet," she would say, "and he has been published and has written a couple of novels. He reads poetry at these little clubs in Montreal and Toronto, but he thinks he has written some songs, and he wants you to hear him."

Leonard's novels, *Beautiful Losers* and *The Favorite Game*, were branded "defiant" and "uninhibited" by Canadian reviewers. In later years Leonard called them an homage to his misspent youth. Mary brought me copies of his books and I was enchanted, but none the wiser about his songwriting skills.

I was in the midst of recording my sixth album, *In My Life*, for Elektra and had already put together a session with Dick and Mimi Fariña before Dick's death, recording "Hard Lovin' Loser." I had fallen ill with mono and hepatitis, which landed me in the hospital. When I was released, Mary arranged for Leonard to come to New York.

I answered the door and found a good-looking, slightly stooped figure, his handsome face wreathed with a smile—a sweet smile, an engaging smile, a rare smile. It was the smile of an intelligent and sensitive artist. I knew in an instant that he was special, and knew that I didn't care if he couldn't write songs!

We embraced, already friends in a way, since we were friends of Mary's. Michael and Linda Liebman were there, and I offered drinks. Leonard asked for a glass of wine, and we talked, getting to know each other. His shyness, I now realize, was probably what kept him from playing his songs that night. Or perhaps he was hoping to seduce me before he allowed me to hear his songs. Well, he had done that, in the first moments we met.

I wasn't expecting a lot, really. It was a shot in the dark. The songs I heard from unknown writers might be fine, but the songs that I took for my own were few and far between. I suppose I had agreed to meet Leonard, really, for Mary's sake, to get her off my case. But what I wasn't expecting was *not* to hear any songs at all that night!

We wound up going out to dinner, laughing and having a lovely time, but still no music. I was curious. Who was this writer who had written songs but did not need to play them? Unusual, that's for sure, in a time when everyone had a guitar and was likely to throw you down, sing their songs, and leave before you even managed to say hello. This reluctance was captivating.

I invited Leonard to come back the next day, which he did. Leonard said he didn't know if he had written songs at all, but that night, with just Michael and me there, he sang them. And what songs they were! He sang "Suzanne" and it was magical.

Then came "Dress Rehearsal Rag," a dark, brutal, authentic song about the contemplation of suicide, the thought of death at one's own hand wedging its way into the place between the eyes and the gut. I knew it, too, belonged on my new album.

I have always been grateful that I did not fall in love with Leonard in the way that I fell in love with his songs. I could have, certainly. He had that charm, that glint in his eyes, that secretly knowing air that always attracted me to the dangerous ones—men who had fantastic sex appeal, were terribly smart and funny, and seemed to slip in and out of other women's lives. I adored Leonard, but thankfully it wasn't the kind of passion that got me into trouble. Instead, his songs would let me fly.

Having already made five albums by the time I met Leonard, I had my pick of songwriters for *In My Life*. Sometimes, as in the case of Tom Paxton, I would hear a song and record it before the actual composer got a record deal and could record it. Many songwriters, including Leonard, Joni Mitchell, and others, would try to build a following for their songs by singing them in clubs, but few had the power of the song-selling machine that throbbed behind Carole King's music and that of other writers in the Brill Building stable. I recorded "Suzanne" and "Dress Rehearsal Rag," Leonard's career took off, and he signed a contract with Columbia.

People have labeled me a folksinger for most of my career, but the eclectic nature of my choices was present in my third album and has continued to this day. Most of the songs I had already recorded by 1966 fell into the category of the unusual, from William Butler Yeats to Bob Dylan, from Pete Seeger to old sea chanties. They would, I hoped, reach my listeners' hearts as well, but I have always chosen for myself first. Leonard Cohen's songs magically combined elements of all those genres and pointed toward the new direction I wanted to take—songs that were more dramatic, with a depth and dimension that were going to make this album stand out from my previous work. Many of the songs were written by composers outside the folk tradition.

Both "Suzanne" and "Dress Rehearsal Rag" appeared on *In My Life,* and I recorded one or two of Leonard's songs on almost every album I made well into the 1990s.

Leonard was naturally reserved and afraid to sing in public. Later he would complain to his lawyer, Marty Machat, that certain people had told him he could not sing.

"None of you can sing!" Marty famously replied. "When I want to hear singing, I go to the Metropolitan Opera!"

But still the nagging feeling that he could not perform well as a singer plagued Leonard. I knew he could sing. He just had to get his feet in the water and do it.

A few weeks after I recorded "Suzanne," I invited him to join me at a benefit I was doing. Jimi Hendrix was going to make an appearance, along with a number of other New York City artists. Leonard was terrified, but I convinced him that even though he had never performed his songs in public, he was going to be fine.

The concert was for the National Committee for a Sane Nuclear Policy at Town Hall on April 30, 1967. I asked Leonard if he would sing "Suzanne."

"I can't sing. I wouldn't know what to do out there. I am not a performer," he said. I assured him I would introduce him and be nearby. By this time my recording of "Suzanne" was out on *In My Life*, and people knew the song.

Leonard's first public singing appearance was festive and historic. He was nervous, and as I introduced him and brought him onstage in front of the enthusiastic full house, I could feel his hands shaking. But when he began to sing, the shaking left his voice and he steadied, and people began to revel in the beauty of "Suzanne." About halfway through the song, blaming what he later said was a broken string, he stopped and walked offstage. I went back on with him and we finished the song together. People went wild.

Leonard never broke my heart, but his songs have, every time I sing or hear one of them. As Leonard says, "There is a crack in everything; that's how the light gets in."

Chapter Twenty-One

In My Life

*There are places I'll remember
All my life though some have changed.*

—John Lennon and Paul McCartney,
"In My Life"

$\mathcal{M}$any nights, after drinking so much, my suicidal thoughts returned. I often called Ralph to say I was afraid I was going to do myself harm, and ask him to put me in a hospital. He refused every time. He told me to think positively, that I was surely going to feel differently in the morning. I did, in fact, feel differently; for another day, or another week, or another month, the thoughts would go away. But they always came back.

Ralph and I were lucky. The excitement and the journey were too wonderful to give up, but the dark thoughts, coming around the corners of many a lonely night, were never far away. I didn't know it was the booze, always the booze, that brought on the darkness.

I was blessed to be working with great musicians. Josh Rifkin came aboard my team in 1966 when I was recording *In My Life* and *Wildflowers* in New York, London, and Los Angeles. I met Josh because he was making records for Nonesuch, part of the Elektra family. He was smart and full of humor, and he created great orchestrations.

A classically trained musician, Josh was a graduate of the Juilliard School and had studied at New York University. Teresa Sterne, who ran Nonesuch Records, had hired him to record, produce, and play some of their more esoteric music, and conduct the many Telemann, Haydn, and Scott Joplin records that Nonesuch released. Josh had reinvented fingering technique on his recordings of Scott Joplin's ragtime piano. Mark and I invited him to New York to talk about the music we were interested in recording. Josh ended up writing the arrangements and conducting the songs for *In My Life* and *Wildflowers*. He also played the famous harpsichord riff on "Both Sides Now," something I believe no one but Josh would have thought of. With Mark's input, I believe—because they talked the language of early music together—it was Josh who suggested that I record "Ecco la Primavera," an anonymous fourteenth-century composition arranged by Francesco Landini, on *Wildflowers*. Josh was sweet, a genius, and a devil of a piano player. We all got along beautifully.

We went to London to get the more authentic sound of the same singers and musicians who had been on the recording of the musical *Marat/Sade*. In the hotel there, I freaked out. I was alone, drinking too much, and, convinced I had been poisoned, called for an ambulance. They were very nice and took me to St. Michael's Hospital, where I was made to throw up, after which I said I was fine. Then I left, against the doctor's advice. He wanted me to stay till morning; I wasn't about to agree to that. I knew better than they what was wrong with me, didn't I? My alcoholism was progressing fast, begetting fear, apprehension, terror, and profound depression.

Paradoxically, *In My Life* was just what we hoped it would be:

the singer-songwriter material my fans expected, plus some totally unexpected selections.

Dylan was represented, of course, with "Just Like Tom Thumb's Blues," but with orchestration by Josh Rifkin that would have knocked the socks off Dylan had he been wearing any. "Hard Lovin' Loser" was by Dick and Mimi Fariña, and the song seemed to be about a guy just like Dick—a mischievous but lovable rogue, someone with an irrepressible sense of humor, and someone, I mused sadly, who was, finally, tragic.

In addition to Leonard Cohen's "Suzanne" and "Dress Rehearsal Rag," I recorded a song by Randy Newman, a newcomer in 1966. Mark Abramson found "I Think It's Going to Rain Today" on a song demo tape. Newman would release his first album, *Randy Newman*, in 1968, and by that time, my recording had become a mini-hit. Soon, Dusty Springfield, Nina Simone, and Peggy Lee recorded versions of it as well. Randy Newman was on his way to becoming a successful singer-songwriter and performer.

Then there was Donovan's "Sunny Goodge Street"; and after that came the even more surprising "Pirate Jenny," from *Threepenny Opera* by Kurt Weill and Bertolt Brecht, and "La Colombe," a translation of a Jacques Brel song that was as bitter a charge against war as any I have ever heard. Finally there was "Marat/Sade."

Marat/Sade, directed by Peter Brook, was a play with songs that ran on Broadway in 1966 and told the story of the French Revolution from a unique perspective. I was intrigued, of course, by the portrait of the insane asylum in which the play is set. There was not a drunken night that went by that I did not think I was headed for a place that might be very like a modern-day version of the asylum of Charenton.

When *In My Life* came out, of course I did a lot of publicity. I got help from Nancy Carlin, the friend whom I'd met through the Baez family. Nancy was coincidentally a pal of Linda Liebman.

Nancy had great ideas about the marketing side of music. For *In My Life*, she designed a bumper sticker that said "Put Judy Collins in Your Life"; and I would see it on cars up and down a seventeen-mile stretch around Big Sur.

Before they both moved to Big Sur, Nancy and Joan Baez were friends from Boston. Nancy had been an aspiring folksinger and sang at little clubs when Joan already reigned as the singer du jour of the college folk crowd.

After *In My Life,* Nancy became involved in other aspects of my career. She went with me on the tour that supported the album and later helped me find songs and work on promotion.

Nancy later worked for Joan Baez as part manager and part organizer of Joan's various projects. She received a producer credit on Joan's album *Diamonds and Rust*. She also started the Big Sur Festival, which ran for a number of years at Esalen on the Big Sur coast, where Joni Mitchell, Joan Baez, Cass Elliot, Stephen Stills, and I appeared for the first and only time together.

She and I often talked about the new direction signaled by *In My Life*, which moved away from the guitars, banjos, and mandolins of my previous albums and incorporated more diverse material. Nancy tried her best to prepare me for what she saw as the possible fallout from my rebellion against the expected. I didn't worry, but I tend to be an optimist about my work.

She was right to worry. The critics got out their long knives.

Richard Goldstein, who had joined the *Village Voice* in 1966 and started writing music reviews, wrote: "Judy Collins should take a deep breath of country air and a long look at her guitar—just her guitar." He went in for the kill: "Judy Collins' transition from Joan Baez's kid sister to Barbra Streisand's chambermaid is regrettable. Judy used to be a formidable folk-warbler, and her successful 'ethnic' purity shows on the new album, *In My Life*."

But he wasn't through yet. "Judy Collins lacks the vocal breadth and emotive depth to sing Brecht well. So do a lot of folk singers. But Judy gives us a version of 'Pirate Jenny' that Lotte Lenya wouldn't tolerate in the shower. Her rendition of incidental music from *Marat/Sade* is like the Emancipation Proclamation carved on a bar of soap. Even if you manage to carry it off what can you do with it but wash your face?"

Fortunately the album did well and contained my very first charting single, "Hard Lovin' Loser." Dick Fariña would have loved that; he was thrilled by the idea that his songs could take over the radio waves and seep into the collective unconscious.

Other reviewers described *In My Life* as one of the most interesting albums of the decade. It went off in its own direction, eventually hitting number forty-six on the *Billboard* pop albums chart. And by the looks of things, it was taking me with it.

Chapter Twenty-Two

My Father

*My father always promised us
That we would live in France.*

—Judy Collins, "My Father"

$\mathcal{M}$Y father told me, in the autumn of 1966, that he was dying. He was depressed. He was drinking hard and couldn't stop. I suggested a shrink, knowing that while therapy had not helped me stop drinking, it had helped me have fewer depressions. I hoped it might help my father.

"It's no damn use when I can't even pay my bills," he said. He had lost his most recent radio program and was trying to sell mutual funds and trying to believe in what he was doing. "Anyway, I don't want to change and look at myself and explore my psyche and my navel and my asshole. That's for you and those half-witted friends of yours." (Which friends he meant I didn't know. Not one of my friends is in any way half-witted, but this is the way Daddy sometimes talked.) "Taking your brains apart and paying a fat fee to bellyache to some Ph.D.? No, I'm a cornball from Idaho, ain't nothin' in that stuff for me!" Daddy would revert to twanging country slang when he wanted to make a point, an educated, erudite man making fun of his past or his intelligence, I could not always tell which.

We were in Boulder, Colorado. My parents had come to a concert of mine earlier that night, and then we went to an old friend's house for some food and talk. There was a lot of drinking—when was there not when we were together? Martinis, bourbon on the rocks, Canadian or German beer for the courageous. My mother usually drank Manhattans, each new glass decorated with a red maraschino cherry perched on the lip like a Christmas gift. Tonight she was drinking Presbyterians, a sort of watered-down highball of ginger ale and bourbon. She was driving, she said, and wanted to be awake. At the concert, my father drank glass after glass of Jack Daniel's, smacking his lips. He shouted merrily at my performance, making a ruckus on my behalf, proud of his daughter. On the one hand, his appreciative shouts and applause always gave me courage; on the other, these public outbursts, especially when he was drinking, usually resulted in Daddy becoming the center of attention, and always scared me to death. I did not want people to look too closely at him when he was "in his cups." He could be unpredictable, too enthusiastic, too loud, too *there*.

Still full of praise for my performance, Daddy greeted new and old friends at the small gathering. Slowly, as the evening progressed, I watched him become silent, surrendering conversation to the others, his lips narrowing, his eyes tightly shut or wide and roaming the room, seeing something inside his head that none of the rest of us saw. He moved about the unfamiliar house, finding the kitchen, the living room, the bathroom, walking, as he always did, as though he could see.

I lost him for a while, then sought him out on the deck, where he had wandered. The cold late summer air was clear and fresh and

I could smell the sage. My father's usually straight back slumped as he sat at a redwood table. He always walked with such a proud stride, compensating for his slight stature.

"Smell that?" he said, knowing me from my walk. "Sage."

"Yes," I said.

I took a seat across from him and reached out for his hand. He raised his head and that bright smile flickered across his face for a moment. He told me again, this time quietly, how good I had been, how proud he was of me. Soon, as I watched him, his face fell once more, again becoming a tight-lipped mask. He seemed to be collapsing into himself as he and I sat, drinks in our hands.

It was quiet except for night birds and the soft wind in the pines. Then he started talking. I was pretty drunk by now as well, as I listened to my father tell me of his deepening depression, telling me that, for him, life was no longer worth living.

There was silence.

I felt my breath freeze in my throat, ice crystals in the air. I tried to speak and my voice cracked. I cleared my throat. "No," I thought, "this can't be happening; this is not in the script. He is supposed to get in and out of these depressions; he is the original cheerleader. He's the one who always brought on the band, the baton twirlers. He's the man."

"Daddy, you're only depressed. It will clear up tomorrow. It couldn't be that bad," I said.

I talked brightly to counter the darkness I felt behind his words. I wouldn't accept, couldn't accept, that he had reached a place that was too dark and too painful for him to overcome.

"You're just drunk," I said. "You know how you sometimes get when you drink." The drunk would pass, I said, and with it the depression. I knew him—he would dry himself out again with Tiger's Milk and Gayelord Hauser, with wise words about fate, the future, and staying the course, as he had done for years, turning his depressions around by a monumental effort of his will—like seeing when he could not.

Chuck could do that. He was the father who brightened our mornings with his call to "rise and shine," the blind man who took on the world with both fists, flinging himself into his career in the radio business as a singer and radio personality in 1937 in Seattle, becoming a star in every town he worked in, making a living to support five kids and his wife with gusto and bluster.

But there was something different about this night, about these words and this man. He had come to the edge. I could feel something in my heart breaking, cracking like the sound of ice breaking up.

There was always the drinking, and we didn't talk about it, except in nervy conversations when more than one of us was drunk. The drinking and the depression, the deep remorse, and even the shouting and staggering around in the kitchen late at night were not new to me or to my family. We knew by then that the dragon my father lived with could breathe fire and death, that it wasn't him talking when he was drinking but the dragon. Though we understood what was the matter with him when he drank so much that he became a stranger, it was still frightening. He was simply a different person, talking wildly, insulting the wrong person, coming on to the wrong woman.

Now he was in one of those confiding moods brought on by booze or sometimes just by his deep need to communicate. I never thought to walk away or not to listen. I was the confidante, the fixer, the oldest. I thought it an honor that Daddy confided in me.

I knew he hadn't been happy in the recent past. People still stopped him on the street, still thought of him as a star. That night, speaking to me in a hushed voice that seemed totally sober in spite of all he was drinking, he kept saying, as he turned the tumbler of whiskey in his hands as though it were a looking glass and he could see the future in it, that his life was hopeless, that he couldn't go on living.

I emphasized all the good things that were in his life. Even though I drank probably as much as my father did and knew that whatever was wrong with Daddy's drinking was what was wrong with mine as well, I was a functioning person with a career and with my demons mostly under wraps. I had certainly learned to manage my drinking from my father, and I believed, although I couldn't see the damage, that I was almost okay with it.

Somehow my parents would have to get back to Denver that night. Mother would drive, and my father, blind as well as drunk, would be her co-pilot and navigator, discussing the route, making sure that she drove at a safe sixty miles an hour. He would not, I knew, fall asleep in the passenger seat. He never passed out.

A few months later, he got sick. His doctors all said there was nothing they could find wrong with him, that he was not that ill.

They were wrong.

Chapter Twenty-Three

Wildflowers

The rain is falling down along with the sky
The colors and remembered suns are falling by

—Judy Collins, "Sky Fell"

cAfter I recorded Leonard's "Suzanne" and "Dress Rehearsal Rag" for *In My Life*, he asked me why I was not writing my own material. I had never really thought of it, and without his question, I might not have ever written anything. So I sat down at my Steinway a few weeks later and put a composition notebook on the music stand, a pen by its side. It was the spring of 1967, a quiet day in New York. I started to do what I always call "noodling," having no idea that many of my songwriter friends employed the same technique. Just sit there long enough, not answering the phone, not going to the refrigerator, not leaving the apartment; keep thinking about your fingers on the keys as you find a line, then a riff on the piano to go with it, then another line, then a rhyme, and your heart begins to beat a certain way, you can recognize that beat. It says, "This is good. Find another rhyme, and then go on with it. Find the melody to the bridge. Find your way from the beginning to the end." It is like being in heaven for a few hours.

Melodies from my years of playing the piano came to me through my hands. They were not the same melodies I had learned when I played the piano, nor were the songs I was writing like the ones I had recorded before. These new songs sprang from some idea of a song that was already in me and now were given permission to be uniquely mine. I was inspired by getting back to the piano, inspired by all the songs I had recorded, but the music was mine, an amalgam of what I had absorbed over time and what came to me from my own muse.

They say that any artist has to first learn from the experts, and I suppose that is what I did. I had recorded songs that I still feel are first-rate. Now I would try, sometimes successfully, other times not, to write songs that I felt could live up to the very high bar I had set for myself. I had to go back to my roots as a pianist to find the melodies and the harmonies for my music. I had to relearn the old exercises, play Hanon and a little Debussy, Chopin and even begin relearning Rachmaninoff. Only then, when my muse was free to wander the keys of my Steinway grand, was I able to carve out the songs that would be mine, different from the others I had recorded, different from anything else I heard in other songwriters.

The very first of these was "Since You Asked," which I wrote in about forty minutes. From that easy entrée, I have learned that some take longer than others.

I have always been grateful to Leonard for asking me that question. I was now a songwriter as well as a singer. I began to play the piano onstage, and to sing my own songs.

There is nothing in the world like that feeling.

IN 1967, it seemed as if every piece of music I heard had Al Kooper attached to it. Al played the organ on several important Dylan recordings, including *Bringing It All Back Home,* and he contributed the memorable organ riff on the chorus of "Like a Rolling Stone." In the mid-sixties Al, who had been in the Blues Project with Andy Kulberg as the bassist, and Steve Katz on guitar, started Blood, Sweat and Tears, a hot jazz-rock band.

I had been friends with Al since I moved to New York, and I always felt close to him. He reminded me of my grandfather Oscar, my mother's father—same lean build and open, loving nature. Al was an iconoclast, my favorite kind of guy. And he looked a little like my platonic flame from high school, John Gilbert.

One night, in the spring of 1967, I was fast asleep when the phone rang at three in the morning. Al said a few words about being sorry to be calling so late and then told me he had met a great songwriter and wanted me to hear her sing an amazing song. He put Joni Mitchell on the phone.

He and Joni had met up at a show he was doing (I think she had a crush on one of the band members). Al said he went home with her when she told him she was a songwriter and had some songs he might like.

"I thought, well, if she can't write songs, she's pretty good-looking! I figured I could only lose a night's sleep out of the deal," he told me later.

My good luck is that when they got to Joni's place, instead of jumping into bed with him, she sang him "Both Sides Now." Al had already been in the music business a long time, and he knew a lot of singers. It was my luck that instead of calling Janis or Buffy or Carolyn or the other Judy (Henske), he called me. He knew I was recording another album, and I was the first person on his mind. I will always be grateful that he chose to dial my number.

After Joni sang me "Both Sides Now," I put the phone down and wept. I had never heard a song that I felt was so beautiful, and it would change both our lives.

The next day, this time with Jac, I heard Joni play the song again. It was still magic, and as her blond hair hung over the guitar as she sang, I wept once more, as I would when I heard many of her songs. She was a muse to me in many ways: her great beauty, the light in her eyes, the sadness I felt in her soul. We all felt that, those of us who fell in love with Joni's music. I needed those songs, as Joan had needed Bob Dylan's songs. Joni's writing was magnificent, and I knew that I could sing them. I looked forward to the process, and tried to forge a relationship with this "Lady of the Canyon."

I thought we were friends. We saw each other in New York, and later I brought her to the Newport Festival for the first singer-songwriter concert that I put together in July of that year, which featured Joni, Leonard, Janis Ian, and Tom Paxton, when I was still on the board of the Newport Folk Festival. We laughed a lot, and I can still hear her tinkling laughter. We sometimes did things together. She came to sing on a session I did in California the following year, when my son, Clark, recorded his song "Flying, I'm Flying." During the thirteen minutes of out-and-out rock-and-roll madness, with Van Dyke Parks playing piano, Stephen Stills on guitar, David Crosby on vocals, and John Haeny recording, Joni harmonized with Clark and me. She was an easy friend, and when I went to her home in Laurel Canyon we sat in her tree house and sang duets.

Joni was born in 1943 in Alberta, Canada. Her father was an officer in the Royal Canadian Air Force. Like me, she had had polio as a child; fortunately, she survived without noticeable damage. As a teenager she started playing the ukulele and the guitar, and moved to Toronto, telling her mother she was going to become a folksinger. A beautiful blonde with a wide smile, she sang in coffeehouses and basket houses in Toronto, and then became pregnant with her ex-boyfriend from the Alberta College of Art and Design. In Toronto she married Chuck Mitchell, her new beau, and began singing with him. Kilauren, Joni's daughter, was born a few months later, and Joni gave her up for adoption several weeks after her birth. (Kilauren Gibb would begin searching for her mother in 1997, and they would be reunited.) In those years, Joni held the secret close and seldom confided about her lost child. It had to be terribly painful. Joni would pay homage to her daughter in the songs "Little Green" and "Chinese Cafe."

By 1967, Joni and Chuck had divorced and she was trying to make it on her own. In New York, Oscar Brand featured Joni on his radio show a number of times. Tom Rush took a shine to Joni and sang one of her songs, "Circle Game," and he talked about Joni to everyone. Even if I hadn't heard Joni sing, I would have heard a good deal about her fairly soon.

When I began to sing "Both Sides Now," I felt I had lived through the song. Joni had written a great song, perhaps one of the greatest ever written. "Both Sides Now," as a composition, has everything: sweep and tenderness, specificity as well as breadth. It speaks to everyone who might hear it, a perfect jewel of a song.

Jac Holzman, Mark Abramson, and everyone at Elektra felt "Both Sides Now" was going to be a hit. It might have been the first time anyone really talked about hits in all my years with Elektra, though I learned that they were always hoping that would happen. I had made and sold many records, and had already been at it long enough to track the evolution of my career, but a big commercial hit—a pop single—had never crept up the charts to the top ten. There was no question that I was going to record the song as soon as possible.

Joni and I had spent time together in New York before she moved to Los Angeles. I remember a night at her apartment when she sang some of her other material for me. The flickering candles and light from cut glass lamps fell across our faces. I felt the pull of her talent. I thought then and think now that she is a genius, a wonderful artist whom I will always admire, creative in every medium in which she works. Joni can be touchy and sometimes distant, but all of us have complicated lives.

At the Newport afternoon concert I arranged for "new singer-songwriters" with Leonard, Joni, Janis Ian, and others. Joni took Newport by storm. Her willowy blond good looks and her songs and stories, in which the ache of loss is so vivid and real, connected instantly with the audience.

Joni and Leonard met for the first time at that concert and began a love affair. Still, everyone was a little off-center. I remember being in bed with a man I did not know who was coming down from an acid trip and wanted me to "comfort him," no sex involved. Leonard sat in the room with us, singing "The Stranger Song" softly to himself, not paying any attention at all to what was happening on the bed. The Chelsea Hotel indeed! I trusted Leonard completely in very intimate situations, and although we never had an intimate exchange of that kind ourselves, he was a constant ally I could take into battle with no fear of betrayal. Joni wrote "That Song About the Midway" about Leonard, or so she says. Sounds right: the festival, the guy, the jewel in the ear.

In the fall of 1967 in New York and L.A., we recorded *Wildflowers*, my seventh album, which included "Both Sides Now." I was a veteran by that time, but this album was a new experience in many ways. Not only did we think we had a real shot at a commercial pop single, but just as important to me, the album included my first original compositions, "Since You Asked," "Albatross," and "Sky Fell."

For the cover of *Wildflowers,* I had some photos taken—in the nude—in the front yard of John Haeny's house, the same little house where I would later meet Stephen Stills. They were my first nude photographs and in those days something unique. We also spent time in a field of wild daisies near John's house and took a few indoor pictures as well. The photograph of me in my green velvet dress in a field of daisies became the cover of *Wildflowers*. The nudes were altogether too daring; they're probably still at Elektra in storage somewhere, giving off heat. We never used them, but I always wonder.

I also wonder whatever happened to the friendship I thought I had with Joni. She disappeared from my life, and in spite of my efforts to reclaim that closeness, there is still a wall I cannot fly or climb over.

But I can say thank you. She gave me a beautiful song, and sometimes that is all one can expect—or, should I say, more than anyone has any right to expect.

The press often referred to my "overnight success" in 1968, when "Both Sides Now" became an international hit. In reality it was years of showing up, one night at a time, one club at a time, maybe singing three shows at some place in Oklahoma, San Francisco, or Texas. That's what it took, but it's also true that everything came together as never before for me with "Both Sides Now"—a perfect song, a perfect arrangement, perfect timing. I had my first legitimate, ubiquitous hit single,

The orchestra that played on "Both Sides Now" gathered at the Columbia Studio in New York, which was known for its great records. Sinatra and many other well-known singers had recorded there. We had a big string section, and Josh had asked to have a harpsichord brought in. I had not known of his idea beforehand, and when he began to play the riff on the harpsichord, I was awed and amazed. It gave a classic-rock feel to the songs, even though the instrument was usually heard in Renaissance and Baroque music. I sang with even more pleasure with the strings behind me and the rest of the orchestra producing an unusual and exciting sound. The musicians said they knew they had a hit when they heard it.

Of course, you knock wood when people talk like that, but they were exactly right. Listening to the song today, I am struck by how much I heard that first time, on the phone, how deeply the song affected me at once, and how remarkable a piece of writing it still is. A classic song has much mystery as well as mastery in its form; it sits still in the mind, throwing light on the past and the future, often bringing tears to our eyes, for it reaches into deep emotional wells that are often forgotten in the rush of the moment. The songs that touch me are on a very high level in terms of form and classic structure, and "Both Sides Now" has all of the requirements to make it irresistible. For me, it was an immediate love affair,

With my first top-ten single on the *Billboard* charts, people were even beginning to answer my phone calls. The important thing about *Wildflowers* is that it was a romantic and daring departure—daring in that the songs were fully orchestrated. It was an artistic decision made in the heart, and the heart won. The album cast the idea of folk music and of Judy Collins in a new light. I had been working toward a fundamental breakthrough for years, and *Wildflowers* announced my arrival on that shore.

In December 1967, as I was reveling in the attention *Wildflowers* was getting—which meant invitations to parties, contracts for many more lucrative concerts, and being besieged by requests from songwriters who wanted me to hear their new songs—I got a phone call from my ex-husband in Vancouver.

"I guess you know that Sue and I have been talking about Clark coming to live with you."

You could have knocked me over with a feather.

"We have talked about sending Clark to military school or sending him to you in New York, and you won."

"Put him on a plane and I'll be there to meet him. I can't wait," I told his father. I immediately prepared for Clark's arrival at the beginning of the year, wanting everything to be perfect. For weeks I felt as though I was walking on air. The long wait was over—I was going to have my boy with me, where he belonged, at last.

Clark was barely off the plane in New York when I took him to the courthouse downtown, where I signed papers from his father that would give me sole custody. I swore to myself that I would never relinquish him again.

In New York Clark grew his hair long, which his father and stepmother would never allow. I enrolled him in a great school, and I had already hired a housekeeper, the grand Dahlia Johnson, from Kingston, Jamaica, who previously had taken care of my son and me during those times when he was visiting me in New York.

And now we began to work out how I could tour and be a mother at the same time. I was thrilled that we were together. The battle was over—but the war had just begun.

Chapter Twenty-Four

Sky Fell

The rain is falling down
Along with the sky
The colors and remembered suns
Are pouring by.

—JUDY COLLINS, "Sky Fell"

ELEKTRA Records was a home for me, both comforting and inspiring. The label exposed me to artists who opened up new worlds, musically and otherwise. One night in his apartment in the West Village, Elektra's founder, Jac Holzman, played Tim Buckley's new album for some friends and me while we were getting stoned on Jac and Nina's hash brownies.

When I met Tim, his sweet air of innocence made me want to shelter him from the world—and from himself. With his tousled, matted hair and tattered denims, Tim was a gem, offering his delicate, scared smile to strangers as we strolled through Washington Square. Born on Valentine's Day, 1947, he was destined to be a star. He was a child—a delightful, teasing playmate, with an angelic voice. But he was also a tortured soul who shot heroin at night while I was safe at home in bed after a night of Jim Beam.

Herb Cohen, who managed Judy Henske and Jo Mapes in L.A., had heard Tim Buckley and told Jac he would be perfect for Elektra. In early spring of 1968, Jac's wife, Nina, put on one of her famous dinner parties for Tim, whose wonderful second album, *Goodbye and Hello,* had been released that year, launching Tim on the road to stardom.

I decided when I first heard Tim perform that I would get myself a Martin twelve-string and see what I could do. I loved his songs, especially "Morning Glory" with its strangeness ("Tell me stories, I call to the hobo") and "Once I Was." Tim's pure, haunting voice, sometimes with the hint of a scream in it, was both electrifying and full of beauty.

We didn't know it was the sound of his heart breaking.

I HAD made enough money in 1967 to give my parents a special gift—a trip to Hawaii, all expenses paid. I hoped it would raise my father's spirits. I was imagining them, Daddy with his bare feet, shouting at the waves, reveling in the sun and the sand, my mother relaxed, at last able to have a respite from all her children and the pressures of her life.

I thought of them in the warmth of the sun when I woke up to a cold day in New York. It was March 17, 1968, St. Patrick's Day—and just one day after U.S. troops carried out the atrocities at My Lai in Vietnam. An hour after I got up, Phil Ochs called me on the phone.

"Get dressed. I'm picking you up in an hour to take you to the first Yippie press conference!" He sounded very excited.

"And top of the morning to you, too!" I answered. Clark and I were drinking green Kool-Aid and putting a shamrock in Clark's coat pocket for the Irish songfest at his school.

Phil was recording for A&M. His album *Pleasures of the Harbor* had come out in 1967 and was doing well. He had been writing and recording since 1962, and had made albums for Elektra before signing with A&M. His songs were inspired, tough, intelligent. But I knew he had been depressed of late, looking gloomy and fancying that everyone in the country was after him for his cutting compositions and his political views. Phil's voice was a bit ragged but upbeat and excited in a way I hadn't heard in a while.

"We're going to the Americana Hotel!" He said he had been on the phone for days, talking up the conference for the Youth International Party, or the Yippies, as they were known. He hung up before I could get any more information from him, but I knew about the Yippies from Nancy Bacal, Leonard Cohen's school chum from Canada. She had been a witness to the earliest beginnings of the Yippie movement over Christmas in 1967, while I was in Colorado with my son and my family. Nancy was house-sitting my apartment in New York and dating Paul Krassner, the writer and publisher of the 1960s antiestablishment magazine *The Realist,* who along with Abbie Hoffman, Anita Hoffman, Jerry Rubin, and Nancy Krushan founded the Yippies.

Nancy told me how she and Paul had headed to the Village to celebrate the year's end and found themselves at the famous Greenwich Village New Year's Eve parade in the company of elaborately and bizarrely costumed celebrants. Abbie Hoffman and Jerry Rubin were stoned on acid, running around dressed in flowered skirts and fancy masks, telling everyone how they were starting a movement that would galvanize the world.

"Yippie! That's what we're going to call ourselves! The Yippies!" they were shouting, out of their minds with joy and high as kites. Nancy, Paul, and the two newly created "Yippies" danced together toward Seventh Avenue amid whirling revelers. The calendar turned from 1967 to 1968 and the war in Vietnam, begun with advisers in 1957, entered its eleventh year.

Phil arrived at my front door that day, all aflutter, to pick me up for the Yippies' press conference. No green, I noticed as he grabbed a homemade muffin off my kitchen table. I asked him who would be there.

"Abbie and Paul, Nancy, Dave [Dellinger], Rennie [Davis] and Jerry [Rubin], John [Froines], Tom [Hayden], and Lee [Weiner], that's who!" he said. "Bill Kunstler will be there, too. Our lawyer."

I wondered aloud why they would need a lawyer. I would learn later that it was essential.

Fiercely political, William Kunstler was already famous for taking on the causes of radical movement groups and individuals. In his career he would defend the Berrigan brothers and the Catonsville Nine, the Black Panther Party, the Weather Underground, the Attica prison rioters, and the American Indian Movement. He was a passionate defender of First Amendment rights and a lovely, sweet man who would represent the Yippies from that very day.

Phil and I took a cab to the Americana Hotel in midtown, where the Yippies had strung a rainbow of balloons and ribbons across one of the big banquet rooms.

"Thank you for coming," Abbie said, giving me a great hug. "You and all of us are about to make history and stop this goddamned war!"

Abbie's wild head of hair was wilder than usual that morning, and he had a wired energy as well. He was wearing a white shirt, à la the Maharishi, Levi's, and a string of beads around his neck.

Abbie was three years older than me. He called himself a political activist and saw his mission as making people realize we had to get out of Vietnam and make love and not war. I had heard him say in radio interviews on WBAI that the Yippies were going to spread banana peels in Chicago. He imagined everyone slipping around and laughing at their antics. He was famous for telling kids to lay off the drugs with needles; "the only dope you need to shoot is Richard Nixon," he would say. Abbie was funny, always, and there was a feeling of an agitated sprite about him. He could be dark in his jokes, but they stung with wry humor. He once noted that you get ten years for possession of dope in the United States but only five for killing a kid, so he suggested that if you were caught dealing drugs, you better shoot a kid quick. Most people did not take Abbie or his form of humorous anarchy very seriously. Some people referred to the group around him as "Groucho Marxists."

Abbie was excited about the Yippie launch and glad to be with his cohorts, most of whom I knew from different rallies and events protesting the war. Of those in the room, I knew Phil Ochs and Dave Dellinger the best.

Dellinger looked like a college professor, his hair cropped short. He was wearing a blue suit and a white shirt, in contrast to Abbie and the rest of the group, who were mostly in jeans. At fifty-three, he had already made difficult decisions in his life and stood up for unpopular causes.

Raised in a prominent Republican family in Wakefield, Massachusetts, Dellinger had turned his back on his family's wealth and political position. During his college days at Yale, during the Depression, he had helped hobos, and had served as an ambulance driver during the Spanish Civil War. During FDR's administration he became friends with Eleanor Roosevelt. He studied for the ministry at Union Theological Seminary in New York, where his resistance to all wars deepened. He refused to show up for his physical when he was drafted in 1941, which landed him in prison as a conscientious objector. Later, Dave became an early and outspoken critic of the war in Indochina.

Dave Dellinger possessed a Gandhi-like serenity. He seemed calm, buttoned down, and unflappable on the outside, but he simmered with political passion. His antiwar philosophy had been an influence on Dr. Martin Luther King Jr. as nonviolent resistance began to take shape in the great leader's thoughts. I had listened to Dellinger's inspiring speeches at antiwar rallies for years, and that day at the Americana we embraced at the table, donuts in our hands and peace on our minds. He represented the cool head of a motley group. The *New York Times* called Dellinger "solid, sober, resolute, selfless, and always brave." A gentle elder statesman in his coat and tie—but always the complete radical—Dave was an inspiration.

That morning at the press conference I sang "Where Have All the Flowers Gone," which everyone knew at least some of the words to. We listened to Abbie and the others talk about their intentions: to change the thinking of those in power, and to do it with music and dancing, with a life-affirming message rather than one of confrontation. As naive as it sounds now, they hoped that the forces of beauty and art would reach people on an emotional level and help stop the war.

Only a few slightly bleary-eyed reporters turned out for this comically named organization. Had anyone known how this tiny group was going to capture the world's attention, the press would have come in droves. Most of the news coverage treated the whole affair as a joke. The *Chicago Tribune* was there, but all they said was: "Yipes! The Yippies!"

These young people—and I was one of them—sincerely believed that they had the power to change the course of history. We stood as firmly for civil rights and free speech as we stood against the war, dedicated to what we saw as the founding principles of America. What could be more patriotic than supporting the Bill of Rights? Underneath all the joyous and seemingly frivolous antics of the Yippies, I identified with the seriousness of their commitment.

I have always felt that how you treat your friends, how you vote, and where you put your money and your energy are the things that count in your personal politics. From the very early days of my career, the music I loved connected directly to political and social currents swirling around me, whether it was voter registration for African Americans in the Freedom Summer of 1964, fighting for civil rights, women's rights, or ending the war in Vietnam. My father would smile in appreciation that his training had been more than effective; these two worlds, music and politics, had forever become one.

Later that month I heard from my mother that Daddy had become ill in Hawaii with undiagnosed pains. He was hospitalized now at St. Luke's, in Denver.

On the phone, Daddy sounded weak but he said he was better. When I talked to his doctors about whether I should cancel my concert plans to go to London that month, they reassured me that my father was not in any real danger. Daddy's fifty-seventh birthday was on April 23, and I would go to Denver after London in mid-May to have a late celebration. I had written a song about him, called "My Father," and I planned to surprise him with it.

Denver John, my youngest brother, was seventeen at the time. He had a week off from high school and I had invited him to come with me on the trip to London, a rare opportunity for sister-brother bonding. All of us have always been close. At home, my siblings were doing well. Holly Ann was a teenager, fourteen; David was twenty-one; and Mike, my oldest brother, was twenty-four. Denver and I were glad to hear Daddy was getting better. We were full of excitement as we boarded the plane for London with my band: Susan Evans on drums, Richard Bell on piano, Gene Taylor on bass, and my road manager, Charlie Rothschild.

But the morning before the scheduled concert in London, Denver John got a phone call. Even now, writing about it, I feel a shiver, and tears begin to well up. Our father had had an aneurysm all along, but no doctor was able to find it; when it burst, he died. Daddy was my mentor, the energy and inspiration for my life, for all our lives. We could not imagine the world without that ball of fire and enthusiasm, that talent, that emotional cheerleader. Now he was gone, never again to touch our faces so that he could see our smiles.

My father's best friend (and my godfather) was Holden Bowler. Daddy and he had made a bet: the one who was left when the other died had to stop drinking. Holden was at Daddy's bedside in the moments before he passed. He reported that Chuck said, "You won, old buddy." A true friend to the end, Holden Bowler kept their wager and never touched another drop.

I canceled my show at the Queen Elizabeth Hall and, in a daze, my brother and I flew home to the States for the funeral. We stopped in New York to pick up Michael and Linda Liebman, both of whom had been close to my family. I called my mom from my apartment as I was packing for the trip, putting my black hat and my best black coat and dress into a suitcase. We wept together over the phone, and then my mother said, "Please, no black. Don't wear black. Now, your father will finally see all the colors in the rainbow."

The roses we laid on my father's coffin were a deep ruby red. I kept a dried bouquet of those blood-red roses for years, faded and fragile, a reminder to me of Daddy's bright, eager smile, his wondrously quick mind, and the rare beauty of the man whose like I would not see again.

> In the darkness he would read to us,
> His fingers thwarting blindness
> With the sound of flesh on paper
> Brushing underneath the fantasy
> Like the sound of wind moving through the house:
> He soothed our fear of the night
> With sighing hands.
> —Judy Collins, "Trust Your Heart"

Chapter Twenty-Five

Smoke and Mirrors

I never knew what you all wanted
So I gave you everything

—BRUCE COBURN, "Pacing the Cage"

I ARRIVED in Los Angeles on June 7, 1968, grieving over my dad's death but eager to start my new album. The prospect of singing new songs, some of them my own compositions, renewed my sense of purpose and hope.

My producer, David Anderle, had put together a band of exceptional musicians for my new album, *Who Knows Where the Time Goes*: Jim Gordon on drums; James Burton, one of Nashville's greatest, on pedal steel; Chris Ethridge of the Flying Burrito Brothers on bass; Buddy Emmons, also a stellar guitar player from Nashville; and Stephen Stills on lead guitar.

John Haeny, who was setting up the engineering for my new album and had recorded *Wildflowers* in the same Elektra studios, had once told me that the canyon neighborhoods of Los Angeles were the place to live—a nonstop scene of drugs and music, where huge talents such as Carole King and Brian Wilson might mosey in for a drink. You might see Van Dyke Parks riding around on his bicycle or Frank Zappa catching up on his grocery shopping at the Laurel Canyon Market in the neighborhood where Clara Bow and even Harry Houdini had roamed the winding roads and breathed in the scent of pine and eucalyptus. Tucked in among the little houses on the hillsides were other stars yet to shine: John Sebastian, the Incredible String Band, and Jackson Browne, among others.

It was there that I met Stephen for the first time at the party John and David threw for me at John's house.

All during the evening, Stephen and I sang songs, trading verses, swapping harmonies. I remember leaning against the window and sneaking a closer look at this handsome man with his eyes of a blue different from mine. They were remarkable, and seemed to spin a myriad of colors within their orbs, more blues than one could have dreamed. Stephen's body was taut as a guitar string, his blond hair falling across his face. He looked at me and whispered that he loved the way I closed my eyes when I sang and that he loved my voice.

We drank and sang together, and I sensed Stephen was an old soul with a vivid imagination. He was just twenty-three, six years younger than I, but I didn't think the age difference would be a problem. I worked to keep in shape, and always worried about my weight; even then I was dieting like mad, hoping to look like Twiggy. I had started exercising before it was fashionable, and I often weighed myself before and after I put on my earrings!

We traded stories, told each other about our lives. He was born in Dallas, Texas, and his family had moved a lot when he was growing up. He had gone to school in the Panama Canal Zone, in Costa Rica, and in Florida, where as a boy he learned to ride horses and fell in love with folk music and the blues. He had attended the University of Florida but dropped out to try his hand at making music for a living. He played guitar, sang, and wrote songs. After a few turns in Greenwich Village at the Cafe au Go Go and the Fat

Black Pussycat, he moved to California, where he formed Buffalo Springfield with Neil Young and Richard Furay. Stephen said that he was still unhappy about the breakup of Buffalo Springfield but it was meant to be.

"I have some great news," he said suddenly that night, looking up from the Martin guitar he had been playing and locking eyes with me. "I'm going to form a new group with Crosby."

David Crosby, an L.A. singer and guitar player, was a longtime friend of Stephen's. They had sung together in Les Baxter's Balladeers in the early sixties before David joined the Byrds, with Jim McGuinn, Chris Hillman, and Gene Clark and had recorded many hits, among them "Mr. Tambourine Man" and "Turn! Turn! Turn!"

"So you and David are free and ready to rock," David Anderle said, looking pleased.

"Yes, and Crosby, at this moment, is producing the second Joni Mitchell album," Stephen said, smiling at me. David had heard Joni first in Coconut Grove, Florida, and produced her first album, *Song to a Seagull,* for Reprise Records after I recorded "Both Sides Now." "David was able to get a second record for Joni. They're over at Wally Heider's recording studio as we speak, probably recording 'Both Sides Now.' Your hit."

"But she wrote it," I said in defense of Joni.

"But you did have the hit—admit it!" Anderle had a right to be proud of "Both Sides Now." He had mixed and remixed the song for months after the album came out and finally got it right for radio, making him at least a partner in the song's success. He turned back to Stephen.

"Is it going to be just you and David?"

"We don't know—but for right now it's just us." I could see that Stephen was both agitated and excited about his plans. I didn't know then that he was always like that, so gifted but so high-strung, often a stranger to the serenity everyone seemed to be searching for in those days.

I overheard John telling Stephen that he had seen me naked on his front lawn one morning when I had had some nude photos taken. I was probably too high to be embarrassed, or maybe I was excited that John had planted this image in Stephen's mind.

We were all a little stoned, drinking wine mostly, though somebody was smoking a joint, I remember. I probably took part in whatever people were passing around, although marijuana always made me paranoid. John knew I liked to drink, so there were plenty of my favorites—Kahlúa and a bottle or two of something sparkling, probably champagne and rosé wine. I didn't bother with Southern Comfort but would have it if there was nothing else. There were bottles of beer, which I never touched. Beer made you fat, I knew from experience. There was a bottle of Jack Daniel's that night at John's, and there were drugs. I didn't understand how drugs worked, actually, and the last time I had taken a pill out of a stranger's hand in L.A. at a rock-and-roll party, the pill turned out to be Thorazine. I spent twenty-four hours rolled into a ball in the corner of my host's living room. So I didn't usually do drugs.

In those years, drinking the way I drank had fallen out of fashion. I pretended to like fine, sparkling pink wines and light drugs, but in reality I would have preferred a good shot or two of bourbon. I certainly had enough liquor that night, so I was feeling no pain.

A FEW days before Stephen and I met, the sunny optimism of the Los Angeles hills had been shattered by another assassination, that of Bobby Kennedy, who not two months before had spoken of healing after the murder of Martin Luther King Jr.

My friend Cookie was spending a few days with me in my

rented house on Mulholland Drive. On June 5, he had been at the Improv, a club in L.A. where the Committee, a group from San Francisco, was performing. In those days the Committee included Carl Gottlieb (who would write the screenplay for *Jaws*), Mimi Fariña, and Rob Reiner. Their presentation on the night of RFK's shooting included as part of the show a number of television sets that were airing local news. The actors had been using the TV as inspiration for their scenes when they realized that the news was broadcasting reports of Kennedy's shooting. Everyone panicked, and Cookie raced to my house on Mulholland Drive.

I was getting Clark settled at our rental house when Cookie rushed in, stabbed the on button of the television set, and spun out a story about the shooting. Scenes of chaos at the Ambassador Hotel played out on the screen. Huddled in front of the screen, watching the chaos, we were mesmerized by this terrible news.

Cookie was unaware that his father, Alistair Cooke, had also been at the Ambassador Hotel to do an impromptu interview with Kennedy for the *Guardian*. Alistair had been let into the now-famous kitchen area by security and was waiting for Pierre Salinger to arrange an interview with the senator.

As Alistair Cooke wrote in his "Letter from America" column:

> There was suddenly a banging repetition . . . like some-body dropping a rack of trays. Half a dozen of us were startled enough to charge through the door, and it had just happened. . . . There was a head on the floor, stream-ing blood. . . . And down on the greasy floor was a hud-dle of clothes, and staring out of it the face of Bobby Kennedy, like the stone face of a child, lying on a cathe-dral tomb.

Cookie stayed the night as we watched the television on and off, waking and sleeping again, and then weeping when the news was confirmed by the papers the next day: Robert F. Kennedy was dead. Sorrow fell over Los Angeles and the rest of the country, gloom hanging like smoke, seeming to hide the sun.

Yet as I prepared to record with my band of minstrels a few days after Kennedy's death, there seemed to be a rustle of conviction that we must do something to heal ourselves and those around us. It was the music that was always our haven and our gift.

*T*HE new band began recording in the charming, wood-paneled Elektra studio. The whole place had the feeling of a comfortable, cozy home—a hippie home, with the same fairy-tale ambiance that pervaded everything about Elektra. The compound was a maze of whitewashed walls and spaces for offices, with a new, state-of-the-art recording studio. There, among the instruments and the brilliantly tie-dyed panels to absorb the sound, you could become lost, have a secret joint, kiss the drummer between takes, or have a nap (perhaps not a solitary one) while you were waiting for the band to return from a break. The offices and the studio were separated by a garden, which was nourished by a small spring spanned by a miniature bridge hanging with purple, orange, and white bougainvillea. Stephen kissed me for the first time in that garden as one of my first songs, "My Father" (with Van Dyke Parks playing piano), wafted out of the studio doors and swirled among the blossoms.

Inside the doorway to the Elektra offices, there stood a painted wooden horse—a pure white pony with roses and filigree around his mane—salvaged from some antique merry-go-round.

As our affair took flight in those heady days, Stephen said this was my merry-go-round, my pony, and we would ride our wild white horse together.

Chapter Twenty-Six

The Swinging, Singing,
Murderous Sixties

Polly, pretty Polly, come go along with me
Polly, pretty Polly, come go along with me
Before we get married some pleasure to see.

—Traditional, "Pretty Polly"

Wᴇ continued to record tracks for *Who Knows Where the Time Goes* in June 1968, and the music flowed quickly and easily. I was in love with the sound of Stephen's guitar and his voice—in love, as they say, with love. After the first day of making music with him it seemed I could not remember a time when I had not known Stephen. He sang and played and drove me around the canyons and beaches of Los Angeles in his Bentley, and I fell deeper into the affair that he would chronicle in "Suite: Judy Blue Eyes."

Something inside
Is telling me that I've got your secret
Are you still listening?

Fear is the lock and laughter the key to your heart
And I love you

The songs for my eighth album for Elektra were exciting, and the band was fabulous. "Story of Isaac" and "Bird on a Wire," Leonard Cohen's contributions, were beautifully played by Van Dyke Parks, with Stephen's guitar wrapping around the piano part; "My Father," the song I had written for my dad three weeks before his death, was poignant, and I couldn't get through it at first without sobbing. How could I have found "Who Knows Where the Time Goes?" in time for this album, when it was so perfectly honed following the death of my father? There had to be an overseeing angel who takes care of these things. I just had to let go and let the music and the love and the wine flow, and everything took care of itself. I was ready to catch the gems when they fell into my lap, and they kept on coming. By now I was officially eclectic and would try my hand at anything that touched my heart.

And while we made music, we were safe in this magical place. The Elektra compound seemed to have sprung full-blown from what had been a vacant lot only a couple of years before. Now it shone brilliantly between the vintage clothing shops in Beverly Hills along La Cienega Boulevard. Just up the hill was Sunset Boulevard, home to Barney's Beanery, a bar and pizza joint where the pictures and memorabilia covering the walls seemed to hold the place together. There was a sign that said "Faggots Stay Out." People were always trying to pull it off the walls, and the offending sign was finally torn down in 1984. A lot of artists and musicians hung out at Barney's—from Clara Bow, Judy Garland, and Errol Flynn in their day to Jim Morrison, Janis Joplin, and Charles Bukowski in ours.

One week I ran into Tiny Tim in the lobby of the Landmark Hotel. Tiny was famous for his version of "Tiptoe Through the

Tulips," which had become hugely successful in spite of the fact that it was an odd version of a hackneyed standard sung by a guy with a high, falsetto voice strumming a ukulele. He had become a regular on television variety shows with his long curling hair, his tall, stooped figure, and thin, haunted face. He had recently been married in a bizarre ceremony on *The Tonight Show* to Miss Vicki. I suggested that since we were both staying there, we should meet at the Landmark pool some afternoon and "hang out." He looked down at me and declared in his high, haughty tone, "Hang? I never hang!"

Perhaps I could have put it differently, but it was certainly fun to hang out at clubs, like the Ash Grove, where Mississippi John Hurt might be on the bill with John Jacob Niles, the clear-voiced troubadour, or Kris Kristofferson might be performing with Sonny Terry and Brownie McGhee. The Troubadour was another legendary club where many artists and entertainers of the era would launch their careers. Over the years Lenny Bruce, the Byrds, Bill Cosby, the Committee, Bo Diddley, Arlo Guthrie, Richie Havens, Gordon Lightfoot, Steve Martin, Roger Miller, Joni Mitchell, Laura Nyro, Mort Sahl, Kris Kristofferson, and Nina Simone appeared there. You could always find a friend in the audience; many of us showed up regularly to watch, to listen, and to learn from one another. After the shows, we would often wind up eating dinner and drinking at the Italian restaurant next door, where the veal rollatini was mouthwatering and the martinis were the size of birdbaths.

At Lawry's steakhouse, you might find Big Brother and the Holding Company having a midnight meal after a concert at the Greek, the six-thousand-seat amphitheater in Griffith Park. A few rock-and-rollers might wind up at Hamburger Hamlet, Sambo's, or maybe the Captain's Table on La Cienega.

Janis Joplin was in her heyday and by then had added heroin to her diet of Southern Comfort. She made a profound impression on the world, and on me. At the Monterey Pop Festival, where we had first met, I stood backstage as the lights swirled around Janis. Her voice was big and raw, hanging over the festival like the moon. By the end of the night, everyone was courting Janis. Her first big album on Columbia was released late that year, and everything seemed to be finally coming together for her. D. A. Pennebaker made a documentary of the Monterey Pop Festival, and Albert Grossman (now managing practically everyone in the business, I thought, except me) had become Janis' manager. She was on cloud nine, in more ways than one.

Heroin was cutting a swath through the music community by then, and Jimi Hendrix was using smack openly, as were Tim Buckley and James Taylor. Janis was certainly not going to be left out of the fun, and by the time of our second meeting at the Troubadour, she was hooked. Al Grossman hated drugs. He told me that when he found out about Janis' heroin use, he took out a $100,000 insurance policy on her life—a fortune in those days. Leonard Cohen, who had an affair with her, captured a sense of her yearning and desperation in "Chelsea Hotel #2."

> I remember you well in the Chelsea Hotel,
> You were talking so brave and so sweet,
> Giving me head on the unmade bed,
> While the limousines wait in the street.

Clark, then nine, spent a few weeks with me that summer in L.A. He played a little guitar and loved being in the studio, harmonizing with me in his sweet voice, hovering around John Haeny during the mixes, and learning his way around. Clark got along well with Stephen, who taught him a few licks on the drums. The two of them even organized the recording of Clark's song "I'm Flying."

"I'm Flying" consisted of Clark's repeating of the phrase over and over, followed by a second line, "Don't you know, don't you know." John Haeny, our engineer, let the tape run for thirteen minutes, with Clark singing, Van Dyke playing piano, Joni Mitchell and me singing harmony, David Crosby somewhere in the background, Jim Gordon on one drum set, Clark on the other, and Stephen on guitar.

Ever the obsessive, John Haeny would pull out a copy he had kept for forty-three years and hand it over to me on a trip I made to Hobart, Australia, where he was living, in 2011.

The image of Clark's little face turned up to Stephen's as they made music will always be with me.

AFTER our recording sessions, Stephen and I made love at his apartment not far from the Malibu beach. While the candles burned, we explored each other's hands and then each other's throats and then each other's hearts. We told each other our dreams and let our passions consume us. I felt safe in Stephen's arms, saved. The anxiety that I usually treated with alcohol was tossed overboard like so much ballast. It was a passionate and lovely love affair.

When Stephen and I had a day off in those early weeks of our romance, we might make love somewhere, my place or his, and then go house hunting—in Malibu, in Laurel Canyon—thinking that one day, perhaps, we would move in together. We would find a beach and gaze at the great Pacific Ocean, basking, dreaming, and planning. On the way back to L.A., Stephen would drive, holding my hand, going too fast, as I sat with my heart in my mouth. But I don't think I ever told him to slow down! We talked about everything: our futures, our love of music, how we would change the world, stop the war, make a difference.

One day we were shown some properties by a beautiful, articulate, deeply tanned real estate agent. While she failed to find a house that we really liked, she decided on a different tack and taught us a mantra that she said would heal our lives and bring us wealth and abundance, joy and happiness. It was Chinese, she said, Buddhist.

"Repeat after me," she said. *"Nam myoho renge kyo."*

We repeated, over and over, *"Nam myoho renge kyo."*

I repeated the chant while the ocean rolled by and killer whales breached the surface. I said it over and over when things were really good with Stephen and me: *"Nam myoho renge kyo."*

I learned that *"Nam myoho renge kyo"* is a Buddhist prayer, or sutra, said to contain the ultimate wisdom. It was created in the thirteenth century by a monk who saw in the prayer a path to spiritual peace.

Stephen and I never settled on a house on the beach that we wanted to buy, but we hoped that if we said the mantra enough times, it might bring us that peace that was promised and help our romance last. We were both in need of peace—me to survive my drinking, and both of us to endure the pace of our fast-moving careers, which would exact a toll on our lives. I found that prayers of some kind for inner and outer peace would have to be renewed every day, every year.

"Nam myoho renge kyo," I chanted, while the whales leapt and the sun shone and then it rained. I knew there was something to that chant.

I still do.

Chapter Twenty-Seven

Hello, Hooray!

Hello, hooray, let the songs begin, I'm ready.

—Rolf Kempf, "Hello, Hooray"

THE title song for *Who Knows Where the Time Goes* was written by the great Sandy Denny, the lead singer for Fairport Convention, an English group that was coming on strong. I first heard Sandy sing "Who Knows Where the Time Goes?" on a little tape player in David Anderle's office at Elektra. She had a brilliantly clear soprano, and when she auditioned for the Fairport Convention, the leader of the group said, "It was a one-horse race really . . . she stood out like a clean glass in a sink full of dirty dishes." I often weep when I hear the song, for this great singer died so young, when she was only thirty-one, after a fall down the stairs at a party in London on April 21, 1978.

Across the morning sky, all the birds are leaving
Ah, how can they know it's time for them to go?

Stephen's sweet guitar work behind the title track pulls back the curtain on its tragic beauty, reminding me of what we've lost.

After Leonard Cohen challenged me to start writing my own material I visited Bruce Langhorne, the great guitarist with whom I had traveled the country and whose opinion I valued. I showed him my book of dreams and dark poems. He gave me a plan: go home and write five songs about a relationship—the beginning, the middle, two more, and then the end. I did just that, beginning with "Since You Asked." The fourth song that I wrote was "My Father," which I added to *Who Knows Where the Time Goes*. I love the descending line that Stephen played behind the opening chords, although to this day I still chuckle and shake my head over it, because when he first played it I said, "That is not right!" Stephen just smiled and said, "You'll see, after a while, that it's perfect!" The great Van Dyke Parks played piano on that recording, and he played like an angel. Two more cuts, "The Story of Isaac" and "Bird on a Wire," were written by Leonard Cohen. I can seldom resist Leonard's songs. Many of his most successful works—"Joan of Arc," "Priests," "Bernadette"—begin with familiar stories, which he elevates to the realm of poetry and theater. In "The Story of Isaac," he uses vivid imagery and a soaring melody to add weight and depth to a scene from the Bible.

> *The door it opened slowly*
> *And my father he came in,*
> *I was nine years old.*

Leonard never failed to satisfy my hunger for great musical narratives. The same was true of Bob Dylan, whose "Poor Immigrant" I also included in this album. Two Nashville greats, Buddy Emmons on pedal steel and James Burton on guitar, joined Stephen in what turned into a magical string trio.

The record also included "First Boy I Loved," by the Incredible String Band, and "Hello, Hooray," by Rolf Kempf. Rolf had sent a tape of this strange, mysterious song to David Anderle at

Elektra, and I fell in love with it the moment I heard it. I included one traditional song, "Pretty Polly," about the cold-blooded murder of a young woman, a classic song of the silver dagger variety, powerful and frightening. I have always been attracted to such songs because they speak to the appalling violence that has been perpetrated against women for so long.

Our record was coming together nicely, but it wasn't quite done. I had to return east in late June to take Clark to camp and to do some concerts. I also had one task that I was dreading: I had to break the news to Michael Thomas that I was in love with someone else. It was an emotional scene and though Michael was hurt and angry, he was as good as could be expected. We spent a night of relatively low-drama tears and tenderness. He had been good for me; he was clever and funny and had a wonderful sense of humor and a way with words. Before I met Stephen, he and I had been very happy together, physically and emotionally.

But falling in love with Stephen was like riding the Cyclone roller coaster for the first time: the wind blew past your face and your hair was in your eyes and you could hardly breathe for the speed and the terror and the thrill. How could I explain Stephen? What was I thinking? I didn't really know how to communicate what had happened to me, but I managed to tell Michael that he had to move out of my apartment and find a place of his own in New York.

"I always knew I hated L.A.," Michael said on that painful night. "Now I know why."

I RETURNED to L.A. as quickly as I could.

One evening, as Stephen and I were driving back from Malibu and the setting light streamed over our sunburned bodies through the windows of the Bentley, we started talking about the rest of the sessions and the progress we had made on *Who Knows Where the Time Goes*.

"I think we need one more song," Stephen said. "What about 'Someday Soon'?"

The song was perfect for me, a Colorado girl at heart, and as soon as he mentioned the title, Ian and Sylvia's gorgeous creation came spilling out of me. I remembered all the lyrics, and we hit the freeway singing together in harmony. We kept on singing as we got to Stephen's place, where we stripped and showered and rinsed off the sand, still singing!

The next day we recorded "Someday Soon." Stephen's playing on this song made my heart leap; the sound seemed to move through his fingers along the neck of the instrument and into the center of my being. He added touches to the guitar part that made it step into its own boots and Stetson and tell the romantic tale of a cowboy stealing the heart of a girl.

Ian and Sylvia Tyson, who wrote "Someday Soon," were Canadians. In the early sixties I got to know them in Toronto and in New York, where they often sang. Sometimes I would spell them at clubs and festivals around the country, doing a set after theirs or opening for them on some stage.

I have always had a soft spot for Canadian writers. There is something expansive and yet intimate about their songs, broad as the northwestern plains and as comfortable as having a cup of coffee out on a pinewood porch with a friend. From Ed McCurdy to Gordon Lightfoot and Leonard Cohen, from Joni Mitchell to Ian and Sylvia Tyson, hearing their songs is hearing the truth. And, as the man says, "when you've heard the truth, the rest is just cheap whiskey."

To this day, when I sing "Someday Soon," it takes me back to Colorado, and I see the lean, clear-eyed cowboys in their Stetson hats at the ranches I worked at in the mountains. I hear the music of

Hank Williams playing at the beer joints on Berthoud Pass where we danced, spinning the night away. The West and dreams of life on a ranch—riding a wild pony, galloping over the landscape—were still in my bones, and in my romantic imagination.

Now Stephen was my one and only cowboy. Loving him, singing with him, knowing that his sweet, solid guitar was there, supporting my voice, I felt like all my wishes were coming true.

Chapter Twenty-Eight

Helplessly Hoping

I am yours, you are mine,
You are what you are
You make it hard

—STEPHEN STILLS, "Suite: Judy Blue Eyes"

*I*N July 1968, while I was back in New York, Cass Elliot had a party in L.A., where David Crosby renewed an earlier friendship with Graham Nash, a singer with the English rock trio the Hollies. At some point in the evening Stephen showed up. In the creative brew that seemed always to be simmering in the canyons of Los Angeles, David, Stephen, and Graham sang together for the first time at that party, and the magic, Cass told me later, was tangible.

David and Stephen began lobbying hard for Graham to leave the Hollies, as well as his recording contract with Epic. By the end of the summer, Graham was in. He relocated to L.A., and the trio Crosby, Stills and Nash would begin its spectacular rise. Graham Nash brought a great deal more than the brilliant voice that filled in the high end of the trio's harmonies. His calmness and his quiet wisdom proved invaluable over the years to come.

Meantime, I myself did not want to pack up and move to L.A., and therein, I think, lay the seeds of trouble in my affair with Stephen. On the surface, things appeared to be barreling ahead full steam, but, as in a beautiful old house bought on an impulse, the cracks began to show. New York had been my home for six years when Stephen and I met. If my heart sometimes still longed for Colorado and the grandeur of the Rockies, I had found my true place among the skyscrapers, hustle and bustle, dirt, noise, and frenzy of the Big Apple.

By now I was playing concerts all over the world, and when I wasn't on the road singing, I was either fine-tuning a record in the studio, as I was doing now in Los Angeles, or planning the next album. I would return to New York at the end of every tour, every weekend of shows, to my son, to my cats, my manager, my therapist, my singing teacher, my friends, and now, not to Michael.

And there were the Sullivanians to contend with, always opposed to steady relationships, always encouraging free love and open marriage. I was seeing Julie Schneider now, after seven years with Ralph. It would not be until I was well out of the camp of my therapists that I had some idea of what had happened to me.

One day I mentioned to Stephen that I was going home to New York and would be talking to my therapist about us, about me, about everything.

"I hate shrinks like I hate bad gas in my car," Stephen said in an angry voice, "and I hate New York!" He stalked into the bathroom and turned on the light. In the coming weeks we continued the argument—about New York, about my therapist, and about my moving to L.A. Of course I needed it all, and didn't want to believe that my life in New York and all the rest could be incompatible with my romance with Stephen.

I always felt that any difficulties Stephen and I had were my fault, but looking back, I am quite sure now that it takes two not to tango. And I was learning that the magic and passion of our romance was never going to be enough to make me want to live in L.A. Even when Elektra had moved its studios from New York to L.A., joining Columbia and Capitol and many other artists, the lure of the West Coast wasn't enough to make me want to leave the city.

I thought if I had to live in L.A., I would crawl into a small hole in some wall and expire—from fear, boredom, sunlight, and bad memories. Los Angeles still held the ghosts of childhood pain for me, of my parents' unhappiness, of my mother running out of our white stucco house in west L.A. at three in the morning in her nightgown, with my drunken, blind father running after her, seeing with his uncanny radar, and dragging her back into the house, where I screamed and hurled myself into my mother's arms, crying, "Don't leave, don't leave!" She never did, but the memory of those bitter nights haunted me.

In New York I tried to contemplate, tried to meditate, tried not to drink so much. I tried to look for God, went to see gurus, met the Maharishi, and heard Krishnamurti speak at the New School in Greenwich Village. I went to my sessions with Ralph and then Julie, attended yoga classes and threw the I Ching (the process of casting coins or reading yarrow stalks, which tells you what ancient reading you have been given), and continued, between antiwar demonstrations and meetings of like-minded activists, to search for serenity and peace.

Following the party line of his group, Ralph encouraged me to see other people, not to have monogamous relationships, and to work on my freedom, my career, my wants and needs.

Stephen had a few things to say about all of this in "Suite: Judy Blue Eyes."

> *Friday evening, Sunday in the afternoon*
> *What have you got to lose?*
> *Tuesday morning, please be gone, I'm tired of you*
> *What have you got to lose?*

Will you come see me
Thursdays and Saturdays?
What have you got to lose?

Stephen was very committed to his own path and profession, just as I was to mine. He had already had a successful career with Buffalo Springfield, and was an amazing musician. I had never heard playing like his. Stephen's guitar was a voice with a personality, changing depending on the song but always finding the right path. Sometimes his sound reminded me of the old blues players, such as Son House in his white shirt and tie. Sometimes Stephen's guitar would take off its tie and two-step in a country manner, as if it were wearing spurs and calling the dance. Then it could be very liquid. It always rippled along, filling the empty places in a song, and in my heart. I think I was always as much in love with Stephen's great talent as a musician as I was with him.

We were both stubborn, and when we fought, we fought hard—about where we were going, what each of us wanted from our relationship. These were arguments that seemed to have no satisfactory conclusion. Afterward, we would kiss and make up and go on with our romance, trying to avoid the subjects that caused pain and to appreciate the wonderful things that were happening in our lives, in our careers, and in our love affair.

ONE day my manager, Harold, called to say that *Life* wanted to do a cover story on me. One of *Life*'s staffers, Irene Neves, thought that my music might stand in meaningful contrast to the violent conflicts—social, cultural, political, and military—that seemed to enmesh America in the turbulent spring of 1969. Irene wanted my face on the cover. It would not be out until May 1969.

"We can call you 'the gentle voice amid the strife,'" she told me. I said I hoped to God it would do some good, but I doubted it would.

Rowland Scherman, the photographer, wanted to have pictures of me with Joni Mitchell, so we made trips to visit Joni at her home in Laurel Canyon. She and I posed in the tree house in her yard, and Joni and I played our guitars in her cabinlike living room, which was filled with sparkling chandeliers and stained glass and kittens (including the calico I had sent her the year before). Cookie was there with Joni and me. Irene and Rowland followed me—and sometimes Stephen—around the country as I performed concerts on my regular autumn schedule. Stephen and I wound up at Carnegie Hall in New York City later that year. There were photos of us together, looking as happy as two lovers could be. But we were grappling with a lot of tension, issues of control, and our age difference.

He wrote me from ten thousand feet above sea level on his way to Mexico to see friends and hang out in the sun for a week. His script wandered across the thin blue writing paper stamped "Eastern Airlines": "I am going to get good and drunk now. Am I only too young to fathom your wretched old self?" I knew I loved him, but I didn't know the answer to that simple question.

Before telling me he loved me, he wrote: "There's only one person on God's green earth that's stronger, tougher, and wiser than you! And that's me."

I knew he was right, and still, I wanted to run.

In November 1968, as the final mixes on *Who Knows Where the Time Goes* were being readied, I got a call from Ulu Grosbard, the director. He wanted to use my song "Albatross," from *Wildflowers,* for *The Subject Was Roses,* which he was filming with Patricia Neal and Martin Sheen. I sent Ulu rough mixes of the new album and he thought "Who Knows Where the Time Goes" would also be right for the movie. He asked if we could produce a more up-tempo version, which brought Stephen and me back to the studio.

The night Stephen and I finished recording, I had a plane to catch to New York. Stephen said he was going to stick around the studio for a little while. I later learned that he gave John Haeny a hundred dollars and told him to "roll tape." Stephen said John could leave and he would turn off the machines when he was finished.

What Stephen recorded that night, alone with his guitar in the darkness, would not be revealed for forty years.

THE passion and intensity of my relationship with Stephen, and its troubles, reached its peak during the fall and winter of 1968, when political and cultural fires raged across America.

Who Knows Where the Time Goes was released in November 1968, and "Someday Soon" immediately hit the charts. I went on the road with my touring band, and for a while even managed to ease up a little on my drinking. That was partly the result of some diet pills given to me by the newest in a long line of doctors.

It would be many years before I could admit that my use of alcohol might have played a role in the breakup of my romance with Stephen. As the friction increased between us, I convinced myself that our quarrels were the necessary fuel of a great affair of the heart. But probably because of alcohol I couldn't tell what was normal from what wasn't, and by now alcohol had resumed its grip on me.

I could not seem to surrender and stay in one place long enough to find out what was going on. I was losing control of our romance, and my life.

The one thing that remained stable and steady in those years, like a long marriage, was my visits to my psychologists. I paid for their cars, their houses, helped send their children to private schools.

On the cover of *Who Knows Where the Time Goes* is a photo by Len Steckler of me peering out from a field of the deepest blue, with my eyes wide open.

I was seeing things clearly out of those eyes, or so I thought.

Chapter Twenty-Nine

Amid the Storm

Oh the prickilie bush
It pricks my heart full sore
If I ever get out of the prickilie bush
I'll never go in it any more.

—Traditional, "The Prickilie Bush"

THE Democratic National Convention, held in Chicago on August 26–29, 1968, would be one of the last massive expressions of the peace movement in the sixties. Before the convention, I spoke to William Kunstler, the lawyer for my friends David Dellinger and Abbie Hoffman, and asked him what he expected to happen there. Harold, still my devoted manager, was busy arranging my tour schedule so that I could get to Chicago that week but was concerned for my safety. He and I wanted Kunstler's sense of what to anticipate.

"I expect the worst," he said, "and pray for the best. The Yippies want to have a presence there, to rally and demonstrate, of course, but the country is so divided on this war." We met at

Harold's office, where I was sitting in his big captain's chair. Kunstler leaned over me with his bristly gray hair flying about his face.

"And we can't seem to get our permits. Mayor Daley is acting as though they are expecting a rebel army in Chicago, instead of these loving kids—these Yippies." I thought about that table of bright-eyed peaceniks gathered for the press conference in the spring. "I admit, I'm worried about the boys," Kunstler finished. William was not only a lawyer but also an activist. He knew that the refusal of Illinois to grant permits for a peaceful gathering was an attack on freedom of speech and expression. If the permits didn't come through, Harold warned me, I would technically be breaking the law as an entertainer performing in a public place without a permit.

A few days before the convention began, I spoke with Abbie Hoffman about all of this.

"If there are no permits," Abbie said, "they're going to bash our heads in if we demonstrate." Allen Ginsberg and a lot of other people, including Harold, had become very uncomfortable about the Yippie plan to go to Chicago anyway. It was clear that the city was not going to welcome the Yippies or any other peaceful demonstrators.

"Daley is spoiling for a fight," Kunstler added, referring to Chicago's mayor, "and the rumor is that the National Guard is going to be there with tanks and guns."

Abbie advised me not to come, and I made the decision: I was not going to go to Chicago if things did not change. I would sit this one out.

Walter Cronkite described Chicago at the start of the Democratic convention as a "police state." By the time the Yippies and all the delegates got to the Windy City, there were riot squads on the street, National Guardsmen with billy clubs at the ready, and a sense that a war, not a political convention, was about to begin in Illinois.

Phil Ochs and Dave Dellinger went anyway, without permits, and put on a Peace Concert with William Burroughs and a few other artists. And the city of Chicago did its worst. In the footage of Chicago's expulsion of the antiwar protesters, you can see people running, being beaten bloody, and being hauled off in police vans.

It would be another seven years before the Vietnam War came to an end; ten thousand more men would be dead. The wide-eyed optimism of so many young men and women who devoted themselves to speaking out against the war would be dashed. Many would retreat into silence; many others would become even more radicalized. It was a dangerous, precarious moment for the nation.

During late November, I had a two-week gig at the Cellar Door, a folk club in the Georgetown section of Washington, D.C., where I was sharing a bill with the Journeymen. I loved working the Cellar Door, singing for the political elite who gathered there, and hanging with the charming owner, Sam L'Hommedieu. Five years earlier, when the club was called The Shadows, I had sung there in the somber week following the assassination of JFK.

One day as I was walking past the smart shops in Georgetown, I saw a young man behind a storefront window, hunched over a potter's wheel. I stood mesmerized, watching him shape elegant bowls and vases, each beautiful in its simplicity. I marched into the store and convinced him to give me lessons on how to throw pots. I spent the next two weeks throwing clay during the day with Jim, the potter, and singing at the Cellar Door at night. By the end of the gig, Jim had me turning out some reasonably decent pots, even if most of them looked a lot like the Leaning Tower of Pisa.

When I got back to New York, I went down to the Lower East Side, where I bought clay, a wedging board, a Randall kick wheel, and a small kiln, and I embarked on my new passion. I was still throwing comically misshapen pots that sagged to one side or the other, but I was keeping at it.

One day Stephen rushed into my apartment. Rugged and handsome, he dropped a bunch of roses wrapped in cellophane on the table and started chattering about a business meeting in midtown. Crosby, Stills and Nash's demo was all the buzz in the music business, and David Geffen, who represented the group, was looking to finalize a contract. I must have looked a disaster in my spattered apron, with bits of clay clinging to my long hair, but Stephen took it all in—the wheel, the kiln, the clay-covered girl, the mess— and smiled. He kissed me on the nose and twirled me about the room, then casually picked up a lump of raw clay from my wedging board, pushed it around for a little while, and put it down. In his hands it had become a sculpted head. His own head, it seemed to me: the nose, the eyes, the tilt, the shape. Beautiful.

We put the sculpted head in the kiln and drank a couple of glasses of wine while the clay cooked. When a bit of clay fell off the side during the firing process, Stephen lost all interest in the now-imperfect head, but I decided to keep it anyway. It was perfect enough for me.

I kept Stephen's sculpture in the window of that apartment and then my next apartment, where I have lived for nearly forty years now. Perched on the sill next to the purple glass vases and the little crystal pot of porcelain flowers that Sandy Denny gave me were the ashes of my beloved cats, Clyde, Sunshine, Moby, Jam, Midnight, and Ruffles. Also there was that sculpted head, which watched over me through the years as I worked and practiced and struggled to become a writer.

But those loving—and lovely—moments between me and Stephen were becoming few and far between. We spent that winter arguing, via long-distance telephone and sometimes in person, about how we were ever going to make our relationship work if

neither of us would give an inch. A sensation of helplessness began
to creep into our life together.

*T*HE following year, in 1969, the Rolling Stones' "Honky Tonk
Woman" dominated the airwaves. While much of the world had
its eyes on the Nuclear Non-Proliferation Treaty, Nixon began the
process of "Vietnamization" in Southeast Asia. In July, Neil Armstrong and Buzz Aldrin walked on the moon. Over the course of
that same summer, the great Judy Garland would die after a lifelong
battle with alcoholism and drug addiction, and the flower-power
generation would produce its defining moment, the music extrava-
ganza of Woodstock.

Nineteen sixty-nine was a triumphant year for me. I spent
much of my time writing, not only composing songs but also keeping journals, recording my dreams, trying to capture my life and
my thoughts on paper. We celebrated Clark's birthday on January
8. Clark was taking drum lessons, and I was continuing my own
lessons every other day with my neighbor Max.

I was still in therapy, which continued to help me survive my
suicidal thoughts, but my alcoholism continued unchecked. I did
not know how near the edge I was walking. I only knew that in
spite of all the success, I was descending into the nightmare of the
booze.

Stephen and I spoke less frequently now, though we still felt
the tug of attraction. We talked late into the night about our yearning to be together. But still I resisted. While our love affair was
cooling down, Stephen's new trio was gaining heat. Ahmet Ertegun
had signed Crosby, Stills and Nash to a deal with Atlantic Records,
and the early buzz on the street was already fantastic. Stephen was
busy scheduling and rehearsing for their initial concert tour to
coincide with the summer release of the album.

George Shearing and me, Denver, 1956.

At the Gilded Garter in Central City, Colorado, 1959—
my second paying gig after Michael's Pub.

LEFT: *In concert, 1960s.*
ABOVE: *Newport, 1967.*

*C*over of my sixth album, *In My Life,* photographed and designed
by Bill Harvey at the Glory Hole, Central City, Colorado, 1966.

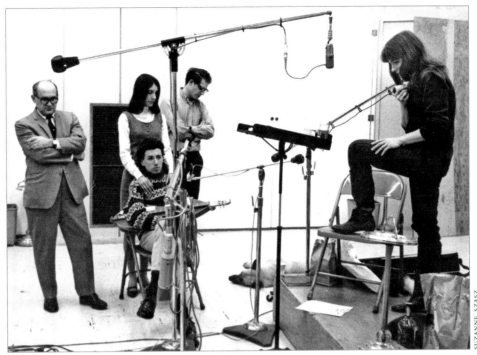

SUZANNE SZASZ

ABOVE *(left to right):* Harold Leventhal, Mimi Baez Fariña, Richard Fariña (seated), and me at a recording session for *In My Life,* New York, 1966.

RIGHT: With "Big Joan" Baez in New York, 1964.

SUZANNE SZASZ

ELEKTRA COLLECTION

Nude shot at John Haeny's home, Laurel Canyon.

With Leonard Cohen,
Forest Hills,
New York, 1968.

ABOVE: Bruce Langhorne and me
at an antiwar rally in the late '60s.

RIGHT: Sketch of me testifying at
the trial of the Chicago Seven in
January 1970.

*A*t the airport with Stephen Stills, 1968.

*J*oni Mitchell and me at Joni's cabin in Laurel Canyon, 1969.

*B*ill Lee and me on
tour in 1965.

*W*ith my singing teacher, Max Margulis.

TOP: With Mimi Fariña, Japan, 1966.

MIDDLE: Pete Seeger, Bob Dylan, me, and Arlo Guthrie at a fund-raiser for Woody Guthrie's Huntington Korea's fund, 1969.

LEFT: In New York with Stacy Keach, winter 1969.

RIGHT: *Stephen Stills and me, winter 1968.*

BELOW: *Singing in Amsterdam, 1972.*

On March 4, 1969, I got a call at home from Joe Papp, the founder of the New York Shakespeare Festival. I had never met Joe, but I certainly knew who he was. Everyone had heard about Joe Papp, the visionary who made Shakespeare accessible to the masses in New York City. His groundbreaking 1956 production of *The Taming of the Shrew*, starring Colleen Dewhurst and presented at the East River Amphitheater on the Lower East Side, had gained him the support of Brooks Atkinson, premier theater critic for the *New York Times*. That was all Joe seemed to need to take the next step for Shakespeare in the Park.

New York City gave Joe the use of the Delacorte, a semicircular outdoor amphitheater overlooking Turtle Pond in the shadow of Central Park's Belvedere Castle. Joe then convinced the city to give him the use of the old Astor Library in the East Village, which was scheduled for demolition, for a dollar a year. He rescued the classic building on Lafayette Street in the nick of time. There he created the New York Public Theater, which would become a world-renowned venue for innovative and exciting work of all kinds for nearly six decades; the building itself was designated a landmark. He also established Joe's Pub at the same location, which did for music what the Public Theater did for the dramatic acts.

Joe sought to nurture contemporary playwrights at the Public, and support a diverse roster of plays. He always surprised New York with his choices, and now he was turning his hand to Ibsen's *Peer Gynt*.

Joe already had a hot team putting the cast together. Gerry Freedman was directing; Joe, Gerry, and Bernie Gersten were producing. As I heard the story, they were sitting around the offices of the Public Theater on a bright March day trying to figure out who they could get to sing John Morris' new songs. Morris had just finished the music for the movie version of *The Producers* and had written other scores for Mel Brooks' films. The cast included

Stacy Keach for the lead, Olympia Dukakis for Anitra, the witchy, many-armed sorceress, and Estelle Parsons as Peer Gynt's mother. All they needed was the long-suffering Solveig.

"You know," Gerry said, "Solveig's songs sound a little like Judy Collins. Who do we know who sounds like Judy Collins?" Bernie, he knew, could probably find what he was looking for among the thousands of singing and acting ingenues in New York.

Joe went straight to the point. "Why don't we ask Judy Collins?"

"She would never do that!" Gerry said with absolute certainty.

"We'll call her and find out" was Joe's reply.

Of course, Gerry was right—at first, anyway. I said no. I wouldn't. Couldn't. *Who Knows Where the Time Goes* had just come out, so there would be concerts to do, and TV appearances. "Someday Soon" had been released as a single and was moving up the charts. I consulted with my friends and my manager, Harold, and they all agreed it would not be a wise move to jump into the theater now, with so much going on.

But I couldn't get the idea out of my head, and after an hour, I called Joe Papp's office back.

"I wonder if I could hear the songs," I told Joe.

"You will love them," he said, "and when you hear them, you will see why you have to do this!" He sent over the four songs written for Solveig. They were love songs, songs of yearning, and they were very beautiful songs. The first real hurdles to my doing *Peer Gynt* had been successfully cleared, and I agreed to give it a try.

"I knew you would come around!" Bernie told me. "We'll have a great time, and you'll love Stacy Keach." He was certainly right about that last part.

March 10, 1969, I went to the Public Theater on Lafayette Street and met with Gerry, Joe, and Bernie. We talked about the play and the plans for the summer. I would meet the other actors in the rehearsals, which would begin in May. I really didn't know what I was getting into, but . . . the Shakespeare Festival? New York? Home, with my son and my friends and my cats? And my therapist? Sounded great to me!

A few days after meeting with Joe Papp, Bill Kunstler called to ask if I would go to Chicago to testify on behalf of my Yippie friends, the boys who were now known as the "Chicago Seven" and who were being tried on charges of conspiracy and inciting to riot. I agreed immediately. The trial was scheduled for September, but Bill wanted to know that he had the witnesses he needed. I told him I would be there. (I would actually not be called to testify until January 1970.)

Somehow, amid all the hubbub, I managed to be in Santa Monica for a concert and saw Stephen. Stephen showed up with gifts at the Holiday Inn where I was staying: a Martin guitar that he had had restored for me and a beautiful song that he had written for me. I heard "Suite: Judy Blue Eyes" for the first time: the story of my life, of our relationship, of the ins and outs of my therapy, and our pain together, his and mine. The sweeping seven-minute song told everything one would have needed to feel the heartbreak, to feel both our hearts break. It was magnificent, and we both wound up in tears.

I think it was meant to win my heart. It certainly won my soul.

But I came away from those hours with Stephen with the unshakable feeling that our breakup was inevitable despite our best intentions. I also left California certain in the knowledge that Crosby, Stills and Nash was poised on the brink of stardom, like a loaded cannon waiting only for someone to spark the fuse. The sweet and the bitter, all at once—as usual, I suppose.

I returned to crowded New York, where horns honked and sirens shrieked, where people lived in apartments and there were no backyards filled with swimming pools and no fires in the hills. I was back at my apartment on the Upper West Side. No more glamorous

Hollywood types driving their Bentleys and Jags to shop on Rodeo Drive, but back to muggings that kept you out of Central Park anytime after six in the evening.

I was thrilled to be home.

On May 1, returning from a tour of the Midwest, as I walked through LaGuardia Airport I spotted on a newsstand my face blazing out from the cover of *Life*. Under the photograph was the headline, lovely and perhaps true in one sense but bitterly ironic in another: "Gentle Voice Amid the Storm." I had just turned thirty.

The real storm was the one in my head and heart. I would have to wait on fate and time to heal me and to help me find the compass that seemed, at the moment, far off.

Chapter Thirty

Stacy, Woodstock, and the Humpback Whales

Farewell to Tarwathie
Adieu Mormond Hill
And the dear land of Crimmond, I bid thee farewell.

—Traditional, "Farewell to Tarwathie"

$\mathcal{A}$T last, at the end of May, I came to a decision about Stephen. I could not take the roller-coaster ride of emotions that characterized our affair. We got rock and roll, we got rhythm, and then we got the blues. Stephen was driven by something I could not see and did not understand. I was driven by something that, apparently, was opposite. Clearly, that ride was almost over.

At the first rehearsal of *Peer Gynt*, I met Stacy Keach. He was handsome, a man in the prime of his life, buoyant, full of energy, sparking with ideas. He met me head-on with that smile of his and lifted me up from the place I had been with Stephen—despairing and sorry, sad and full of regret. I seemed to wake up.

In the Ibsen story I play the woman who waits, true and faithful, for Peer Gynt, the gadabout and free spirit who is off roaming the world to find himself. These days, we'd put Solveig into a twelve-step program for co-dependency, and sooner rather than later! Of course, Ibsen and Grieg didn't see things that way. The romantic songs and the setup for romance—first in the rehearsal hall, where we danced in loving awe around each another, and then in the park, with its birds and water and light—were the perfect conditions for love.

I had invited Stacy to dinner at my apartment, and very quickly we began our affair. When he took me in his arms I felt the friction in my life ease. He was brilliant and creative, but solid, too, with his feet on the ground. We both were involved with other people, but felt at once that something important had happened between us.

Stacy Keach is a courtly man, two years older than me. He had been born in Savannah, Georgia, and always called himself "junior," to distinguish himself from his father, Stacy senior, a director and drama teacher who earned a name for himself in Hollywood radio and movies. Stacy graduated from UC Berkeley in 1963, attended the Yale School of Drama, and earned a Fulbright scholarship to the London Academy of Music and Dramatic Art in England.

He had already established himself in the world of New York theater by the time we met. He had worked with Morgan Freeman in George Tabori's *The Niggerlovers* in 1967. It was Morgan Freeman's first acting job, and Morgan always said he learned more about acting from Stacy than from anyone. Stacy had played Lyndon Johnson in the Barbara Garson play *MacBird,* a satire about the president we all loved to hate, alongside William Devane and Rue McClanahan. The play was an early stepping-stone in the careers of all of these actors, who were all friends of Stacy's. Stacy loved theater and theater people. He would introduce me to many of the actors in the New York community: Jane Alexander, James Earl

Jones, Rene Auberjonois, and Sam Waterston, as well as Laurence Olivier, Ralph Richardson, and the great Jason Robards.

Stacy was a man in the full bloom of his early career, handsome, lively and generous, levelheaded and ambitious, a man of great charm, both on and off the stage.

I felt that I could talk to Stacy, be his friend, and find solace with him. Our love felt complete, imbued with respect and genuine caring.

And I thought: "Here is the man who is going to solve all my problems." On the white horse, of course!

I really did the best I could to be the partner he might have wanted. I would wait, follow, adhere, and love him from afar, from close up, from wherever I was. It was the real thing. Again.

We rehearsed *Peer Gynt* throughout May and into June, then opened in Central Park in July in that greenery-filled fantasy conjured in the Delacorte Theater. And I sang John Morris' songs, which had sold me on doing the show in the first place.

*A*ND where was Stephen? I hadn't heard from him for a month after our last unsettling talk about our broken love affair, but I knew he was rehearsing for his tour with David and Graham, putting in the hard work that would ensure fame and fortune after the phenomenally successful release of the new Crosby, Stills and Nash album.

When I met Stacy, I was beginning the last mad charge into hell, the final descent into alcoholic oblivion. Yet everyone still said, even those who knew me best, "You don't look like an alcoholic! You're too successful, too put together!"

We had not really had any closure, Stephen and I, and perhaps that was best. Every time we tried to find some adult way to end things, we ended up hurting each other. I was drinking, and I would do what I wanted. Someday we would speak again, and perhaps find a way to be friends. I hoped so. Meanwhile, at least that June, Stephen was still hoping and writing crazy, love-filled, disjointed letters. One night in New York I came back from rehearsal and dinner with Stacy to find Stephen hovering near the entrance to my apartment building. He apologized but said we had to talk. I was determined not to. I was unkind. I was in my own world. I had moved on. I did not understand that one couldn't just speed past the wreckage of the heart free of pain and regret. There was a price to all this bungling of relationships, and eventually I would have to pay, as everyone must.

Peer Gynt closed on August 15, 1969, the weekend that history was being made in Bethel, New York, at Max Yasgur's farm at Woodstock. I had not been invited to sing, and so I missed the debut of "Suite: Judy Blue Eyes" sung by Crosby, Stills and Nash. Instead, I headed to Williamstown to see a production of *The Cherry Orchard* with Olympia Dukakis, who had played Anitra in *Peer Gynt*. Stacy, my sister Holly, another friend, and I rented a car and drove first to Yasgur's farm, which was on the way to Williamstown. There we paused to say hello to Bill Graham at the production office on the highway outside the festival grounds. He invited me to go to the stage in the helicopter to watch the festival up close. I thought about all those artists who *had* been invited to Woodstock—from Richie Havens to Joan Baez to Crosby, Stills and Nash—and said thanks but no thanks.

We proceeded to Williamstown, where Olympia was brilliant, and certainly didn't think we had missed anything by not joining the mud and the crowds at Yasgur's farm!

On the way home, I finally thought of a way to get the sound of humpback whales into the world.

I had been given a tape made in Bermuda by the biologist and environmentalist Roger Payne. He had come backstage during one of my performances of *Peer Gynt* and presented me with the first recording ever of the singing humpback whales. He asked me to think of something to do with these great half-ton leviathans, to find a way to make their songs known to the world.

In a way, it was not far from the kinds of requests many song-writers had made of me over the years. Driving back from Williamstown to New York, I knew what I would do. I would sing a traditional whaling song, "Farewell to Tarwathie," a cappella, in duet with these magnificent creatures. It would be the first time humpback whales were heard by most of the world.

I said, over and over, the mantra I had said in California as the black and white killer whales leapt through the Pacific: *"Nam myoho renge kyo."*

I HAVE always thought that some angel of fate intervened to make sure I was not there when Stephen, David, and Graham played "Suite: Judy Blue Eyes" for the first time at Woodstock. It would not have been right for me to be there, singing or not.

And then in September 1969, I heard "Suite: Judy Blue Eyes" for the second time, on the radio, riding in a cab in New York City. It sounded nothing like the solo version Stephen had played me months before. This was different. I leaned forward and asked the driver to turn up the sound and then, sitting back as the city poured by the cab's windows, I was moved to tears all over again.

The driver looked at me strangely as I managed to get the door open and literally staggered from that cab after paying my fare. I was sober, stone cold sober, and very much in shock.

The song would rock the country and the world into a new place where rock and folk came together. The gorgeous harmonies of David, Stephen, and Graham, along with Stephen's shimmering guitar work merging with insistent rhythms, created a truly new sound. Hearing it the first time was a totally dazzling experience. "Suite: Judy Blue Eyes" was the single that would spearhead a fresh new sound in popular music, and I knew after I heard it that first time I would have a hard time getting over it—the affair, the breakup, what the song meant about my addiction to the therapists who told me it was not in my best interests to commit to anyone. I am not blaming them; I was the one who threw the dice and then backed away from the table. Stephen knew exactly what he was doing; he was that smart and that gifted. In a way it was his revenge, served hot, and it was magnificent.

My love affair with Stacy was just beginning to blossom. We continued through that autumn to spend all our time together when I was not on the road. Clark and Stacy bonded and became close friends. We got iguanas and made trips to the park and the zoo. For Christmas that year, Stacy gave me a husky puppy, Smokey, a little black and white fluff ball with a red ribbon around his neck. We had the perfect holiday.

Stacy moved in with me, and we soon realized we were going to need a new apartment.

Our hearts were entwined, our lives as well. And our good fortune in finding each other was clear as a bell to both of us.

Chapter Thirty-One

The Art of Antiwar

The Democratic convention is about to begin in a police state, there doesn't appear to be any other way to describe it.

—WALTER CRONKITE, *CBS Evening News*

SEPTEMBER 24, 1969, marked the beginning of the trial of Abbie Hoffman, Jerry Rubin, David Dellinger, Tom Hayden, Rennie Davis, John Froines, Lee Weiner, and Bobby Seale. Within two weeks, the trial had become a circus. Bobby Seale called the judge, Judge Julius Hoffman, a "fascist dog," a "pig," and a "racist," among other epithets. Seale was verbally harassed by the judge, tied to his chair, gagged, and denied permission to defend himself. Seale's lawyers made a deal for a separate trial, and the Yippies became known as the Chicago Seven.

The convention itself had been a disaster. Now, outside the courthouse in the Windy City, the National Guard was called in as demonstrations grew for and against the defendants. I flew to Chicago on January 23, my mother's birthday. She told me on the phone that she was proud of me and wished she could be with me.

I checked into a hotel near the courthouse. I felt nervous but believed in what I had come to do.

I met with William Kunstler that night and he and I spoke about what Judge Hoffman might ask me and what direction the testimony might take. I was inspired by this devoted, brilliant man who had championed so many good causes.

I woke up the next morning feeling like a patriot, full of anger about the war, indignant about the trial, and eager to take part. After all, this was a democracy, and I was simply going to have my say. At the courthouse, I sat in the echoing halls waiting to be called. I was determined to speak eloquently.

But I didn't say half of what I wanted to say. By the time the clerk came to escort me into the courtroom, I had forgotten everything and just wanted to get through the ordeal one way or another and let them know that they had the wrong guys and the wrong war, and the country was mad as hell and wasn't going to take it anymore.

I felt like Alice having just fallen down the rabbit hole and drunk from a little bottle and become so small. I saw the boys—men, really—all in a row: Abbie, David, Rennie, Tom, and the others. The judge sat in his black robe looking sinister, as though he might reach out, grab me, and stuff me where no one would ever find me. I could go to jail if I told him something he didn't like and wound up in contempt. A vision of the prison in Joliet flashed through my mind—I had once slept with an ex-con from Joliet, and he had told me about the conditions there—and the thought made me shiver. The boys really could go to jail, I thought.

I stood up when my name was called and approached the bench, where I laid my hand on the Bible. I had not seen a Bible since the Methodist church my family attended in Denver. The book seemed almost alive in the hand of the clerk, accusing, hiding its meaning behind its black cover. Was Christ really against the war? Was He for peace? All the songs I had sung for peace were in my throat. I wondered that none could prove my point.

The look on the judge's face told everyone that he wanted to get this witness off the stand as quickly as possible. The defendants were wearing what looked to me like clothes of shining silver, purple, and bright green. They seemed dressed for a party. The look on the judge's face said it all, the unspoken implication being: "You're a misfit, Collins, a singer." Kunstler looked tired but strangely elegant. He opened with a few questions about who I was and what I did for a living.

MR. KUNSTLER: Would you state your name, please?

THE WITNESS: Judy Collins.

MR. KUNSTLER: What is your occupation?

THE WITNESS: I'm a singer. I sing folk songs.

MR. KUNSTLER: Now, Miss Collins, I call your attention to March 17, 1968, at approximately noontime on that date. Do you know where you were?

THE WITNESS: I was at the Americana Hotel in New York City attending a press conference to announce the formation of what we have now come to know of as the Yippie Movement.

MR. KUNSTLER: Who was present at that press conference?

THE WITNESS: There were a number of people who were singers, entertainers. Jerry Rubin was there. Abbie Hoffman was there. Allen Ginsberg was there, and sang a mantra.

MR. KUNSTLER: Now, what did you do at that press conference?

William and I had discussed the night before how my testimony might go. Over dinner with his staff at the hotel restaurant he had said he wanted me to talk about the Yippie press conference. He needed to instantly get the attention of the jury and judge as to why I had attended it. I told him I was sure I had been invited because I was a singer, as well as an active participant in the peace movement.

"And what might you do as a participant in the peace movement?" he had asked me.

"Well," I'd said, "I might sing something, like 'Where Have all the Flowers Gone.'"

"Then," he'd said, smiling and smacking the table and grabbing my hand, "that is what you must do! You must show them by singing it, not just saying it!"

So in court the next day, that was what I did. I started to sing.

"Where have all the flowers—"

Outraged, the judge interrupted, "Just a minute, young lady."

But I went on singing.

"—where have all the flowers gone?"

Then I felt a hand come over my mouth as the court clerk, on the judge's orders, stopped me. It was as if my breath had been taken from me, and I was gagged, silenced. I stood, dazed and frightened. I had indeed fallen down that dark hole. No one had ever done such a thing to me in my life. I struggled to regain my balance.

In my mind, I kept seeing the gag going on Bobby Seale, the straps wound around his wrists and his body to keep him still and from talking in his own defense. For all I knew, they were coming with the tapes and the ropes for me.

DEPUTY MARSHAL JOHN J. GRACIOUS: I'm sorry. The judge would like to speak to you.

THE COURT: We don't allow any singing in this court. I'm sorry.

THE WITNESS: May I recite the words?

Mr. Kunstler: Well, your honor, we have had films. I think it is as legitimate as a movie. It is the actual thing she did, she sang "Where Have All the Flowers Gone," which is a well-known peace song, and she sang it, and the jury is not getting the flavor.

The Court: You asked her what she did, and she proceeded to sing.

Mr. Kunstler: That is what she did, your honor.

The Witness: That's what I do.

The Court: And that has no place in a United States District Court. We are not here to be entertained, sir. We are trying a very important case.

Mr. Kunstler: This song is not an entertainment, your honor. This is a song of peace, and what happens to young men and women during wartime.

The Court: I forbid her from singing during the trial. I will not permit singing in this courtroom.

Mr. Kunstler: Why not, your honor? What's wrong with singing?

Mr. Foran (prosecuting lawyer for the City of Chicago): May I respond? This is about the fifth time this has occurred. Each time your honor has directed Mr. Kunstler that it was improper in the courtroom. It is an old and stale joke in this courtroom, your honor.

Now, there is no question that Miss Collins is a fine singer. In my family my six kids and I all agree that she is a fine singer, but that doesn't have a thing to do with this lawsuit, nor what my profession is, which is the practice of law in the federal district court, your honor, and I protest Mr. Kunstler constantly failing to advise his witnesses of what proper decorum is, and I object to it on behalf of the government.

The Court: I sustain the objection.

I told the court that violent demonstration had been the furthest thing from the minds of these young men when they formed the Yippies and said that I was sure Rennie, Abbie, David, Tom, and the others had been provoked.

It seemed to me that the Illinois National Guard, practicing what the Ohio National Guard would perfect just a few months later at Kent State, had decided to assert its authority from the very start, to strike these peaceniks to the ground without waiting for provocation.

Why were these young men being penalized for wanting peace? Violence against people who think we should not kill one another is surely one of the most disturbed of human behaviors.

Walter Cronkite was so right. Chicago had felt like a police state, and in some ways I feel even today as if the peace movement never recovered from it.

William Kunstler invited Phil Ochs to testify in Chicago and, having learned from our experience with my singing, urged Phil to read the words to "I Ain't Marching Anymore," which he did, without any interference from Judge Hoffman. However, as Phil exited the courthouse, he sang the song to the crowd of reporters, and later his impromptu performance was broadcast on the *CBS Evening News with Walter Cronkite*. That always amused Phil, as he knew Cronkite was responsible for making sure that CBS included his song in its news coverage that night.

The jury, at the end of February, found two of the defendants, John Froines and Lee Weiner, innocent of all charges. The other five, Abbie, Dave, Rennie, Tom, and Jerry, were convicted of crossing state lines with an intent to incite a riot. On February 20 they were sentenced to five years in prison each and a $5,000 fine. Abbie, in addressing the judge after sentencing, suggested he try LSD and said he could set him up with a dealer to provide the drugs.

Kunstler immediately appealed the verdict, and a long and

painful two and a half years followed as they waded through the legal process to find out if they would, in fact, have to serve jail time. Their lives, their hopes, their dreams, were held hostage, even if the men were not literally incarcerated.

On November 21, 1972, the convictions were overturned by the United States Court of Appeals for the Seventh Circuit on the grounds that the court had violated their rights. Leaving the courtroom, Rennie Davis said he was going to move next door to the prosecutor (Tom Foran) and "bring his sons and daughters into the revolution." Jerry Rubin gave Judge Julius Hoffman his book inscribed, "Julius, you radicalized more young people than we ever could. You're the country's top Yippie!"

Meanwhile, the war in Vietnam raged, and the collateral damage from the trial proved tragic. Phil Ochs seemed to be falling apart in the wake of the convention. That sweet and troubled man often drank too much, like the rest of us, and suffered remorse because of it. He had been entangled in some of the violence stirred up by the police, who swung batons at peaceful protesters and chased young people as though they were criminals. In the aftermath, the CIA hounded Phil, harassing him, tapping his phone. He began to call himself "John Butler Train" and to say "Phil Ochs has been killed by the CIA in a mugging in Tanzania while he was on tour." He took to wearing a white suit—his Mafia suit, he called it—and referred to himself as "a cross between Elvis Presley and Che Guevara."

After 1970, Phil began using pills to sleep, and booze to counter his extreme mood swings. I think the FBI and the CIA drove him out of his mind. But that didn't stop him from writing, recording, performing. Friends feared he was becoming a danger to himself, and he increasingly spoke of suicide.

Phil Ochs hanged himself on April 9, 1976.

Abbie Hoffman, co-founder of the Youth International Party, died in 1989 after being diagnosed with bipolar disorder. He had swallowed 150 phenobarbital pills, and his death would also be ruled a suicide.

David Dellinger spent the years after the Chicago Seven trial writing and teaching until his death in 2004. He dedicated his last book, *Revolutionary Nonviolence*, to "all the veterans of the Vietnam War—those who fought it and those who fought against it."

Chapter Thirty-Two

Amazing Grace

Amazing grace
How sweet the sound
That saved a wretch like me.

—Traditional, "Amazing Grace"

"Amazing Grace" was born in a period of political strife in England and the United States, and perhaps my latter-day version served as a kind of tonic during another time of social upheaval.

In late January 1970, I became involved in an encounter group with a number of friends in New York. It began when I met Candy Jackson at a dinner party. Candy was a tall, handsome, and articulate recovering addict who had fled from Synanon, the West Coast sober community for drug users. Candy had been hired to run the encounter groups at Phoenix House, an in-house treatment center for drug addicts and alcoholics on the Upper West Side in New York.

In the course of the evening's conversation he learned that some friends and I were planning to meet and discuss buying property in Vermont. Like New Englanders from an earlier century, we would find a way to live together, sharing property, money, and the fruits of the land.

Candy said, "Before you do that, you have to encounter each other, see what you are all made of."

Candy came to our first meeting, and after we let him give his spiel, none of us ever talked again about buying land. We "encountered" one another, with Candy leading us, for the next two years. He had found a gold mine: neurotic Upper West Siders who needed to tear one another to pieces and would pay him to help us do it. Insane, now that I think of it. Perhaps we should have known better, but in fact, there were some surprising things that came out of those sessions.

For one thing, Candy nailed me on my alcoholism and dared me to stop drinking. I took the dare and stayed away from alcohol for two months. I started again, of course, but Candy had pierced through my wall of denial . . . for the moment. And while it was all right for me to call myself an alcoholic, and for me to tell my therapists that I was an alcoholic, God forbid anyone else should point it out!

Mark Abramson and Jac Holzman were part of the group, and Mark proved himself to be so effective in drawing out other people's concerns that Jac asked him to lead a group of Elektra executives at a weekend retreat. That was Mark's first involvement with any kind of group therapy; later, after he moved to upstate New York, he helped run therapy groups for inmates at a nearby prison. It was said of him that he was an excellent therapist. I was not surprised.

One night, members of the group were at one another's throats. Mark said to me, "You should sing something. We are losing it here; everybody has to calm down." I sang "Amazing Grace," thinking that at least it was a song some of us knew. The next morning Mark called me.

"We have to record that song," he said.

And so we did.

Mark and I decided that this next album—my ninth for Elektra—had to have a flavor that was spiritual in its nature. We would not have used that term, but we were searching. "Farewell to Tarwathie," with the singing whales, was the first step in the right direction, and with "Amazing Grace," I knew we had found the defining song, the spiritual center, of the album, which we called *Whales and Nightingales.*

We recorded several other traditional songs, among them "Simple Gifts," a Shaker song that Aaron Copland adapted for *Appalachian Spring,* and "Gene's Song." I was taught this little gem by Evelyn Beers and her husband, Bob, who started the Fox Hollow Folk Festival in Petersburgh, New York, in 1966. The Beers were fascinated by folk crafts, such as the little walking man on a string that you gently bounce on a thin board of balsa wood, which makes him "dance." Evelyn supplied the rhythm for this charming folksong with those little dancing feet.

Other songs on the album came from contemporary composers and songwriters, including Jacques Brel, Joan Baez, and Bob Dylan. "Nightingales I" and "Nightingales II" were my compositions, and Josh Rifkin orchestrated them both beautifully.

All of the songs on this collection emerged, I believe, out of my personal ideas about faith. They explore the power of nature in our lives, the idea that all life is sacred, and the idea that the planet, in its beauty and fragility, is being hunted, like the great whales, to depletion. That spring marked the first celebration of Earth Day, a signal event in raising environmental consciousness.

The album culminates with "Amazing Grace." I learned the song from my maternal grandmother, Agnes Byrd. I had known it for most of my life, but I was not familiar with the story of John Newton, the English slave-trading captain who wrote the song. He had nearly died in a shipwreck. He became a minister and, years later, wrote "Amazing Grace."

We recorded "Amazing Grace" in St. Paul's Chapel on the campus of Columbia University. I brought in a group of friends to sing in the choir, some professional, but mostly amateurs: Eric Weissberg, Harris Yulin, Stacy Keach, and my brother Denver John. I loved the haunting echoes bouncing around the chapel, lending an otherworldly quality to the song.

But an a cappella hymn? People at the label were getting a kick out of this, knocking it around, playing it for one another, delighted, but with no thought of its becoming anything but a good filler on the album. They were as shocked as I was when it turned out the universe had other plans. This recording of "Amazing Grace" dominated the radio waves, the album flew out of the stores, and within weeks it became a worldwide sensation.

It seemed that people had not tired of prayer or of hymns or of church. They just needed the music.

Chapter Thirty-Three

Easy Times

Easy times come hard for me
And oh, my darling
Time again to dream
That you are comin' home.

—Judy Collins and Stacy Keach Jr., "Easy Times"

During the years we were together, Stacy kept busy all the time, creating unique and memorable characters in many films and Broadway shows. Meanwhile, I was out touring and making records or at home, trying to take care of Clark. Stacy gave one of the most thrilling performances I have ever seen as Buffalo Bill in Arthur Kopit's play *Indians*. He transformed the theater into the Wild West. You could smell the dust and the manure, feel the puff of the gunpowder as it streamed off Annie Oakley's six-shooter. We were still living in my old apartment on West 79th Street, although we'd soon find a new place farther uptown. Stacy would come home from his performances drenched in sweat, mopping his face, his hair plastered to his forehead, and his handsome eyes dark with fatigue.

Stacy won rave reviews in *Hamlet*, first at the Long Wharf Theater in New Haven and then at Joe Papp's New York Shakespeare Festival. Then he landed the lead role in the spring of 1970 in a movie directed by Frank Perry about Doc Holiday, called *Doc*. Frank was planning to shoot the film in Almería, Spain, and asked Stacy about his thoughts on the cast. Of course Stacy wanted Harris Yulin, his good friend and an amazing actor, to play Wyatt Earp. Faye Dunaway was cast as Doc's common-law wife. And one day Stacy and I were driving out to the Hamptons, talking about who should play the kid. I knew my brother Denver John, who had been in a theater company in Vermont and was very gifted, would be perfect for the part. Stacy agreed, and Frank gave Denver a screen test, his first and last. (Denver makes his living on the other side of the camera now, shooting music videos and movies and filming television specials. He also directs and/or shoots all my television productions.)

In June we took Clark and his friend Josh Klein, son of my therapist, with us for a few weeks to Almería, which has often stood in for the parched and jagged territory of Texas in American westerns. The crew and the stars and their guests ate langoustine and drank *cerveza* and went to the bullfights in a little town on the coast. I loved watching Stacy play Doc Holliday under Frank Perry's direction. The "barbed, grisly dialogue" of *Doc*, as the *New York Times* described it, was written by Pete Hamill.

Faye Dunaway had starred in *Bonnie and Clyde* and *The Thomas Crown Affair* and had co-starred with Marcello Mastroianni in *A Place for Lovers,* during the production of which they became lovers. Marcello came to Spain and found Faye involved with Harris Yulin, and I remember that everyone on the set was abuzz when the handsome, charismatic Mastroianni arrived. But she was not having any of it. He later was said to have confided that he never spent an unhappy moment in Faye's arms. Faye flew to Madrid, he said, and met another man.

Stacy was Faye's leading man in *Doc*, and I was there, very much in her way, although Stacy and I had a deal that I would make myself scarce when he and Faye had their love scenes. She later told me that it was awkward for her that I was there.

"I *always* have an affair with my leading man," she said. "Except that in *Doc*, you cramped my style, because I couldn't have Stacy!" We both laughed, but it hadn't seemed very funny in Spain.

Jimmy Webb wrote the music for the movie and told me that when Frank Perry flew out to Los Angeles to talk about the score, they spent four days drinking a quart of tequila each day and wound up with a sound track that resembled a scruffy Mexican band imitating Tito Puente.

It was really a vacation for me, watching the filming, being with Clark and my beloved brother Denver John, laughing in the light of the bonfire that always burned as seafood was grilled over the coals at night, for the cast and everyone who was swabbing down with aloe after baking beneath the Spanish sun. It *was* like the West, not just on film—hot and dusty and full of sharp colors—but we were blessed with a lovely hacienda where the shutters made lovemaking cool and comfortable in the afternoons.

Also, I knew I was falling more and more in love with Stacy. That was such a good feeling—to be totally involved with a man I admired and got along with. Almería was an escape for me in a way, a restorative time-out from the relentless daily pace of my life. But after a few weeks, Stacy's work on the film wrapped up, and we flew back home.

I got Clark into school and returned to the road.

CLARK began having troubles, acting out, and at the end of the year Stacy and I hunted for a new school for him. His therapist felt he would be better-off at a boarding school, and I had to say I agreed. I could not guess that he had the illness he inherited from my family genes. The alcoholism was alive and rampant in him, and he had started using drugs. No doctors in my life, most of whom he saw at some time or another, identified his problem as drug-related.

In January 1971, Clark was packed off to a boys' school in Maryland. Three weeks into his first semester, he had a sledding accident and went into the hospital for life-saving surgery. I spent two weeks with him in Baltimore at the hospital thanking God for his surgeon, who had done a delicate operation to repair his skull. At first we did not know if he would live or die, and he hovered, it seemed, for ten days. Then I saw his eyes open and a gleam come into them. He told me later that he had made a decision to come back, to live his life. I will be grateful for that miracle all my days.

After Clark spent some time at New York Presbyterian Hospital doing rehab and getting healthy again, his therapists said he would be better-off not living at home, and helped me find a school in Vermont where he would have much closer supervision and get the scholastic help he needed. By now he was eager to get back into classes. But, of course, he took his addictions with him.

In the spring of 1971 Stacy and I went to Stockton, California, where Stacy rented a house near one of the canals while he played the lead in *Fat City*, directed by John Huston. I rented a piano, went swimming every day, and tried to quit smoking. I had smoked since I was fifteen, but now I could feel it taking a toll on my voice and on my health. I had always exercised, but now when I swam or worked out, I could feel my lungs fighting for air.

That summer I became bulimic. Just like that. No run-up, no warning. One day, out of the blue, my eating disorder emerged in full bloom. In retrospect, I might blame lots of life crises, but of course my drinking was getting worse and worse. When I stopped smoking, the food addiction moved right in. Through my difficult future recovery from alcoholism and my subsequent sobriety, food is still the thing about which I have to be most vigilant. An eating disorder is a killer, mysterious and perplexing, but as a friend of mine says, as long as you are breathing, there is hope.

I had been addicted to sugar since childhood. My mother was a great cook, and desserts, especially fudge and divinity (the latter a wicked white thing made with cream of tartar, sugar, sugar, and more sugar, and some whipped egg whites), were her specialties. I spent my bus change on sugary treats when I was on my way to my piano lessons, and I loved to steal my father's beloved chocolate-covered cherries out of his drawer.

From the age of about eighteen I had tried every diet I could find. I visited fasting farms and joined self-help groups to stop eating. Starting when I was twenty-three, I exercised every day. I ran and swam; I did crunches, took yoga, and practiced the Royal Canadian Air Force exercises. (All of this while I was, by now, putting away a half-quart of booze every day.) Now, more than a decade later in California, as I prepared to swim daily in our beautiful pool to stop smoking, I thought I had invented bulimia, or at least restored it from Roman history, dragging it from the past to my personal aid.

I was never very overweight, but the illness of the food disorder thrived, and it would be eleven years before I would be given a solution.

Fortunately, one addiction of mine would prove beneficial, and at times probably saved me: my need to be surrounded by my friends. Even from Stockton, I did my best to keep up with my friends in New York and around the country. I had made friends with a couple—from St. Louis, Judy and Peter Weston—when I worked at a club there. One day Judy and I had a great conversation on the phone, and the minute we hung up, I went to the piano and wrote a song called "Song for Judith." I changed the name of the song to "Open the Door" and put it on my album *Living*, which was released in 1972 and consisted of songs I had recorded from my 1970 and 1971 concert tours:

> *Sometimes I remember the old days*
> *When the world was filled with sorrow*

It's interesting how the lyric seems to be set sometime in the future, when I would be able to look back at my younger, troubled self. Perhaps I knew then, somewhere deep inside, that I would someday find some answers.

Chapter Thirty-Four

The Mogul and the Movie Star

Isn't it rich? Are we a pair?
Me here at last on the ground, you in midair.

—STEPHEN SONDHEIM, "Send in the Clowns"

IN 1972, Elektra Records released a new album of Judy Collins hits from the previous decade. Jac and I had made the choices and planned the cover, conceived by Nancy Carlin and photographed on the beach in front of her friend Betty Beard's house in Malibu. *Colors of the Day* came out that spring and included "Someday Soon" and "Both Sides Now," plus "Amazing Grace" and my own "My Father," "Since You Asked," and "Albatross." The songs that had gone onto the charts did so again, and the album went platinum; it still is in print. Later, Bill Clinton, in his 1992 run for president, referred to it as his favorite album and then proceeded to name every song, which impressed me no end!

That same year, I was part of an event organized by Shirley MacLaine, a gathering of women to support Senator George McGovern in his run for president. McGovern supported the issues that we were fighting for, including withdrawal of all forces from

Vietnam. It was a high-profile, exciting event, culminating in a performance at Madison Square Garden in New York City that included Gloria Steinem, Shirley, Carly Simon, and others. We sang, spoke, and raised money for the candidate, who had been a member of the Kennedy administration and a great advocate of women's rights as well as having a strong liberal agenda.

In spite of my events and touring schedule, I was drinking more than ever. Sometimes, when Stacy was away on a shoot, I felt as if I was floating on another planet. He and I decided we needed to have our own apartments, and he took a place a couple of blocks away near the American Museum of Natural History. I continued to try to get Clark, now thirteen, through the ups and downs of his early adolescence. His school in Vermont seemed to be the right place for now. We had great visits and summers and school breaks together. Our relationship, always close, became closer and more supportive and loving. Clark made efforts to stay in touch with his father, but I didn't see Peter for years. We had a very distant and cool relationship. But I knew things about him, from Clark, and from my former sister-in-law, Hadley. Peter now had a doctorate and taught William Blake at the University of British Columbia in Vancouver. Once, in the women's bathroom at the school, graffiti was found on the wall that said: "Peter Taylor is God!" It was signed "The girls in the 9 a.m. Blake class." Clark was very proud of his father, and did his best to keep the door open for him.

One night in the spring of 1972, I got a phone call from Jac Holzman. I had been with Elektra for eleven years by then, and we had done well by each other. Elektra had nurtured me, produced and promoted my albums, and I felt secure in my recording career. I was not ready for the news I was about to receive.

"Dear," Jac said, "I am leaving Elektra as of tomorrow."

I was devastated and angry. I depended on Jac's support and was shocked he hadn't told me he was thinking of leaving the company. "Amazing Grace" was still charting all over the world, but I was nervous about the new album I was making and I needed Jac's confidence and support.

He said he had made a deal with Steve Ross to buy him out but leave him in charge of a great deal of the technical aspects of the Warner-Elektra-Atlantic companies, such as the development of cable—Jac was always ahead of the curve in technology. He said that he was leaving the company in good hands and I would be meeting David Geffen, the new president of Elektra (who would be merging his own company, Asylum, with Elektra), at Lillian Roxon's funeral the next day. He would introduce us. At a funeral!

Lillian Roxon's death had been another shock. Lillian had died of asthma the week before Jac made his announcement to me. Her funeral was a gathering of rock and folk musicians and independent film people. She was mourned by everyone who knew her personally and by many who did not.

I did meet David Geffen that day; I knew of him because he had helped Stephen when Crosby, Stills and Nash was getting together. Jac did the honors, and it was all very cordial, but I was screaming inside. The entire event was so bizarre and unprecedented that I did not speak to Jac for two years, although we have made our peace and he is still one of my closest friends. And to give him credit, he was certainly right about David Geffen, who turned out to be a fine executive at Elektra, and who helped me enormously, both in making my forthcoming album, *Judith*, and with his friendship over these many years.

*I*N 1972, I would join Robert Jay Lifton and others to put on an event that involved a petition to Congress for "Redress of grievance," to make the public statement that Congress needed to take responsibility for funding what I and many other people felt was an illegal war in Vietnam.

I spent months reaching out to everyone from my friend Sister Corita, the Catholic activist, who was sick and could not come to the event, to the actor Carroll O'Connor, who said he was amazed that I had the chutzpah to call him, and declined flat-out.

We were insisting that Congress answer accusations that they had sanctioned the American invasion of a sovereign country, Vietnam, and had made the American people pay for a war that was disastrous and could not be justified.

Many artists, writers, and intellectuals agreed to participate, and those who showed up in the halls of Congress in 1972 included Tennessee Williams, Joe Papp, Francine du Plessix Gray, Ida Turkel, and Cynthia Macdonald, among others. Many of us were arrested and spent the night in jail.

Garry Wills was there, and in his book *Outside Looking In,* he writes of how a friend called him and said, "You have written about many antiwar demonstrations. Isn't it time to put the rest of your body where your mouth is?" I shared a cell with Francine, Ida, and Cynthia. When we were arrested, Garry said he was told by Ida Turkel that "Judy Collins gave their cell great music." I was singing "Amazing Grace."

I wouldn't have called it fun, but certainly it felt good to be with other like-minded women. My friend, the poet Cynthia Macdonald, who taught at Sarah Lawrence at that time, and I had always found it difficult to make dates with our schedules, so we loved being together, even in a cell!

I remembered having heard that Jane Fonda had had all her sleeping and vitamin pills taken from her at one of the political events she participated in, and so I dumped my loose pills down the toilet bowl in our cell. Sad to say, along with the pills, I dropped the amethyst ring my grandmother had left me.

As I sat in jail, ever the optimist, I was sure our actions would help bring the war to a quick end. But of course the war continued to rage.

*L*ATER that spring, I had a brainstorm, an idea that would not go away, and would eventually help me get through the growing turbulence in my relationship with Stacy. It also gave me a focus that took my mind off my drinking.

Before discovering folk music, of course, I had studied classical piano with Dr. Antonia Brico, and I had learned bits and pieces of her moving and inspirational life story over the years. I decided to make a film about her life. I bought an 8 mm Rollei movie camera and then realized that I needed at least a 16 mm camera to do the job properly. And I could use someone who knew about film to help me! I dug deeply into my small savings, reached out to a couple of friends in the film industry, and before you knew it, I was on my way to making sure no one was ever going to forget Antonia Brico.

Writers should write about what they know, a common bit of wisdom has it, and I knew a lot about this woman. She was a pioneer, a heroine, and a mentor to me. By 1972, I was enmeshed in the women's movement and had joined women's consciousness-raising groups in New York, including one that my friends Gloria Steinem and Marlo Thomas had started with other women friends from *Ms.* magazine. These women, too, were enthusiastic about Brico, as I had shared her story with them. They helped give me the courage to try something entirely different for me: producing and directing a film.

I wrote the treatment and talked it over for months with Max, whose power as a teacher and a mentor had motivated me to tell this particular story. I then put together a team, starting with my co-director, Jill Godmilow, a talented New York documentary filmmaker who would share the directorial credits with me on *Antonia: A Portrait of the Woman,* which would later be nominated for awards at Sundance and other festivals for many films, including *Waiting for the Moon.* Jill suggested a gifted cinematographer, Coulter Watt, with whom she had worked before on documentary films. Coulter is a painter as well as a cinematographer and had an eye for beauty that would fulfill my dreams of what this movie should look like.

I would focus on interviews with Brico, and on her conducting her own orchestra in Denver. I also wanted to feature one of her students who might replicate my own experience with Brico. We found Helen Palacus, a student much like myself, who was playing a concerto with the orchestra. We were able to film the rehearsals, we could show Brico at work with one or two of her most promising pupils and reveal her pioneer spirit and her deep love of and talent for the music she conducted. Brico would talk about her life during the interviews in her studio.

As a student of Brico's between the ages of ten and sixteen, one of the things I did was to spend occasional Saturdays with her in her downtown studio. We would lunch on sliced chicken, grapefruit, and almond-vanilla cake, listening to the weekly live opera broadcasts from the Metropolitan Opera in New York. Sitting in that room, surrounded by the statues of Beethoven, Mozart, and Jean Sibelius, I felt as if I was absorbing the inspirational elements of this extraordinary woman's life.

I later read about everything she had done, drawing on clippings from around the world and newspaper interviews. I listened to Brico speak of how her mother—who had become pregnant by an Italian sailor and been cut off by her family for her sins—could not afford to raise her; how her mother went from Amsterdam to Rotterdam to have her baby; and how that baby was whisked off to America, to San Francisco, by foster parents, who had no rights to take her. Brico was beaten by her foster mother, and finally she ran away from home to live with a friend. It was at Berkeley that she decided to become a conductor. When she found Yogananda, the Indian guru, in New York City, he helped her to go to Germany, where she attended Berlin's State Academy of Music, and there she was finally able to pursue her dream.

When she graduated, she conducted the Berlin Philharmonic, startling the critics with her power and musical charisma. After her conducting debut in 1929, a critic from one of the Berlin papers wrote that she "possesses more ability, cleverness and musicianship than certain of her male colleagues who bore us in Berlin!" Back in the United States, San Francisco and the Hollywood Bowl fought to have her conduct her debut concert, and both claimed her as their "Cinderella."

Brico was the only woman orchestral conductor in the United States for decades. She worked with major symphonies around the world, including Sibelius' orchestra in Finland, and the London Philharmonic. During World War II, she formed her own all-women's orchestra in New York, which performed weekly at Carnegie Hall.

In 1945, she went to the Aspen Summer Music Festival. She knew Albert Schweitzer was going to be there to speak about Bach and perform in a Bach concert. She introduced herself, and he invited her to come to Africa and study Bach with him. Like many before him, Schweitzer must have been amazed that Brico actually showed up, pith helmet and mosquito netting in her suitcase along with clothes for a month in the jungle. She never would have turned down an offer to study Bach with a master, even if it meant traveling halfway around the world!

This was a journey I had to make, not just to find Antonia but also to find, again, that girl who had been snatched from the arms of Rachmaninoff by the Gypsy Rover.

When we finished the film, Jill and I put our time and energy into marketing and promotion. *Antonia* opened the Women's Film Festival at the Whitney Museum in New York, winning much acclaim, and was nominated for an Academy Award in 1974. CBS featured a piece of the film as well as an in-depth interview of Brico by Mike Wallace.

The release of *Antonia: A Portrait of the Woman,* as well as its nomination for an Academy Award, sparked a second wave of interest in Brico's career. She conducted concerts all over the world, reclaiming her stature and earning accolades, able to make a comfortable living, perhaps for the first time in decades.

I was, most of all, gratified that I had helped tell the story that had fascinated me all my young life. I find her story inspiring for women all over the world who wish to follow their dreams.

*A*s we were finishing *Antonia,* I became part of a coalition organized by my friend Cora Weiss, called Women Strike for Peace. In February we traveled to France to attend the Paris peace talks between the North and South Vietnamese and the United States. There were a hundred of us, people from all over the United States, all ages, all genders, all colors. Cora arranged through the State Department to get us into the conference, which was no small feat. We flew over in a crowded, very uncomfortable chartered plane. My friend John Gilbert's father, a Unitarian minister, was on the trip; the only other person I knew on the plane was Cora. I remember two young African American men in the group who spent the flight taunting us for being white and privileged and useless. I needed that like a hole in my heart.

We went to the U.S. embassy first, where, in the cold February weather of Paris, we were given not even a cup of tea. The ambassador did not want anything to do with busybody American peaceniks. Next we went to the South Vietnamese embassy. They gave us tea but were only slightly friendlier than the Americans. Finally, discouraged and depressed, we headed for our final visit, to the North Vietnamese embassy, where they rolled out the red carpet and gave us a bust-out party. And once again, when we got home from these travels, the war that we wanted so much to see ended was still going on, and did for another three years.

But you keep working, keep taking actions, and keep hope burning.

Chapter Thirty-Five

The Last Gasp

It's four in the morning, the end of December
I'm writing you now just to see if you're better.

—LEONARD COHEN, "Famous Blue Raincoat"

THE school in Vermont that Clark attended was effective for a while. But Clark's addiction did not subside. We struggled in the dark, fumbling for help. And in 1974, when he was fourteen, I started to look for a new school, some solution for his growing problems. I sent him off to Windsor Mountain, in Lenox, Massachusetts, where we had gone for an interview and were told by the headmaster that Windsor Mountain—a prep school housed in an elegant stone mansion—worked well for young people who might have issues with substance abuse. In other words, they were aware, and they would take care. Of course, it is impossible to police an addict, no matter how glamorous your facility is, if he is not at the same time getting help to stay away from drugs. It worked for a few months.

〜

*B*Y the time *Antonia* was released in 1974, Stacy and I had been together for the better part of five years. In the last couple of years both of us had started seeing other people.

While we were doing press for *Antonia,* I started seeing Coulter, my cinematographer on *Antonia,* on and off, and spending time with Stacy as well. When the reviews of the movie appeared, I began seeing Jerry Oster, a reporter for the *Daily News.* Jerry had given the film a rave review and showed up to interview me. For a short time there were three lovers in my life. So very sixties! In the seventies!

Alcoholism was about to devour me, but it hadn't slowed down my work and productivity. After completing *Antonia,* I began my fourteenth album, *Judith.* I had convinced David Geffen to arrange for Arif Mardin of Atlantic to produce the album, luring him to Elektra when normally he would not have done a project outside of Atlantic. I had heard some of Arif's work and fallen in love with his arrangements and especially his production of a song on a Danny O'Keefe album, "Angel, Spread Your Wings." I felt Arif would do an amazing production of a song I had written in 1973 about Duke Ellington called "Song for Duke."

Arif was a treasure, a multitalented Turkish American who had been producing artists for Atlantic Records for decades. I did not realize his deep history when we started to work together. He had produced Aretha Franklin for years as well as the Bee Gees and Bette Midler.

He was a gentle, sweet, sophisticated man who had been raised in Istanbul and came to the States to attend the Berklee College of Music in Boston. He began working with Ahmet and Nesuhi Ertegun in the early days of Atlantic Records. His gentle way of conducting record sessions, his ease with all kinds of people, from musicians to managers to agents and groupies, was comforting and professional. I got to know his wife, Latife, his children, Julie and Joe, and his friends and extended Turkish family.

Arif was the producer on *Judith,* and I wanted Phil Ramone to engineer; it was an unusual request, since Phil usually produces. Ramone is another legend in the business, a robust, engaging presence, and the man who produced Billy Joel, Carly Simon, Paul Simon, Luciano Pavarotti, Madonna, and Rod Stewart, among others. One of his most famous gigs was producing Marilyn Monroe's version of "Happy Birthday" for JFK's birthday on May 19, 1962.

One of my most important choices for *Judith* was "Send in the Clowns," which I'd discovered in Stephen Sondheim's musical *A Little Night Music.* Jonathan Tunick would do the orchestration. I was also ready to record a couple of my own songs.

By now, I had begun to have serious vocal problems again. I had to warm up for an hour in order to sing, and even then it was touch and go. We got the album made, but only with a huge effort. I never would have succeeded without them. They babied me through, letting me sing in the morning, because after lunch and the wine that went with it, I could sing no more until the next day. It was humiliating, and all caused by alcohol.

There was a quartet of musicians in New York at that time who made up my regular recording band—Tony Levin, Hugh McCracken, Steve Gadd, and Eric Weissberg. Along with Arif and Phil, they carried me through this difficult recording period.

Arif added just the right touches to *Judith.* He suggested the Rolling Stones' "Salt of the Earth." The great Jimmy Webb shows up on *Judith* as well, with "The Moon Is a Harsh Mistress." Arif's wife recommended "Brother, Can you Spare a Dime?" by Jay Gorney and Yip Harburg. An Upper West Sider, Yip was always trying to convince me that I should sing "Over the Rainbow," too, which he'd written with Harold Arlen, but I didn't feel it was right for me then. Judy Garland was still very much alive in people's memories, and the image of her singing while sitting on the edge of the stage, everyone's heart in her hand, felt sacred. I did finally record it almost thirty-five years later.

We added Steve Goodman's classic, "The City of New Orleans." Steve, a kind, loving, courageous man, plays on this rendition, along with a rollicking group of friends and colleagues. He first came to notice when he walked up to Arlo Guthrie in a bar and asked if he could sing him a song. Arlo said, "Yes—if you buy me a beer, you can sing the song for as long as the beer takes to drink." They ended up sitting at the bar together while Steve sang "City of New Orleans" ten times or more, while Arlo wrote down the words and learned the melody.

But the chart-topper from *Judith* was "Send in the Clowns." Nancy Bacal, Leonard Cohen's close friend from Canada who became a very close friend of mine, had sent me the cast recording of *A Little Night Music* the year before, and this song completely took hold of me. I didn't care that two hundred other people had already recorded it. I knew I had to sing it. It is probably my most frequently played song, instantly recognizable from the sweet and sad counterpoint of the English horn in the background. I treasure the letter that Stephen Sondheim wrote me, thanking me for giving him his first top-ten single.

After learning "Send in the Clowns," I was finally able to see my way clear to "I'll Be Seeing You," one of my father's favorites from the Great American Songbook. Sammy Fain, who wrote the song with Irving Kahal, used to tell me when we ran into each other at events at the Songwriter's Hall of Fame and around New York that of all the people who had sung it, he liked my version best.

I said, "Oh, Sammy, I bet you say that to all the girls!"

By now I had grown more confident about my own songwriting. On *Judith*, I included three new compositions, each of which came out of its own place deep within me. It is not always clear what or who inspires a song, but I am very certain of what triggered the writing of "Houses." I spent three months out on Long Island in 1972. Stacy was around some of the time, and my son was with me as well. I would practice the piano dutifully every day, and then I would write in my notebooks. One day that summer I got a call from Stephen. We had remained friends, but we hadn't spoken in quite a while. He must have been a little bit lost in his own world just then, and I know what that feels like. He spent about an hour telling me what was going on in his life. I listened, laughing at the appropriate times, but I also crossed my eyes, my fingers, and my toes, knowing he couldn't see me. I tried to break in a few times to respond or say something, but he finally hung up without asking me how I was, how I felt, or even what I was doing. Later that night I had a dream in which I told him everything that had happened to me. And the next day I wrote the song.

> *You have many houses, one for every season*
> *Mountains in your windows, violets in your hands*
> *Thru your English meadows your blue-eyed horses*
>   *wander*
> *You're in Colorado for the spring*
> *When the winter finds you*
> *You fly to where it's summer*
> *Rooms that face the ocean, moonlight on your bed*
> *Mermaids swift as dolphins paint the air with*
>   *diamonds*
> *You are like a seagull, as you said*
> *Why do you fly bright feathered sometimes*
>   *in my dreams*
> *The shadows of your wings fall over my face*
> *I can feel no air, I can find no peace*
> *Brides in black ribbons, witches in white*
> *Fly in thru the windows, fly out thru the night.*

Duke Ellington and I were represented by the same agent in Europe and the United Kingdom, a wonderful man named Robert

Patterson. One day in New York in 1974 I got a call from Robert and his wife, Sybille, asking me to come to the Plaza Hotel for drinks and dinner. When I got there, they explained that Duke was terribly sick and that he was going to call in a few minutes to talk to Robert about canceling his upcoming tour in the United Kingdom. We began our dinner, and the call came. Then Robert passed the phone to me. I remember standing near the long velvet curtains by the window, looking out at the lights in Central Park twinkling through the trees. Duke's voice was weak, but he spoke to me so kindly, and asked me about my upcoming record, about my touring. How did I like working in Europe? Did I have family? Wasn't I glad I was a musician so I could lead this kind of life doing what I loved and making people happy?

The next week Duke died, never having left the hospital. I made my way in the rain to the viewing in the mortuary in Harlem, stood in line for hours, and then touched the great Duke's hand as he lay in his casket. I went to the funeral with Sybille and Robert, and sat in the front row in the Cathedral of St. John the Divine. Ella Fitzgerald sang, as did Sarah Vaughan, and the Billy Taylor Quartet played. I have always thought the Duke gave me, in our conversation, some courage to face the trials that were barreling toward me like an oncoming train.

I wrote "Song for Duke" after the funeral:

> *The people stood around the church*
> *Ten thousand people there, they say, or more*
> *Black and white and rich and poor*
> *They were there to say goodbye.*

That same week my son Clark overdosed at Windsor Mountain School in Massachusetts. We had hoped the staff and the environment might help him stay away from drugs. But once again we failed to treat his problems effectively, because no therapist understood that his problems were not emotional but the result of a genetic tendency to addiction that had been handed down to him. From the hospital in Pittsfield, he and I went down to Maryland to look into Sheppard Pratt, an institution for people with all kinds of mental illnesses. They had no substance abuse program then, and at that time I still didn't understand that my son's problems were the same as my own. I thought his drug use was somehow different from my drinking and there were no rehabs anywhere to be found.

But Clark did well at Sheppard Pratt, and we had a good series of therapy sessions together. I spent a lot of days traveling to Maryland to be with him. The day we were scheduled to meet with his father, Clark ran away. He wound up somewhere on the coast of Maryland. He called me to say that he would let me know where he was going, but he didn't want me to try to find him.

I wrote "Born to the Breed" while my heart was aching to find him.

Clark was sixteen.

"Love the one you're with," Stephen sang, and perhaps it is just that simple. My therapists certainly believed and reinforced that whenever they could: see a lot of people, don't get stuck in a rut with the same person. It all suited my personality and my lifestyle, but I burned with guilt when affairs ended, and never found myself happier afterward. I just felt alone.

When Stacy and I parted in 1974, we remained friends, and we are still bonded in blood, since my sister, Holly, was married to Stacy's brother, Jim Keach, for a number of years, and their son, Kalen, is Stacy's nephew as well as mine.

During this period, Nancy Carlin sent me "Bread and Roses," for which Mimi Fariña wrote the music, inspired by a poem written by James Oppenheim about the 1912 strike by female textile workers in Lawrence, Massachusetts.

As we go marching, marching, in the beauty of the day
A million darkened kitchens, a thousand mill lofts gray,
Are touched with all the radiance that a sudden
  sun discloses
For the people hear us singing: Bread and Roses!
  Bread and Roses!

Bread and Roses became the title of my 1976 album, also produced by the team of Arif Mardin and Phil Ramone.

The album itself pays tribute to a broad range of composers and artists, from Duke Ellington to Elton John, as well as some old English folk songs I had picked up along the way. It also contains a song, "Plegaria a un Labrador (Prayer to a Laborer)," by the great Chilean songwriter and theater director Victor Jara, often called the Bob Dylan of Chile. Jara was murdered, along with so many others, during the 1973 Chilean coup d'état. He was arrested for his leftist activities and because he was a guitarist who played songs of the people as well as antigovernment material. His ribs and hands were broken before he was shot to death in the Chile Stadium in Santiago. I went to a screening of a documentary about Jara's life at the New York Film Festival in 1976. I met his widow, Joan Jara, a dancer and activist who had worked hard to challenge the Pinochet regime. Joan later sent me a tape of the song and a note that said: "My husband loved your songs, and I know he would have wanted me to get this to you." I recorded the song last, just before the album was released in November 1976.

ONCE *Bread and Roses* was complete, I began to lose all my inspiration and motivation. My thoughts of light and laughter and inner peace seemed to dissipate and then disappear entirely. I was emotionally and spiritually dying, although I battled to keep up a respectable image of recording and touring.

David Geffen had left Elektra in 1975, turning over control of the company to Joe Smith. Joe was good for me, supported my albums, and followed through on the marketing of *Judith*, which had been made on Geffen's watch. Joe did what he could for *Bread and Roses*. When the double album *So Early in the Spring* came out in 1977, catapulting "Send in the Clowns" back into the *Billboard* top ten, Joe made sure that *Judith* got an additional promotional boost as well.

*T*HE Vietnam War ended in April 1975, and we celebrated as helicopters lifted American civilians and some Vietnamese men and women from the embassy in Saigon, stragglers hanging from the underbellies of the Hueys as they flew to the safety of ships waiting offshore. Rejoicing filled the streets. The war, and with it the anger and angst that had filled our lives for a decade and a half, was over.

*B*Y 1977, I was seeing double much of the time. I began to plan the rest of my life with Jerry Oster—or at least what might be left of my life, for by that time I was very busy dying.

"Out of Control" was one of the few songs I wrote about being over-the-moon in love, but the title could have referred to just about any aspect of my life: over the top, but going under.

I was weepy and wilting with heartbreak and despair. My field of vision had narrowed to what seemed like a slit. Clark was in and out of schools and even jails and institutions by this time. The only thing that really thrilled me was that he had come home to live with me in New York. He went to high school, finished his degree, and stayed sober. I was desperately trying to keep it together. And then Jerry left.

I was a wreck, but one of the things I had done over the years since my affair with Stephen was to keep in touch with him. From time to time we would talk, and the closure that we initially had not had took place slowly over time. It was as though the relationship was tied to my staying alive through the worst of my drinking. I could hang on to him in the storm.

I went to Miami in February 1976 and stayed with Stephen and his mother, Ti, and his sister Hannah in his beautiful house on a canal. Stephen's marriage to Véronique Sanson, the French singing star, had ended and she had moved back to France, leaving her son, Chris, with Stephen. Every night Stephen would come home from the studio, where he was recording a new album. He and David and Graham had gone their separate ways two years before, each making his own solo album after their enormous successes in the late 1960s. Stephen had a couple of very successful singles during those years, "Love the One You're With" as well as "Change Partners," very much in tune with my romantic pursuits at time.

I would wait up for my ex-beau, swimming in his pool, hanging out with Ti and Hannah. They must have thought a ghost had descended upon them, and a drunken ghost at that! I would drink all day, not ready yet to give it up, and then drive alone to the beach, where I would pass out in the sun for a couple of hours. These were very dark times for me. Ti and Hannah and Stephen were very patient and very kind, hoping, I am sure, that any minute I would pack up my bags and fly back to New York, leaving them in peace.

I could no longer go without drinking for even a few hours; in truth, I hadn't been able to do so for three years. I was totally losing my voice and, for the first time in my career, canceling concerts, sometimes several weeks' worth at a time. In 1977 I was diagnosed with a hemangioma, an abnormal buildup of blood vessels, on my left vocal cord. (In drinkers, hemangiomas often appear on the face, as bright red cheeks or nose.) If I performed one concert, I would become immediately hoarse afterward and have to cancel the rest of the shows in the run. I would then go on a course of prednisone, which is a very strong steroid; and in a few days, my vocal cord would be better and I would try again. Meanwhile, I would hole up in a local hotel with the ten or eleven people who were on tour with me—pianists, drummers, road managers, everyone on salary, of course—and we would all swim in the hotel pool and sleep and eat, and I would drink. Constantly, every hour, every day. Vodka was my drink of choice then. I was convinced it was undetectable, not knowing it was seeping out of the pores of my skin, announcing my illness to everyone around me.

Then I would try another ragged attempt at singing. Friends of my mother called her in tears to tell her that they had heard me in Portland, San Francisco, or Chicago, and that her daughter's career was over, that her voice was a tattered remnant of what had taken her to stardom. Even my scheduled appearance on *The Muppet Show* in May 1977 in London had to be rescheduled. I called Jim Henson to tell him that I was really too ill to come to London and do the show. We had known each other since the early seventies, when he asked me to appear on *Sesame Street*. I still find it hard to believe that drinking made me cancel on Kermit and Oscar and Snuffleupagus!

Jim understood. He told me to get well, and postponed my appearance until the fall, when I finally did *The Muppet Show*. I was barely able to sing, but I made it through. A few days later I was back in New York for surgery to remove the offending capillary on my vocal cord.

The doctor told me that the surgery was still new, a laser technique that had had both good and not-so-good results, but he said I really had no choice. He believed that the operation would give me perhaps a fifty-fifty chance of being able to sing again. I had no choice but to surrender and pray for the best. I couldn't imagine what would happen to me if I couldn't sing.

I drank late into the night at the hospital before the surgery, putting away more than a quart of vodka. A few friends—the few I had left—joined me. At six in the morning the next day, the nurses came in and sniffed around the hospital room, where I had a half-gallon bottle of vodka, nearly empty, in the bedside table. They said it smelled like booze. Had they known how drunk I had been the night before, they would not have operated when they did—anesthetics and alcohol are a deadly combination.

The surgery was a success, but my life, I thought by now, was a complete failure. I was nearing my bottom, and by 1978, I knew I hadn't far to go. I had had so much success in my career, and yet I had only one request—that I should be allowed to drink myself to death.

Chapter Thirty-Six

The Drinking Decades

This life . . . feels like a real fight—as if there were something really wild in the universe which we, with all our idealities and faithfulness, are needed to redeem.

—WILLIAM JAMES, "Is Life Worth Living?"

By 1978 I had been drinking for twenty-three years. For the last four years I had been drinking round the clock. I could not stop for family, for fame, or for the future. I could not stop for my son, for my voice, or for my work. I couldn't stop for God or for my soul. I had come to the end—the end of love, I was sure, and the end of the bright road that had been my life. The road was gone, the lovers were gone, the music was gone—for me, the poetry, the charm, the hope, the beauty, all seemed gone from the world. Alcoholism was bred in my bones. Drinking was my birthright, like my smile. It was in my history, in my family, and in my heart, and by the time I was twenty, it was part of my body chemistry. The smell of its deep stain seeped out through my body. I felt in my alcohol-soaked heart that it was there for good.

From the beginning, I knew I was in trouble with booze. By the time I was fifteen I had taken my first drink. Very soon, by the time I was in my late teens, the drinking was in charge, and I knew, from the compulsion I felt to have more, that the enemy—the one that had my father by the throat—was at my own neck. It was never going to let go. Even then, I knew that if it had its way, it would kill me.

I had thought about killing myself during the years that I drank. I would have hanged myself if I had had the courage. If I had owned a gun, had more pills, or lived on a higher floor, perhaps I would not be here. Like so many of my peers, I did not know what was wrong with me. I thought it was the world, the politics, the way things did not go in ways I preferred.

The darkness in my life was something most people knew nothing about. They thought of me as successful, and I appeared to be well balanced. I got to work on time, I maintained a career touring, recording, doing television. When I was interviewed, I spoke as though I had something to say, something to share. When I look into the eyes of my old self on some of the YouTube videos, I see the beast behind my pale, quiet face.

Successful? I was succeeding in spite of my illness, as my father had done for so long. Oh, I didn't have mansions or dozens of cars or jewelry, which were not my thing. But I had something much more valuable to me: a career in which I could be creative and make a living at what I loved. Many of my records had become hits, some of them around the world. I sang in some of the most famous concert halls in the world.

Nothing stopped me—not the despair, not the sickness, not the disgrace. I was utterly serious about drinking. I had many love affairs, but if the truth were known, the affair with alcohol was the one that counted.

Many of the people I had known in the music business had died of the disease of alcoholism by then, or from some other, equally merciless addiction. The road was hard, the life was hard, but if you are an alcoholic, some part of you still thinks you can beat it.

I read every self-help book I could get my hands on. Not one of them said anything about alcoholism being an illness. I spoke to my therapists about being an alcoholic, but I was always assured that if we got to the bottom of my problems, I wouldn't have to drink anymore.

At times I would have a drink during a therapy session. After fifteen years of Sullivanians, I tried new therapists. One said I would not be a candidate for AA, since it was low-class—they had those men in raincoats at the meetings. Another doctor told me she knew about AA, but for me, a one-on-one approach would probably be the best alternative. That gave me comfort, for I knew that somewhere in the course of AA I would have to stop drinking. I would do the one-on-one thing, whatever that was.

I had always worked hard at controlling my drinking; it was a matter of honor. Hell, it was a matter of making a living. I knew I was more miserable than I should have been, and all the pills I could get—those for sleeping, those for waking up, for slowing down, for losing weight—were scheduled around the times of the day when I would have to drink to keep up the level of alcohol in my body.

Where had the time gone? Where were the beautiful promises of my childhood, of my career, of my parents? It looked very much as though Sweet Judy Blue Eyes was down for the count. There had been a time when the dream was bright. My memory, strangely undamaged, told me the story, over and over again, like the recollection of some far-off place, some fabled paradise to which I yearned to return.

Chapter Thirty-Seven

Resurrection

"We are lost."
"No, it will turn out well."
"How will it?"
"I don't know. It's a mystery."

—MARC NORMAN and TOM STOPPARD,
Shakespeare in Love

IT was April 1978, and in New York the spring was lush and bright with forsythia, its branches flowing over the old stone bridges in Central Park.

I wound a silk scarf around my head, hiding as best I could behind sunglasses and wearing a long dark coat that was too warm for the weather. I took a cab across the park, past bright patches of Japanese plum trees, but I was unmoved by all that color, feeling nothing of the promise of spring. I was on my way to an appointment with yet another doctor—a last resort, I thought. If this one didn't know how to help me, I would go home to another of the long, dark, harrowing blackouts I had been having day after day, night after night.

I had called my beloved sister, Holly Ann, to come to New York to help me get through whatever it was I was going through. She brought her young son, Kalen, whose bright ten-month-old face, smiling at me over the cereal-spattered table of his high chair, was the only thing I could look at that made me want to go on living. In a few days I would turn thirty-eight.

That day I had an appointment with Dr. Stanley Gitlow, who had been suggested to me by a man I will call Joe, a well-known actor and well-loved man about town. This felt like the last stop on the line. I had known Joe by reputation—a few times a year he would be in a highly public brawl somewhere in a bar, and instead of seeing his startlingly handsome face shining out of the pages of the *New York Post* or the *Daily News*, I'd see a different Joe, a man full of rage, beaten about the eyes, fists out, clamoring for more of his opponent's blood. Or at least that was the way I viewed it, and it gave me courage, made me feel I was not alone in this struggle.

I was never photographed knocking someone over, but I felt a kind of unholy bond with Joe. He was doing what I wished I could do, acting out on impulses I understood. He was showing them, getting even, and, like me, probably not even remembering where he had been until he was told the next day. My own rampages didn't make it into the gossip pages, even when they were very public, like the time I slugged a New York City police officer at Madison Square Garden. The cop hadn't wanted to let me back into the VIP seats at a 1977 Dylan concert, and I took offense.

I had called Joe in Los Angeles, where he was working on a movie. On his dime, he called me back, and we talked for about forty minutes. I was half or more in the bag, moving toward my afternoon blackout, and I wrote down everything he said in a big drunken scrawl. He told me where to go and what to do and whom to call. He said there were answers, and that they involved people who were doing what I needed to do—not drink. He said I must see Stanley Gitlow, and that Stanley would know what to do.

I heard the truth in Joe's voice. He told me how sick he had been, and how desperate. He talked about the miracle, as he described it, that had come into his life.

The flowers in the boxes in front of Stanley Gitlow's office on Fifth Avenue, tulips in deep purple and red, were nodding. I walked into his office, where he sat behind his desk, a handsome and dapper-looking man in his fifties. The thought occurred to me that I could have been dating him. I nearly turned around and walked out. He looked too good to be true in his white coat, a stethoscope hanging around his neck. He smiled at me, a bright, wonderfully winsome smile.

His smile was the only hopeful thing in the room, as I began to tell him what I was feeling, what I thought was my problem. I discussed the years of therapy and the years of drinking. I told him who I thought I was—an artist, a singer, a mother, a lover. By the time I told him my lover had left me, I was sobbing, lost in my melodrama. I said I didn't know what was wrong with me.

I said I knew I was dying, some days quickly, sometimes slowly. I said I plowed miserably from day to day, pulling myself from one blackout, one despairing morning, to the next. I told Stanley that despite all the success, I felt my life might as well be over. I contemplated suicide every day, I said, and if I were capable of pulling a trigger, I would have.

"Stop!" he said, interrupting my soap opera. He was smiling, as though I had just told him an amusing anecdote instead of the beginning of the end of my life. "Don't say another word. I know what is wrong with you, and I know what you can do about it!" He kept smiling.

I froze. No one had ever told me he knew what was wrong with me and that there was something I could do about it. Of all the doctors and shrinks I had seen in the twenty-three years since I had started drinking, not one had ever said these words to me.

"You have an illness," Gitlow said, "and it is going to kill you.

But there is a solution." No one had ever spoken to me about an "illness."

"Of course," Gitlow continued, "you can keep drinking, wait a couple of years, and check yourself into an institution with your wet brain and throw away the key." I didn't say a thing. This particular option was already on my to-do list, anyway.

"Or," Gitlow went on—and here his kind eyes sparkled and he leaned closer to me and looked me in the eyes—"since you seem to be a bright girl under all those tears, you could check yourself into rehab and start to get your life back."

The strange thing is that I absolutely knew I was hearing the truth. For some reason, after all the high-priced doctors who prescribed pills, or who told me we would work on the psychological problems and then the drinking would solve itself; after all the god-awful hangovers and the promises to myself not to let my life deteriorate into an endless stream of blackouts; after finally deciding I was never going to stop drinking of my own free will, the window of hope opened in that office. I was going to get a chance to have the life I had been missing out on for years.

Early on the morning of April 19 I flew to Reading, Pennsylvania. My assistant, Janet Matorin, and my accountant, Saul Schneider, were with me on the plane, two of the last people who were still able to deal with me. I did not know where Clark was. We had not talked for a few days, and he was on his own dark, troubled road, doing drugs, dealing heroin, sleeping with a gun under his pillow. He might have weighed 130 pounds, ten pounds less than what I weighed. The money I was giving him for school had been spent on drugs. He was nineteen. I was thirty-eight.

When we landed in Reading, a tall young man who, to my surprise, recognized me immediately met us. I said I had to use the restroom and hurried off to drink the large jelly jar full of vodka that I had stuffed into my huge shoulder bag before I left my apartment that morning. I was already quite drunk, and the ten ounces of vodka put me in a happy, giddy, joyful mood that would last all of about ten minutes while they drove me up to Chit Chat Rehabilitation Center for Alcoholics (now called the Caron Foundation).

The young man let me off with my luggage at the door of a pretty white house at the top of a hill. A drunk farm—this was where I had landed. Me, the hope of my family, the hippie gone silver and platinum, was bloated and sweating, even in the cool air of the Pennsylvania morning. I could not walk, talk, think, or function without a quart of vodka in my system. And there I was in the springtime of my life, with my suitcase full of books, my typewriter, my up and down pills for getting me through the day.

In the pale green trees the birds were singing and the sun was bright on the flowers around the farmhouse. Residents smiled at me from the white-painted rocking chairs on the porch and in the reception rooms. When I reached my room in the detox section the kind nurse told me she would take the vitamins, the sleeping pills, the books, the typewriter, the empty jelly jar. She showed me where I might shower, and where I would sleep. And then she said, softly, tenderly, "Now, why don't you let us drive?"

On April 19, 1978, I took my last drink, God willing. In the Valium-aided withdrawal that followed, I felt I could hear tulips pushing through the dark earth.

For the first few nights I woke up in the night to the screaming, open mouths of my demons, howling through the quiet hills around me. The faces of my friends, my son, my sister and brothers hung over me, shining like beacons during the few hours I slept. Between daily meditation meetings we listened to Father Martin talk about the disease of alcoholism in his film *Chalk Talk* as we detoxed, sweated, hurt. I ached as I listened to Joni Mitchell sing, over and over again, the songs from *Don Juan's Reckless Daughter*. Most days I sobbed my eyes out, seeing flowers and hearing music as though for the first time, weeping over my own sad, broken drinking story. But the sounds that were most real came from the stories of other alcoholics.

From the time I was two or three, I yearned to know how everyone else did it—how they smiled when they wanted to cry, how they went on when they wanted to stop and fall to their knees and say, "I give up." In my childhood, politics and debate and music were as much a part of our upbringing as booze. (We were privately convinced that people who did not drink must be illiterate!) But now, in Pennsylvania, I listened, and I began to learn. And though the details were often different, the feelings and the sorrow were the same.

One morning a few days after my arrival at the drunk farm in the hills of Pennsylvania, I walked past the mirror and for the first time in years looked into my own eyes without flinching.

Chapter Thirty-Eight

Miracles and Menaces

Be ahead of all parting, as though it already were
behind you, like the winter that has just gone by.
For among these winters there is one so endlessly winter
that only by wintering through it will your heart survive.

—Rainer Maria Rilke (translated by
Stephen Mitchell), *The Sonnets to Orpheus*

My life began again when I got sober, as though I had been re-born, as though all the years before had been a warm-up for the real thing. I could think, act, be present, and feel joy as well as pain. The deep fear and all the bitter resentments began to lift, and as the big change sank in, a myriad of other remarkable results began to follow. The constancy of habit—training, showing up, doing my work in spite of what might have been going on in my life—began to bring me the kind of joy and satisfaction that had always eluded me on the deepest levels.

The hemangioma surgery I'd had earlier had been successful, a near miracle. A tiny white scar was all that was left of the trouble, though it took me a couple of years to get back the full strength of my voice.

Three days before I had my last drink, in April 1978, I had been asked to go on a blind date with a man recommended to me by a friend of mine. Jeanne was dating his business partner and thought he was so wonderful she had to introduce me. I told her I was not in the mood, having been jilted by Jerry Oster, but she insisted, and I agreed to meet him at a fund-raiser, at Patrick O'Neal's restaurant, the Ginger Man (which he had renamed the Ginger Person for that evening's gathering in support of the Equal Rights Amendment).

I walked in, trying to look sober. This was going to be my final party before going off to the drunk farm to get clean. I was going to try to get in as much drinking as was humanly possible before I landed at Chit Chat.

A pair of blue eyes looked across at me in the restaurant. Louis Nelson greeted me and smiled. He was handsome, calm, and smart, with an open spirit. Not a singer, not an actor. I was drunk, but I was dazzled.

I knew only a little about Louis. He was an established and successful designer, having put the color in Head skis—the rainbow colors that took over from all the black in the 1960s. Because the color had drained out of my life, this seemed like a sign to me.

Louis pulled my chair out for me. I was shocked. I thought, "What does he want?"

Stephen Sondheim was there, as were Gloria Steinem and Patrick O'Neal. The night was festive. We were all hopeful that a women's rights bill might be passed in Congress.

At the end of the evening Louis hailed a cab for me, then got in after me. I was pleased and surprised. Louis took me home, walked me to my door, and kissed me on the cheek.

Then he left.

I called him the next day, and he called me, and then I called him again. I wanted to tell him where I was headed, but instead I hemmed and hawed. I was going away, I said. I was sick, I said, and I was right.

I called him again the day before I left for Chit Chat. I thought about him on the flight to Pennsylvania, and when I came home, Louis called me. In July we went out to dinner.

On the inside of the wedding rings we wear is the date we met, April 16, 1978, the day the angels sent Louis. We have seldom been apart since our first real date, when we went to Orsini's for dinner, except every now and then when he's unable to join me on a concert tour. We talked all night over our chicken and mush-rooms while waiters hovered, hoping we would leave. He saw me home and again left me at the door, promising to return, which he did.

Into my life came the things I have always been looking for. Louis and I are friends, lovers, confidants. We read and talk; we go to the movies. We love all our cats, including the most recent, Rachmaninoff, Coco Chanel, and Tom Wolfe. And we laugh a lot. He is a loving, creative, talented man. He knows how to listen and has helped me in every way with my career and music.

When Louis and I had been together for eighteen years, we were married at the Cathedral of St. John the Divine in a wedding that celebrated our joys with five hundred of our friends and fam-ily. It was a sober wedding—not a drop of booze was served—and everyone seemed to have a wonderful time! It was a celebration of our life together, our devotion to each other, and the fact that since I met Louis, I have never looked back, never deceived him, never been unfaithful.

Louis was the one I had been looking for all along.

CLARK was nineteen and in the middle of a long stretch of drug use when I got sober. He was kicked out of Sarah Lawrence, then was accepted by Columbia, where he took Chinese calligraphy and semiotics. For five more years he fought the madness of his addiction, but in 1984, Clark finally surrendered and flew to Minnesota to go to Hazelden, the recovery center for addicts and alcoholics. His life changed at once, it seemed, and he began to live a happy, useful life, free of drugs and alcohol. He started to thrive, finding love. He and his wife, Alyson, had a beautiful baby daughter, Hollis, who is the apple of my eye. She is so like her father in every way—she looks like him, laughs as he laughed, walks and talks like him, a subtle reminder in every movement that she is her father's child.

But in 1992, the bottom fell out of Clark's recovery. On January 15 Alyson found him in his Subaru station wagon, dead from asphyxiation. He had been drinking, and he made a tape of his last words.

I feel the agony of that loss every day of my life. I adored my son. At times I wanted to kill anyone who may have been in any way responsible for the pain he was in. But I had to let go of blame and anger, for if I held on to it, it would destroy me.

When he got sober in 1984, Clark had begun to write me letters. The only letters I'd previously received from him were scrawls from camp, the kind moms often get:

> Dear Mom,
>   I am having a good time—I caught a fish, here
> is a picture of the fish.
>   Love, Clark

It is always difficult to describe to someone who did not know him the beauty that was in Clark. People who spent time with him always felt it. There was a joy and tenderness in this attractive, tall, redheaded boy, a quality of caring for others. He was a good friend with a great heart and a smile and the ability to tear at your emotions with his laughter and tears.

He wrote me when I was seven years sober and he was celebrating fourteen months of sobriety.

St. Paul, Minnesota
Rainy Tuesday
April 23, 1985
Dear Mom,

Thank you for your wonderful and thoughtful letter. I mean thoughtful in the sense that it's nice that you found time to write and in the sense that there are some things to think about in there.

Congratulations on your birthday. I can remember when you first got sober and boy I couldn't believe you really did it! Then when you started trying to help me, I thought you were crazy! But you were actually being restored to sanity. You've changed so much. You've become a directed person in a way that you never were. I always had the feeling before you got sober that you couldn't manage your life. (I'm not trying to be funny!) You were so vague and lacking in a true center, running around frantically, worried and unhappy. Now you have a calm centeredness and a directedness that is truly beautiful. Your strength and faith, found in (spirit), were something I couldn't discount. They were such tangible facts that I couldn't dismiss your sobriety as some kind of unhealthy fanaticism. I saw proof that sobriety works and I believe, as I've told you before, that a seed was planted in my heart—a belief in the possibility of joyful, rewarding sobriety.

I know that my relapses must have caused you

*a lot of pain. I know I've made an effort with this
amend. But I think that I somehow know better
what kind of grief we feel to see someone return to
active addiction now that I've seen a few of those
and one suicide.*

*And Mom, it must be really awful when it's
close family.*

*Life is good. I love you and I thank you for
being a swell mom.*

Love, Clark

I wept when I found this letter again many years after he had
sent it, many years after his death—a letter from the grave. Like the
touch of his hand, like the dreams I have of him that have come in
startling numbers over the years since, they reassure me that I am
not separated from him in any but a physical manner. He is here
in his daughter's beautiful bright eyes, in how his name comes up
often in the world, in the memory of his sweet soul. I will never be
apart from him.

When Clark died, I dug myself out of the pit of despair again,
Louis by my side all the way. Each day I chose not to drink. And I
chose not to take my own life.

I make these choices anew every day, one day at a time, and
on many days it remains the only thing I do that feels right. I find
great comfort in talking to other suicide survivors—great peace, in
fact, in telling them that there is a gift in every loss and that they
can survive. I tell them my story, and tell them what I do, and hope
that it helps. That way I can keep Clark's legacy alive, and keep my
own heart busy so that it will not break, though the breaking heart
can be a healing heart as well.

When my son died, I began to understand what heartbreak
really was. It turned out I hadn't had a clue.

In Judaism, it is taught that there are three stages of grief to be endured. First there is weeping, for we all must weep for what we have lost. Second comes silence, for in the silence we understand solace, beauty, and comfort from something greater than ourselves. Third comes singing, for in singing we pour out our hearts and regain our voice.

Chapter Thirty-Nine

The End of the Storm

When the snow flies
And the night falls
There's a light in the window,
And a place called home
At the end of the storm.

—JUDY COLLINS, "The Blizzard"

I HAD four more albums left on my Elektra contract when I recorded *Hard Times for Lovers*. It was the first album I made as a sober woman, and it would be an amazing experience.

Charles Koppleman and Gary Klein, who had just finished working on Dolly Parton's album *Here You Come Again,* were my producers. Charles is a man who loves great songs, and we had chosen a gathering of beauties, from Hugh Prestwood's title track to Glenn Frey and Don Henley's ballad "Desperado," to the Rodgers and Hart classic "Where or When." Elton John's "Sweethearts on Parade" added an ironic and perfect look at stardom and what it is and is not. I had learned the lesson well and loved this beautiful song of Elton's, who was, though I did not know it, in his own struggle with addiction and success.

Louis and I and my band all headed to L.A. to record, where Charles had set us up in a huge suite at the Beverly Hills Hotel. My rooms were filled with flowers. Being in L.A. again terrified me, and in the studio I felt tentative, frightened that the presurgery hoarseness and laryngitis from the hemangioma would return, even though my surgeon had assured me that everything was fine.

I brought Max Margulis out to California to stay with me for a few days, to listen and help. I knew I did not have the old power and intensity back. It was enough, however, to know I was singing well. I felt tremendous relief.

I fought, as usual, for the right sound on my voice, agonizing over the mixes with Armin Steiner, our engineer and, back in New York, remixing with another engineer to get what I wanted out of the recordings. Every day I was getting stronger, and by the end of November I was finally ready to tour.

My first live concert after we completed *Hard Times for Lovers* was in a huge auditorium in Hartford. There were seventeen people on that tour, among them some of the best musicians in the business: Tony Levin on bass, Ken Bichel on keyboards, Hugh McCracken on guitar, Warren Odes on drums, and a trio of backup singers I called the "Fallen Angels," darling young men who now are either sober or dead. I strode out onto the stage, into the lights, and it all came together.

I have been trained to perform, to do live shows. Perhaps I needed the big sound of a theater with a fantastic audio system, but whatever it was, it was all there. The lingering fear was gone, the voice was everything it had not been and could be now—richer, bigger, more intense, and healthy.

The crowd roared as I finished the set, and Gary Klein, my line producer on *Hard Times,* who had suffered through the sessions in California and gotten the best he could from my singing, ran in from the wings. He threw his arms around me.

"My God, where did that voice come from?" he said, nearly in tears. "Finally, the Judy Collins I knew and loved is back!" I blushed, and he went on, "Why didn't you sing like that on the record?"

I had to tell him that it had not been possible then, but time was healing me, and the live concert had shown me where I could go. The feeling was amazing, as it had been years before the hemangioma had begun. Now I could come home to the voice I had prayed was still there. I was finally back where I belonged.

PART of the pulse of a musical career is the periodic firing up of the artistic urges, which of course interact with the business demands. The clock ticks on through the years, pointing the way to a new adventure in learning new songs, writing them, putting thoughts and energies into focus. It is something that drives me, as it does any artist, to keep trying to do the best work I can.

Between 1979 and 1983 I made two more albums, *Times of Our Lives* and *Running for My Life*. Sober, I had begun to write songs again, and on those albums there were many more of my own compositions. To be writing songs again was heavenly.

But I struggled with the next album, *Home Again,* which featured Dave Grusin as producer. Dave had Academy Award nominations for the scores of *Heaven Can Wait, Tootsie,* and *The Champ,* among others, and was a good friend as well as a colleague. In the mixes, in which I was watching over every song, I wanted, as usual, to make all the vocals crystal clear and not to have them drowned out by the instrumentation.

The record included "Shoot First," which I co-wrote with Dave, and another of my songs, "Dream On," as well as the title track, "Home Again," by Michael Masser. I sang "Home Again" with T. G. Sheppard, a fine country singer from Nashville.

By 1984 Elektra had changed presidents again, and the new man in charge, Bob Krasnow, wanted a "new look" for Elektra, which meant getting rid of the old guard—including my own particular genre of artists. In the preceding twenty-four years, my albums had achieved gold and platinum status in the industry (meaning many had sold over a million copies), I had had dozens of *Billboard*-charting songs, and I had been nominated for a half dozen Grammys, receiving Song of the Year Grammys for "Send in the Clowns" and "Both Sides Now."

Even all that success was not enough, and after *Home Again* was released, Elektra and Bob Krasnow did not renew my contract. For the first time in twenty-four years, I was without a record label.

I was devastated, and that led me to start my own label, Wildflower Records. In setting it up, I tried to emulate my old mentor, Jac Holzman, and I often think, "How would Jac do this?"

OVER the past four decades, Stephen and I, after those difficult years when we were in love and then parted, have somehow remained friends, and we continue to see each other from time to time.

In 2007, someone found that old quarter-inch tape Stephen had made in the studio the night in 1968 after we recorded "Who Knows Where the Time Goes," and sent it to Graham Nash. Graham returned it to Stephen, who arranged for it to be released on Rhino Records as *Just Roll Tape*. Many of the songs about the fractured fairy tale that was our musical and personal relationship were on that tape, sung in his sweet, steely voice, accompanied by his poignant guitar playing. Stephen had recorded them in the dark in that white villa of a studio at Elektra, where not even John Haeny was a witness.

Just Roll Tape contains the original acoustic versions of some of the most beautiful songs ever written, including, of course, "Suite: Judy Blue Eyes." There's also a song on it I had never heard before, called simply "Judy." My eyes filled with tears as I listened for the first time. The songs on this CD are rare jewels, a revelation. How strange that the world—and I—would have to wait decades to hear these raw, early versions of songs that Stephen had written, many for me. I wonder, would it have made a difference to our love affair if I had heard this recording of them then? Perhaps. They were amazing, and Stephen was amazing. But he had his secrets, too; this recording was one of them.

I called him after I listened to the songs.

"It's like getting a valentine forty years later," I said. I could hear his smile over the phone. I knew it was time to find out more about this man who had such an important place in my psyche.

In an interview after *Just Roll Tape* was released, Stephen said: "There are three things men can do with women: love them, suffer for them, or turn them into literature. I've had my share of success and failure at all three." Of course, our original romance was too hot to handle, too much for me. He was too young, and I was even younger in a way, shackled in many ways by my dependence on the Sullivanians, and of course by my drinking.

On my next trip to California I had dinner with Stephen and his wife, Kristen, and my granddaughter, Hollis, who was then twenty-one. Stephen has seven children and he and Kristen have been married for fourteen years. One of his sons, Henry, was then thirteen years old. During dinner, Stephen and Kristen told us that Henry had begun to do some sculpting in clay. They thought it was odd, for Henry's talent for sculpture seemed to have come out of the blue.

I reminded Stephen of the head he had sculpted all those years ago and told him I still had it. He had totally forgotten. When I went home to New York the next day, I wrapped the delicate clay sculpture in bubble wrap and sent it off to him. I had a hard time parting with it, but I am glad I gave it back to the man who fashioned it, so his son can see how wonderful it is and know his father's talent flows in his blood.

In October 2009, Stephen and I recorded a song together for my 2010 album *Paradise*. Stephen was in town for a silver anniversary of the Rock and Roll Hall of Fame, and we were working in my home studio on the Upper West Side, singing Tom Paxton's "Last Thing on My Mind." He wore a two-toned blue shirt, telling me, "This dark blue is for my eyes, and this light blue is for yours."

I was wearing tight black jeans and a cashmere sweater. My feet were bare, and Stephen kept looking quizzically at them while we rehearsed the song.

"I remember those bunions," he finally said between takes, nodding down at my feet. All this was happening while Louis, my wonderful, loving husband, took pictures of the two of us.

"You used to warn me I was going to get bunions on my feet if I kept wearing those tight cowboy boots. So I had the bunions taken off," he said. He looked at my feet again. "I see you haven't done a thing with yours!"

"How romantic!" Louis said, and we all laughed.

The thunder is loud and the lightning flashes as I make my way home from my concert in upstate New York. The rain is still falling, but I know it will take more than thunder and lightning to keep me from finishing with a flourish. The inner wars, and the outer ones, go on while I pray and struggle; sometimes in the middle of a dark night of the soul I wonder how they became my wars to fight. And then I hear a voice that says, "Why *not* me?"

Louis and I live a peaceful, loving, sometimes quiet life amidst the success and drama of our careers. We love spending time together; we laugh together, and when trouble comes, we weep together. Our romance is better than ever after thirty-three years. Louis' presence in my life is a miracle and a gift after my long, dark descent into madness and alcoholism. I feel incredibly blessed.

Throughout my life there have been kind strangers and flashes of good fortune. I've been given the beauty of dawn and dusk in hundreds of cities around the world. I think of the great songs that have carried me along, songs I have sung with you, and for you, all over the world—songs that have carried all of us in rough seas as well as tranquil times, songs that have healed our hearts and kept us going.

After all these years, I still believe that music can change the world, and as long as there is music, the dreams will never die.

Acknowledgments

I am indebted to John Glusman, my brilliant editor at Crown Archetype, who has been inspiring, patient, and wonderfully insightful. He has brought *Sweet Judy Blue Eyes* to fruition, talking me through the most difficult places, seeing around corners that I couldn't see, and finding a way to keep the goal in sight; he has waved his incredible magic editing wand over the text, getting the arc of the story just right, bringing it all back to the music, where it belongs. Thank you, John, for all the care and time you have put into bringing *Sweet Judy Blue Eyes* home, and for your love of the songs and the people in the book. You have made all the difference.

I am very grateful to Shaye Areheart, who saw what this book could be and had faith in the story I wanted to tell. You have been a part of *Sweet Judy Blue Eyes* from the first, and I thank you.

Thanks to my agent, Susan Raihofer, who has been enthusiastic all along about *Sweet Judy Blue Eyes,* even when I wavered. Your belief helped me take the book in the direction it had to go, and it gave me courage all the way along, with your enthusiasm and your fine editing of the original material, and your ability to laugh! That laughter did a lot to ease the occasional frustrations that are bound to arise when you are working on a project for many years!

David Sobel was upbeat, cheerful, and professional during many months over many long distances as I toured in the United States and overseas and we worked together on the first drafts of *Sweet Judy Blue Eyes*. Thank you for introducing me to digital editing; I will never go any other way!

Thanks to Tina Constable, the publisher of Crown Archetype. You rock in the publishing world, doing it the old-fashioned way, with care and attention and commitment. Thank you!

Thanks to Domenica Alioto for all your help with the photos as well as all the important details that have gone into bringing this book to publication.

Thanks to Mary Choteborsky, for all your help.

Thanks to Barbara Sturman for the lovely inner book design, and for finding me the most elegant of dingbats!

In the years I have spent writing this memoir, I have reached out to many people I had not seen or spoken to for years, as well as many friends with whom I have been in close touch over the decades. Friendships have been renewed and refreshed and, in some cases, brought to a new level of intimacy.

My thanks to Fred Weintraub for your humor and stories about the many people we both knew in the old days, some who are gone and some who are still here. And, as we found each other again, after forty-five years, thanks for welcoming Louis and me into your home and letting us get to know you and your wonderful wife, Jackie. I treasure the renewal of an old and trusted companion on this social and musical journey.

Special thanks to Loretta Barrett, for always being there.

Jac Holzman has been so much a part of my life for fifty years, and I thank him for his constancy and for providing a model of professional and personal integrity that has made all the difference in my recording life as well as in my understanding of friendship. You were amazing, and still are.

Thanks to my family—to my mother, Marjorie, and father, Chuck; to my son, Clark: gone but never forgotten. And to my sister, Holly Ann; my brothers Denver John, David, and Michael; as well as my granddaughter, Hollis.

Thanks to my friends, who love and support me in the dark as well as the bright places on the journey.

My gratitude and thanks to Katherine De Paul, who has run my business, making it all look easy, for nearly seventeen years now. Your support and professionalism is a guide and an assurance that all will be done with care and attention to detail. You amaze me every day with your ability to wear many hats and be exceptionally effective in each and every one. I salute you as the "major doma" who keeps all the wheels oiled in this career I have always called a circus. You are amazing

Additional thanks to Lorna Owen, Alan Silverman, Arif Mardin, Russ Walden, George Williamson, John Haeny, Susan Cheever, Scott Bercu, Peter Shukat, Jonas Herbsman, Lisa Napfel, Ken Waissman, Emily Goldstein, Gloria Grossman, John Smith, Erica Jong, Julia Cameron, Emma Lively, Murial Lloyd, Ron Gallen, Maria, Robert Hall and the Hall Family, Jane Cecil, Barbara Quinn, Doris Dallow, Penny Schwartz, Suzanne Seeley, Molly Jong Fast, Pia Lindstrom, David Braun, Eugene Kokot, Scott Morris, Kenny Di Camilla, Charlie Rothschild, Jerry Mundis, Peter Yarrow, Charles Nurnberg, Jeremy Nurnberg, Charles Koppleman, Gary Klein, Josh Rifkin, Danny Fields, Rachmaninoff, Coco Chanel, and Tom Wolfe.

And thanks to my audiences over all of these more than fifty years. You have bought my records and CDs, come to my shows, written letters to me, and lifted me from the sometimes grueling effects of travel into the warmth of your appreciation. You give me wings.

Always, I thank my beloved husband and partner of thirty-three years, Louis Nelson. You are my special angel, sent by the spirits that guide me. I am grateful for all the years we have had together, and for your understanding and humor, your generosity in sharing me with the public, and your letting the past be a part of our present, at least some of the time.

I love you.

Discography

1. A Maid of Constant Sorrow

Elektra, November 1961. Produced by Jac Holzman.
1. Maid of Constant Sorrow. 2. The Prickilie Bush. 3. Wild
Mountain Thyme. 4. Tim Evans. 5. Sailor's Life. 6. Bold Fenian
Men. 7. Wars of Germany. 8. O Daddy Be Gay. 9. I Know
Where I'm Going. 10. John Riley. 11. Pretty Saro. 12. The
Rising of the Moon.

2. Golden Apples of the Sun

Elektra, July 1962. Produced by Jac Holzman.
1. Golden Apples of the Sun. 2. Bonnie Ship the *Diamond*.
3. Little Brown Dog. 4. Twelve Gates to the City. 5. Christ
Child Lullaby. 6. Great Selchie of Shule Skerry. 7. Tell Me Who
I'll Marry. 8. Fannerio. 9. Crow on the Cradle. 10. Lark in the
Morning. 11. Sing Hallelujah. 12. Shule Aroon.

3. Judy Collins 3

Elektra, 1963. Produced by Mark Abramson and Jac Holzman.
1. Anathea. 2. Bullgine Run. 3. Farewell. 4. Hey, Nelly Nelly.
5. Ten O'Clock and All Is Well. 6. The Dove. 7. Masters of War.
8. In the Hills of Shiloh. 9. The Bells of Rhymney. 10. Deportee.
11. Settle Down. 12. Come Away Melinda. 13. Turn! Turn!
Turn! (To Everything There Is a Season).

4. The Judy Collins Concert

Elektra, July 1964. Produced by Mark Abramson.
1. Winter Sky. 2. The Last Thing on My Mind. 3. Tear Down
the Walls. 4. Bonnie Boy Is Young. 5. Me and My Uncle. 6. Wild
Rippling Water. 7. The Lonesome Death of Hattie Carroll.

8. My Ramblin' Boy. 9. Red-Winged Blackbird. 10. Coal
Tattoo. 11. Cruel Mother. 12. Bottle of Wine. 13. Medgar Evers
Lullaby. 14. Hey, Nelly Nelly.

5. *Judy Collins Fifth Album*

Elektra, 1965. Produced by Jac Holzman.
1. Pack Up Your Sorrows. 2. The Coming of the Roads.
3. So Early, Early in the Spring. 4. Tomorrow Is a Long
Time. 5. Daddy You've Been on My Mind. 6. Thirsty Boots.
7. Mr. Tambourine Man. 8. Lord Gregory. 9. In the Heat
of the Summer. 10. Early Morning Rain. 11. Carry It On.
12. It Isn't Nice.

6. *In My Life*

Elektra, 1966. Produced by Mark Abramson.
1. Tom Thumb's Blues. 2. Hard Lovin' Loser. 3. Pirate Jenny.
4. Suzanne. 5. La Colombe. 6. Marat/Sade. 7. I Think It's Going
to Rain Today. 8. Sunny Goodge Street. 9. Liverpool Lullaby.
10. Dress Rehearsal Rag. 11. In My Life.

7. *Wildflowers*

Elektra, 1967. Produced by Mark Abramson.
1. Michael from Mountains. 2. Since You Asked. 3. Sisters of
Mercy. 4. Priests. 5. A Ballata of Francesco Landini: Lasso!
di Donna. 6. Both Sides Now. 7. La Chanson des Vieux Amants.
8. Sky Fell. 9. Albatross. 10. Hey, That's No Way to Say
Goodbye.

8. *Who Knows Where the Time Goes*

Elektra, 1968. Produced by David Anderle.
1. Hello, Hooray. 2. Story of Isaac. 3. My Father. 4. Someday
Soon. 5. Who Knows Where the Time Goes. 6. Poor Immigrant.
7. First Boy I Loved. 8. Bird on the Wire. 9. Pretty Polly.

9. *Recollections*

Elektra, 1969. Produced by Mark Abramson.
1. Pack Up Your Sorrows. 2. Tomorrow Is a Long Time. 3. Early Morning Rain. 4. Anathea. 5. Turn! Turn! Turn! (To Everything There Is a Season). 6. Daddy You've Been on My Mind. 7. Mr. Tambourine Man. 8. Winter Sky. 9. The Last Thing on My Mind. 10. The Bells of Rhymney. 11. Farewell (Fare Thee Well).

10. *Whales and Nightingales*

Elektra, 1970. Produced by Mark Abramson.
1. Song for David. 2. Sons Of. 3. The Patriot Game. 4. Prothalamium. 5. Oh, Had I a Golden Thread. 6. Gene's Song. 7. Farewell to Tarwathie. 8. Time Passes Slowly. 9. Marieke. 10. Nightingale I. 11. Nightingale II. 12. Simple Gifts. 13. Amazing Grace.

11. *Living*

Elektra, 1971. Produced by Mark Abramson.
1. Joan of Arc. 2. Four Strong Winds. 3. Vietnam Love Song. 4. Innisfree. 5. Song for Judith (Open the Door). 6. All Things Are Quite Silent. 7. Easy Times. 8. Chelsea Morning. 9. Blue Raincoat. 10. Just Like Tom Thumb's Blues.

12. *Colors of the Day*

Elektra, 1972. All songs produced by Mark Abramson, except "Someday Soon," "Sons Of," "Who Knows Where the Time Goes," and "My Father," produced by David Anderle.
1. Someday Soon. 2. Since You Asked. 3. Both Sides Now. 4. Sons Of. 5. Suzanne. 6. Farewell to Tarwathie. 7. Who Knows Where the Times Goes. 8. Sunny Goodge Street. 9. My Father. 10. Albatross. 11. In My Life. 12. Amazing Grace.

13. *True Stories and Other Dreams*

Elektra, 1973. Produced by Mark Abramson and Judy Collins.
1. Cook with Honey. 2. So Begins the Task. 3. Fisherman's Song. 4. The Dealer (Down and Losin'). 5. Secret Gardens. 6. Holly Ann. 7. The Hostage. 8. Song for Martin. 9. Che.

14. *Judith*

Elektra, 1975. Produced by Arif Mardin.
1. The Moon Is a Harsh Mistress. 2. Angel, Spread Your Wings.
3. Houses. 4. The Lovin' of the Game. 5. Song for Duke. 6. Send
in the Clowns. 7. Salt of the Earth. 8. Brother, Can You Spare a
Dime? 9. City of New Orleans. 10. I'll Be Seeing You. 11. Pirate
Ships. 12. Born to the Breed.

15. *Bread and Roses*

Collector's Choice, 1976. Produced by Arif Mardin.
1. Bread and Roses. 2. Everything Must Change. 3. Special
Delivery. 4. Out of Control. 5. Plegaria a un Labrador (Prayer
to a Laborer). 6. Come Down in Time. 7. Spanish Is the Loving
Tongue. 8. I Didn't Know About You. 9. Take This Longing.
10. Love Hurts. 11. Marjorie. 12. King David.

16. *So Early in the Spring*

Elektra, 1977. Produced by Mark Abramson, Judy Collins, David
Anderle, Arif Mardin, Jac Holzman, and Ann Purtill.
1. Pretty Polly. 2. So Early, Early in the Spring. 3. Pretty Saro.
4. Golden Apples of the Sun. 5. Bonnie Ship the *Diamond*.
6. Farewell to Tarwathie. 7. The Hostage. 8. La Colombe.
9. Coal Tattoo. 10. Carry It On. 11. Bread and Roses. 12. Marat/
Sade. 13. Special Delivery. 14. The Lovin' of the Game. 15. Both
Sides Now. 16. Marieke. 17. Send in the Clowns. 18. Bird on the
Wire. 19. Since You've Asked. 20. Born to the Breed. 21. My
Father. 22. Holly Ann. 23. Houses. 24. Secret Gardens.

17. *Hard Times for Lovers*

Elektra, 1979. Produced by Gary Klein.
1. Hard Times for Lovers. 2. Marie. 3. Happy End. 4. Desperado.
5. I Remember Sky. 6. Starmaker. 7. Dorothy. 8. I'll Never Say
Goodbye (theme from the movie *The Promise*). 9. Through the
Eyes of Love (theme from the movie *Ice Castles*). 10. Where or
When.

18. Running for My Life

Elektra, 1980. Produced by Judy Collins.
1. Running for My Life. 2. Bright Morning Star. 3. Green Finch and Linnet Bird. 4. Marieke. 5. Pretty Women. 6. Almost Free. 7. I Could Really Show You Around. 8. I've Done Enough Dyin' Today. 9. Anyone Would Love You. 10. The Rainbow Connection. 11. This Is the Day. 12. Wedding Song.

19. Times of Our Lives

Elektra, 1982. All songs produced by Lewis Hahn and Judy Collins, except "Great Expectations" and "It's Gonna Be One of Those Nights," which were produced by Lewis Hahn, Arif Mardin, and Judy Collins.
1. Great Expectations. 2. The Rest of Your Life. 3. Grandaddy. 4. It's Gonna Be One of Those Nights. 5. Memory. 6. Sun Son. 7. Mama Mama. 8. Drink a Round to Ireland. 9. Angel on My Side. 10. Don't Say Goodbye Love.

20. Home Again

Elektra, 1984. Produced by Dave Grusin and Larry Rosen.
1. Only You. 2. Sweetheart on Parade. 3. Everybody Works in China. 4. Yellow Kimono. 5. From Where I Stand. 6. Home Again (with T. G. Sheppard). 7. Shoot First. 8. Don't Say Love. 9. Dream On. 10. The Best Is Yet to Come.

21. Amazing Grace

Telstar, 1985. Produced by Tony Britten, Keith Grant, and Judy Collins.
1. Amazing Grace. 2. Day by Day. 3. Bridge over Troubled Water. 4. I Don't Know How to Love Him. 5. Both Sides Now. 6. Abide with Me. 7. Just a Closer Walk with Thee. 8. When You Wish upon a Star. 9. A Child Is Born. 10. The Rose. 11. Day at a Time. 12. Oh Happy Day. 13. Morning Has Broken. 14. Send in the Clowns. 15. The Lord Is My Shepherd. 16. Jerusalem.

22. Trust Your Heart

Gold Castle Records, 1987. Overall U.S. production by Judy Collins.
1. Trust Your Heart. 2. Amazing Grace. 3. Jerusalem. 4. Day by Day. 5. The Life You Dream. 6. The Rose. 7. Moonfall. 8. Morning Has Broken. 9. When a Child Is Born. 10. When You Wish upon a Star.

23. Sanity and Grace

Delta, 1989. Produced by Judy Collins, Rupert Holmes, Keith Grant, and Tony Britten.
1. History. 2. Lovin' and Leavin'. 3. Sanity and Grace. 4. Daughters of Time. 5. Born to the Breed. 6. Moonfall. 7. Morning Has Broken. 8. When a Child Is Born. 9. Jerusalem. 10. The Life You Dream.

24. Fires of Eden

Sony, 1991. Produced by Judy Collins.
1. The Blizzard. 2. Fortune of Soldiers. 3. Test of Time. 4. Fires of Eden. 5. Home Before Dark. 6. The Air That I Breathe. 7. City of Cities. 8. Dreaming. 9. Queen of the Night. 10. From a Distance. 11. The Blizzard (reprise).

25. Judy Collins Sings Dylan . . . Just Like a Woman

Geffen, 1993. Produced by Judy Collins and Alan Silverman.
1. Like a Rolling Stone. 2. It's All Over Now, Baby Blue. 3. Simple Twist of Fate. 4. Sweetheart Like You. 5. Gotta Serve Somebody. 6. Dark Eyes. 7. Love Minus Zero/No Limit. 8. Just Like a Woman. 9. I Believe in You. 10. With God on Our Side. 11. Bob Dylan's Dream.

26. Come Rejoice! A Judy Collins Christmas

Wildflower/Rhino/Mesa, 1994. Produced by Judy Collins and Alan Silverman.
1. I'll Be Home for Christmas. 2. Away in a Manger. 3. Joy to the World. 4. Song for Sarajevo. 5. Cherry Tree Carol. 6. Good King Wenceslas. 7. All on a Wintry Night. 8. Come Rejoice.

9. Little Road to Bethlehem. 10. Silent Night. 11. A Christmas Carol. 12. Charlie and the Bells Medley: White Christmas/ Happy New Year. 13. Let It Snow. 14. Amazing Grace.

27. *Shameless*

Atlantic, 1995. Produced by Judy Collins and Alan Silverman.
1. Bright Morning Stars. 2. Melody. 3. Mountain Girl.
4. Shameless. 5. Risk. 6. Bard of My Heart. 7. Wheel Rolling.
8. Lily of the Valley. 9. Let's Pretend. 10. Song for Sarajevo.
11. Wind, Water, Fire and Stone. 12. Kerry Dancers. 13. Raised on Rock and Roll.

28. *Voices*

Solo, 1996. Produced by Judy Collins and Alan Silverman.
1. Since You've Asked. 2. My Father. 3. Albatross. 4. Weaver Song (Holly Ann). 5. Secret Gardens. 6. Houses. 7. Open the Door. 8. Born to the Breed. 9. Trust Your Heart. 10. The Life You Dream. 11. The Blizzard. 12. Sailor's Life. 13. Voices.

29. *Christmas at the Biltmore Estate*

Elektra, 1996. Produced by Judy Collins.
1. Joy to the World. 2. Silver Bells. 3. Santa Claus Is Coming to Town. 4. Jingle Bells. 5. Hark! The Herald Angels Sing. 6. What Child Is This? 7. The Twelve Days of Christmas. 8. Come Rejoice. 9. The Holly and the Ivy. 10. All on a Wintry Night. 11. The First Noel. 12. I Saw Three Ships. 13. The Night Before Christmas. 14. O Come, All Ye Faithful.

30. *Forever: An Anthology*

Elektra, 1997. Produced by Judy Collins, David Anderle, Mark Abramson, Arif Mardin, Jac Holzman, Lewis Hahn, and Gary Klein.
CD #1: 1. Someday Soon. 2. Who Knows Where the Time Goes. 3. Chelsea Morning. 4. Suzanne. 5. Born to the Breed. 6. Maid of Constant Sorrow. 7. Since You Asked. 8. Bread and Roses. 9. In the Hills of Shiloh. 10. City of New Orleans. 11. The Fallow Way. 12. Grandaddy. 13. My Father. 14. La

Chanson des Vieux Amants. 15. In My Life. 16. Marat/Sade.
17. Send in the Clowns.
CD #2: 1. Both Sides Now. 2. Desperado. 3. Master of War.
4. Fisherman's Song. 5. So Early, Early in the Spring. 6. First
Boy I Loved. 7. Albatross. 8. Hard Lovin' Loser. 9. In the Heat
of the Summer. 10. Pirate Jenny. 11. Turn! Turn! Turn! 12. Salt
of the Earth. 13. Farewell to Tarwathie. 14. Spanish Is the Loving
Tongue. 15. Nothing Lasts Forever. 16. Walls (We Are Not
Forgotten). 17. Bird on a Wire. 18. Amazing Grace.

31. *Both Sides Now*

OnQ Music, 1998. Produced by Judy Collins and Alan Silverman.
CLASSIC FOLK: 1. The Times They Are A-Changin'. 2. Barbara
Allen. 3. Both Sides Now. 4. Black Is the Color of My True
Love's Hair. 5. Plaisir d'Amour. 6. Morning Has Broken. 7. Cat's
in the Cradle. 8. Leavin' on a Jet Plane/Take Me Home Country
Road. 9. Loch Lomond. 10. Let It Be. 11. Blowin' in the Wind.
12. Amazing Grace.
CLASSIC BROADWAY: 1. Don't Cry for Me Argentina. 2. How Are
Things in Glocca Morra? 3. My Heart Stood Still. 4. I've Grown
Accustomed to His Face. 5. Embraceable You. 6. Bewitched.
7. Till There Was You. 8. Younger than Springtime. 9. I Can't
Get Started. 10. They Say It's Wonderful. 11. My Funny
Valentine. 12. Send in the Clowns.

32. *Live at Wolf Trap*

Wildflower, 1999. Produced by Judy Collins.
1. Someday Soon. 2. Mountain Girl. 3. Both Sides Now. 4. City
of New Orleans. 5. Gypsy Rover. 6. She Moves Through the
Fair. 7. My Funny Valentine. 8. Kerry Dancers. 9. Danny Boy.
10. My Father. 11. Bird on a Wire. 12. Send in the Clowns.
13. Amazing Grace. 14. Beyond the Sky. 15. Who Knows Where
the Time Goes.

33. *All on a Wintry Night*

Wildflower, 2000. Produced by Judy Collins.
1. I'll Be Home for Christmas. 2. Come Rejoice. 3. Away in a
Manger. 4. Joy to the World. 5. In the Bleak Midwinter. 6. Song

for Sarajevo (I Dream of Peace). 7. Good King Wenceslas. 8. All on a Wintry Night. 9. Let It Snow. 10. Silent Night. 11. A Christmas Carol. 12. Cherry Tree Carol. 13. The Blizzard. 14. The Wexford Carol.

34. *Judy Collins Wildflower Festival*

Wildflower, 2003. Produced by Judy Collins.
1. Cat's in the Cradle. 2. Kingdom Come. 3. Silly Little Diddle (Tom Rush). 4. Wings of Angels. 5. Close the Door Lightly (Eric Andersen). 6. Blue River (Eric Andersen). 7. Someday Soon. 8. St. James Infirmary (Arlo Guthrie). 9. Mooses Come Walking (Arlo Guthrie). 10. Home Before Dark. 11. Open the Door. 12. City of New Orleans. 13. Thirsty Boots. 14. Will the Circle Be Unbroken?

35. *Judy Collins Sings Leonard Cohen: Democracy*

Elektra, 2004. Produced by Judy Collins.
1. Democracy. 2. Suzanne. 3. A Thousand Kisses Deep. 4. Hey, That's No Way to Say Goodbye. 5. Dress Rehearsal Rag. 6. Priests. 7. Night Comes On. 8. Sister of Mercy. 9. Story of Isaac. 10. Bird on the Wire. 11. Famous Blue Raincoat. 12. Joan of Arc. 13. Take This Longing.

36. *Portrait of an American Girl*

Wildflower, 2005. Produced by Judy Collins.
1. Singing Lessons. 2. That Song About the Midway. 3. I Can't Cry Hard Enough. 4. You Can't Buy Love. 5. Pacing the Cage. 6. Sally Go 'Round the Roses. 7. Voyager. 8. Drops of Jupiter (Tell Me). 9. Wedding Song (Song for Louis). 10. Checkmate. 11. Liberté. 12. Lincoln Portrait. 13. How Can I Keep from Singing.

37. *Judy Collins Sings Lennon and McCartney*

Wildflower, 2007. Produced by Judy Collins and Alan Silverman.
1. And I Love Her. 2. Blackbird. 3. Golden Slumbers. 4. Penny Lane. 5. Norwegian Wood. 6. When I'm Sixty-Four. 7. Good

Day Sunshine. 8. Hey Jude. 9. We Can Work It Out.
10. Yesterday. 11. I'll Follow the Sun. 12. Long and Winding
Road.

38. *Paradise*

Wildflower, 2010. Produced by Judy Collins and Alan Silverman.
1. Over the Rainbow. 2. Diamonds and Rust (with Joan Baez).
3. Once I Was. 4. Weight of the World. 5. Last Thing on My
Mind (with Stephen Stills). 6. Dens of Yarrow. 7. Kingdom
Come. 8. Emilio. 9. Ghost Riders in the Sky. 10. Gauguin.

Index